Social Economics

CESifo Seminar Series

edited by Hans-Werner Sinn

Social Economics

Current and Emerging Avenues

Joan Costa-Font and Mario Macis, editors

CESifo Seminar Series

The MIT Press
Cambridge, Massachusetts
London, England

Set in Sabon LT Std by Toppan Best-set Premedia Limited. Printed and bound in the United States of America.

Library of Congress Cataloging-in-Publication Data

Names: Costa-i-Font, Joan, editor. | Macis, Mario, editor.
Title: Social economics : current and emerging avenues / edited by Joan Costa-Font and Mario Macis.
Description: Cambridge, MA : MIT Press, [2017] | Series: CESifo seminar series | Includes bibliographical references and index.
Identifiers: LCCN 2016024354 | ISBN 9780262035651 (hardcover : alk. paper)
Subjects: LCSH: Economics--Sociological aspects. | Economics--Psychological aspects.
Classification: LCC HM548 .S59 2017 | DDC 302--dc23 LC record available at https://lccn.loc.gov/2016024354

10 9 8 7 6 5 4 3 2 1

Contents

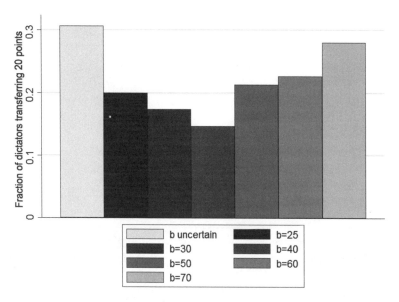

Figure 2.2
Percentage of transfers—asymmetric vs. symmetric information (within-subjects). The figure depicts the share of subjects A who transfer. Bar 1 refers to transfers under asymmetric information without reward. Bars 2–7 depict transfers for each level of benefit under symmetric information without reward. $N = 75$.

for benefit levels from $b = 25$ to $b = 70$, only 20 percent, 17 percent, 15 percent, 21 percent, 23 percent, and 28 percent of all subjects are willing to transfer money, versus 31 percent under asymmetric information.

Table 2.2 depicts the results of an OLS regression with the individual transfer decision as the dependent variable. As independent variables we include the benefit levels under symmetric information. The omitted category is the decision under asymmetric information. The regression confirms what figure 2.2 has already pointed to. Fewer prosocial decisions are made under symmetric information compared to the case of asymmetric information. The differences for benefit levels below 60 are statistically significant.[6]

From figure 2.2 and table 2.2 it is clear that, on average, subjects are more willing to transfer when they do not know the exact value of b. This difference is due to a combination of several effects. First, we observe *heterogeneous* transfer patterns as predicted by *different* social preference theories. We can assign each dictator to one of four patterns[7]: selfish subjects who do not transfer for any benefit level (60 percent of all subjects), subjects who transfer for all values of b and whose behavior is

Table 2.2
Dictators' transfer decisions ($N = 525$).

	(1)
Transfer when benefit = 25 (= 1)	−0.107** (0.0525)
Transfer when benefit = 30 (= 1)	−0.133*** (0.0480)
Transfer when benefit = 40 (= 1)	−0.160*** (0.0469)
Transfer when benefit = 50 (= 1)	−0.0933* (0.0474)
Transfer when benefit = 60 (= 1)	−0.0800 (0.0496)
Transfer when benefit = 70 (= 1)	−0.0267 (0.0539)
Constant	0.307** (0.0539)

Standard errors are in parentheses. The table reports results from an OLS regression. Dependent variable is the individual transfer decision. Explanatory variables are the benefit levels under symmetric information. The omitted category is the asymmetric information case. Standard errors are clustered at the subject level. Level of significance: * $p < 0.10$; ** $p < 0.05$; *** $p < 0.01$.

thereby in accordance with a concern for efficiency as well as maximin preferences (7 percent), subjects whose behavior is in line with an efficiency concern but not with maximin preferences (20 percent), and subjects whose behavior is in line with inequality aversion (13 percent).[8]

When b is known, different subjects transfer for different values of b. For low values of b, subjects whose behavior is consistent with inequality aversion transfer. They do not transfer, though, when the benefit reaches a certain threshold. In contrast, subjects whose behavior is in line with an efficiency concern transfer starting from a certain threshold. As figure 2.3 shows, the share of individuals with inequality aversion or efficiency concern changes with the value of b.[9]

The second element that leads to higher transfers under asymmetric information is as follows. As is implied by the social utility functions, most individual transfers are not negatively affected by risk. According to these functions, all subjects who transfer under $b = 40$ and $b = 50$ should also transfer under asymmetric information. We observe eight such subjects (this number does not include 7 percent of subjects who always transfer, regardless of b), all of whom transfer under asymmetric information. Hence, every subject who should behave prosocially according to social preferences chooses to do so. Moreover, we observe eleven subjects who transfer either under $b = 40$ or under $b = 50$ under

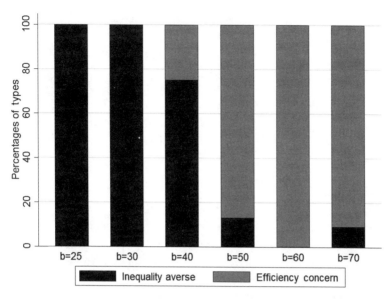

Figure 2.3
Transfer patterns for different values of b. The sample is restricted to those subjects whose behavior follows the prediction by either efficiency concern or inequality aversion. The exact level of b is known. One subject only transferred at $b < 40$ but also for the value of $b = 70$ under symmetric information. We assigned this subject to pattern "inequality aversion."

symmetric information. For these subjects, both decisions—transfer and no transfer—would be in line with social preferences under asymmetric information. In fact, seven of these eleven transfer. Finally, we find 16 subjects who are not egoists but who transfer *neither* for $b = 40$ *nor* for $b = 50$, so they should not transfer under an expected value $b = 45$. Eight of them transfer nevertheless. Thus, we find some evidence for a certain increased prosocial behavior under asymmetric information and no evidence for a negative effect of asymmetric information.

Together, the evidence that subjects are not negatively affected by asymmetric information and the evidence that the parameters of our experiment are such that two different types of subjects separate for known transfers under symmetric information but both transfer when the information is asymmetric can explain the higher number of transfers under asymmetric information.[10]

As a consequence of the above results, earnings for subjects B are substantially higher when A decide under asymmetric information. Each value of b is equally likely, and the unconditional decision to transfer

(0.31) is the same for all values of b. Under symmetric information, each value of b is also equally likely as before. Yet, as subjects make a transfer decision for each value of b, the conditional probability may vary over b and is smaller than the probability under asymmetric information. Hence, players B have a higher chance to obtain a transfer: 31 percent under asymmetric information versus 21 percent under symmetric information.[11] And their expected transfer is 40 percent higher: 10 points under symmetric information versus 14 points under asymmetric information.[12]

Heterogeneity
The driving force behind our results is the heterogeneity of social preferences. For the different values of b the share of individuals who transfer varies. There are more individuals who transfer for lower and higher values than for intermediate values. This pattern is in line with social preferences. For low values, inequality-averse individuals transfer; for higher values, efficiency-concerned individuals do so.

When conducting the experiment, we also gathered some background information on participants, most notably field of study, age, and gender. The experimental lab in Mannheim gathers this information through ORSEE (Greiner 2004), an automatic tool used to administer subject pools.

In the following, we investigate how transfer patterns under symmetric information of the data do vary with gender. In figure 2.4 we present transfers under asymmetric information and symmetric information separately for women and men. The first bar represents the shares of women and men who transfer when the benefit level is not known, the second for a benefit level of 2.5, the third for 3, and so on. It becomes clear that patterns are different. In fact, women show a transfer pattern that is closer to inequality aversion: More women transfer for low values of b. For men it is just the opposite: They are more likely to transfer for higher values of b, a behavior that is in line with efficiency concerns.

With the exception of the benefit level 40 these differences are significantly different (t-test, $p < 0.05$).

Interestingly, men and women are similar with respect to their behavior under asymmetric information. This difference is also not statistically significant. Still, more women tend to transfer under asymmetric information than men. But note that there are some women who are concerned with efficiency and who drive this effect.

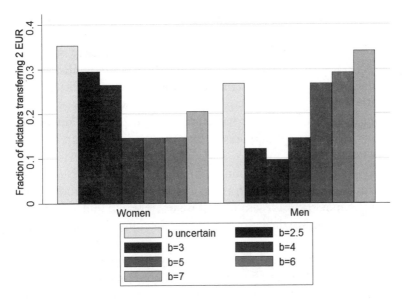

Figure 2.4
Transfer patterns and the role of gender. The figure depicts the share of subjects A who transfer. Bar 1 refers to transfers under asymmetric information without reward. Bars 2–7 depict transfers for each level of benefit under symmetric information without reward. N = 75.

2.5   Discussion and Conclusion

Our analysis reveals a connection between different and seemingly unrelated findings. It has been observed that women tend to care more about inequality and men more about efficiency. Our experiment supports this finding in another setting.

This finding is important because it relates to experiments that indicate the significance of social preferences for political decisions. The experiments by Tyran and Sausgruber (2006), Höchtl et al. (2012), and Sauermann and Kaiser (2010) highlight the relevance of inequality aversion for redistribution decisions. But, as is illustrated by the findings of Paetzel et al. (2014), many political decision have multiple dimensions (e.g., redistribution and efficiency) at the same time. The experimental evidence suggests that both inequality aversion and preferences for efficiency may affect prosocial behavior. Our findings reinforce that the composition of individuals is crucial. At the same time, we can link these differences to gender.

Moreover, it has been established that women tend to be more risk averse if private payoffs are considered. Our experiment is one of the first pieces of evidence that risk attitudes regarding the payoffs of others do not demonstrate such differences.[13] If there is uncertainty whether the transfer from the dictator would imply more equal or more efficient allocation, all socially concerned players, regardless of sex and type of concern, choose to take a risk and make a transfer, even if this implies an allocation they would not support under symmetric information. In addition, both sexes do not use the uncertainty as an excuse not to transfer as one may suspect from the results reported by Dana and Weber (2007). As a result, we observe more transfers under asymmetric information than under symmetric information, and we observe that under asymmetric information both women and men tend to transfer under different certain payoffs for recipients.

It is clear that these results are preliminary and require more testing in the future. But still we think that this link is very interesting, and it will be informative to reconsider explanations of gender differences on social preferences and risk preferences in the light of our results.

In future work, we hope to extend this line of research toward strategic interactions and voting settings in order to explore the robustness of our findings in more settings, to check whether the effect of preferences hinges on dictators' being pivotal, and to find out whether our findings can be replicated in large groups.

Acknowledgments

We thank Dirk Engelmann, Hans Peter Grüner, participants in seminars at the University of Mannheim, and participants in the CESifo conference on social economics for helpful comments and suggestions. We thank Philipp Barteska and Paul Voss for excellent research assistance. We gratefully acknowledge financial support from the Deutsche Forschungsgemeinschaft through grant SFB 884 (Political Economy of Reforms).

Appendix

Descriptive Statistics
Descriptive statistics are presented in tables 2.3 and 2.4.

Table 2.3
Dictators' transfer decisions—summary statistics, sessions *AsymInfoFirst*
($N = 45$).

	Mean	Standard deviation	Median
First part			
Transfer (= 1)	0.36	0.48	0
Second part (with reward)			
Transfer (= 1)	0.4	0.5	0
Third part (with reward)			
Benefit = 25: Transfer (= 1)	0.24	0.43	0
Benefit = 30: Transfer (= 1)	0.22	0.42	0
Benefit = 40: Transfer (= 1)	0.22	0.42	0
Benefit = 50: Transfer (= 1)	0.27	0.45	0
Benefit = 60: Transfer (= 1)	0.33	0.48	0
Benefit = 70: Transfer (= 1)	0.33	0.48	0
Fourth part			
Benefit = 25: Transfer (= 1)	0.18	0.39	0
Benefit = 30: Transfer (= 1)	0.18	0.37	0
Benefit = 40: Transfer (= 1)	0.18	0.39	0
Benefit = 50: Transfer (= 1)	0.24	0.43	0
Benefit = 60: Transfer (= 1)	0.27	0.45	0
Benefit = 70: Transfer (= 1)	0.31	0.47	0

Further Results

In this subsection we briefly discuss the effect of the reward and compare in more detail sessions *AsymInfoFirst* and sessions *SymmInfoFirst*.

Reward   The introduction of a reward in parts 2 and 3 has a positive effect. More subjects choose to transfer money. (See figure 2.5.) Mirroring the positive effect, when the reward is withdrawn, we observe a negative effect. The willingness to transfer decreases. The results of an OLS regression (table 2.5) confirm that the reward has a positive effect and

Table 2.4
Dictators' transfer decisions—summary statistics sessions *SymmInfoFirst*
($N = 30$).

	Mean	Standard deviation	Median
Fourth part			
Transfer (= 1)	0.23	0.43	0
Second part (with reward)			
Transfer (= 1)	0.2	0.41	0
Third part (with reward)			
Benefit = 25: Transfer (= 1)	0.27	0.45	0
Benefit = 30: Transfer (= 1)	0.23	0.43	0
Benefit = 40: Transfer (= 1)	0.2	0.41	0
Benefit = 50: Transfer (= 1)	0.27	0.45	0
Benefit = 60: Transfer (= 1)	0.27	0.45	0
Benefit = 70: Transfer (= 1)	0.23	0.43	0
First part			
Benefit = 25: Transfer (= 1)	0.23	0.43	0
Benefit = 30: Transfer (= 1)	0.17	0.38	0
Benefit = 40: Transfer (= 1)	0.1	0.31	0
Benefit = 50: Transfer (= 1)	0.17	0.38	0
Benefit = 60: Transfer (= 1)	0.17	0.38	0
Benefit = 70: Transfer (= 1)	0.23	0.43	0

that it is statistically significant. Moreover, we do not find a "crowding-out effect" at the individual level.

Order Effects   When we compare the subjects' behavior in sessions *AsymInfoFirst* and *SymmInfoFirst*, we find small differences though none being statistically significant. In sessions *SymmInfoFirst* subjects transfer less in all treatments and the effect of asymmetric information is not so strong. (See figures 2.6 and 2.7.) The reasons are that we observe a smaller percentage of subjects with prosocial preferences and

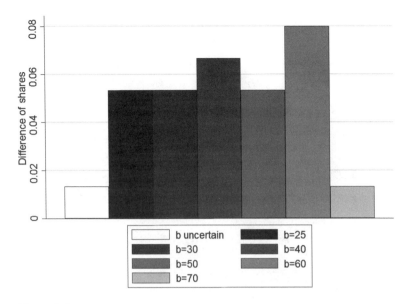

Figure 2.5
The effect of reward on transfers. Bar 1 depicts the difference between the shares of individuals who transfer under asymmetric information with reward and the share of individuals who transfer under asymmetric information without reward. Bars 2–7 depict the differences between the shares of individuals who transfer under symmetric information with reward and the share of individuals who transfer under symmetric information without reward for each level of benefit. $N = 75$.

Table 2.5
Dictators' transfer decision—reward ($N = 1,050$).

	(1)
Transfer when benefit = 25 (= 1)	–0.0867** (0.0430)
Transfer when benefit = 30 (= 1)	–0.113*** (0.0388)
Transfer when benefit = 40 (= 1)	–0.133*** (0.0334)
Transfer when benefit = 50 (= 1)	–0.0733* (0.0401)
Transfer when benefit = 60 (= 1)	–0.0467 (0.0406)
Transfer when benefit = 70 (= 1)	–0.0267 (0.0446)
Reward (= 1)	0.0476** (0.0197)
Constant	0.290*** (0.0462)

Standard errors are in parentheses. Table reports results from an OLS regression. Dependent variable is the individual transfer decision. Explanatory variables are the benefit levels under symmetric information. The omitted category is the asymmetric information case. Standard errors are clustered at the subject level. Level of significance: * $p < 0.10$; ** $p < 0.05$; *** $p < 0.01$.

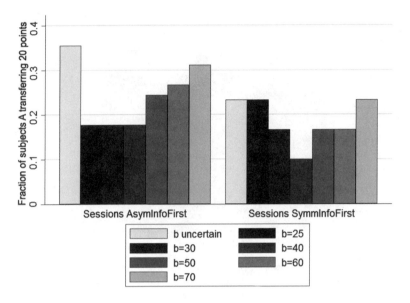

Figure 2.6
Percentage of transfers—sessions AsymInfoFirst versus sessions SymmInfoFirst. The figure depicts the share of individuals in the role of A who transfer for sessions AsymInfoFirst and sessions SymmInfoFirst. Bar 1 refers to transfers under asymmetric information. Bars 2–7 depict transfers for each level of benefit under symmetric information.

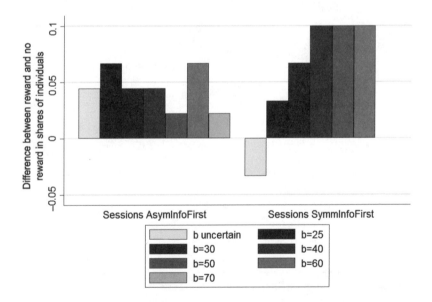

Figure 2.7
The effect of reward on transfers—sessions *AsymInfoFirst* versus sessions *SymmInfoFirst*. Bar 1 depicts the difference between the shares of individuals who transfer with reward and the share of individuals who transfer without reward under asymmetric information. Bars 2–7 depict the difference between the shares of individuals who transfer with reward and the share of individuals who transfer without reward for each level of benefit under symmetric information.

that we observe a different composition of types. There are relatively more subjects with inequality aversion and fewer with efficiency concern. As a result, we have relatively fewer subjects who transfer under $b = 40$ or/and under $b = 50$. Hence, it is not surprising that the average willingness to transfer under asymmetric information is not so strong in the robustness sessions. This result also serves as a nice illustration of the complex interaction between heterogeneity of types and asymmetric information. Regarding individual behavior, the reaction to asymmetric information is very similar in sessions *AsymInfoFirst* and sessions *SymmInfoFirst*.

Notes

1. For surveys of the literature, see Bowles and Polanía-Reyes 2012 and Gneezy et al. 2011.

2. The probability is 1/10 for the high reward and 9/10 for the low reward. In all sessions, $r = 5$ was drawn.

3. Subjects B had no decision to make in the experiment, but we elicited their beliefs about what they thought subjects A would do.

4. Note that neither Fehr and Schmidt (1999) nor Charness and Rabin (2002) discuss the possibility of risk regarding the others' payoffs, and that it is not obvious how to implement it within their framework.

5. We focus on the main results. The effects of changing the order as well as the effect of the reward are discussed in the appendix.

6. We also estimated a random-effects model (not reported here). The results were very similar. Furthermore, we did a Wilcoxon signed-rank test. For benefit levels 30 and 40 the null hypothesis can be rejected at the 1% level, for $b = 25$ and $b = 50$ at the 5% level, and for $b = 60$ at the 10% level.

7. The assignment is based on behavior under symmetric information.

8. We have 150 pairs and therefore 75 dictators; 40 are selfish, 15 behave according to efficiency concern, 5 according to either efficiency concern or maximin preferences, and 10 according to inequality aversion.

9. By definition the patterns for other groups are degenerate. Subjects transfer either for all values of b or for none.

10. Given that we observe higher transfers under asymmetric information, it is also clear that the type of information asymmetry we introduce is not sufficient to make subjects behave more selfishly because there is more "moral wiggle room," as is reported in Dana and Weber 2007.

11. Probability to obtain a transfer is equal to $\frac{1}{6}(20+17+15+21+23+28)\% = 21\% < 31\%$.

12. $E[b] = \frac{1}{6}(0.2 \cdot 25 + 0.17 \cdot 30 + 0.15 \cdot 40 + 0.21 \cdot 50 + 0.23 \cdot 60 + 0.28 \cdot 70) = 10 < 0.31 \cdot 45 = 13.95$.

13. To the best of our knowledge, only Bradler (2009) considers gender as an explanatory variable in risk attitudes toward others; she does not find a significant effect.

References

Andreoni, James, and Lise Vesterlund. 2001. Which is the fair sex? Gender differences in altruism. *Quarterly Journal of Economics* 116 (1): 293–312.

Bolle, Friedel, and Philipp E. Otto. 2010. A price is a signal: On intrinsic motivation, crowding-out, and crowding-in. *Kyklos* 63 (1): 9–22.

Bowles, Samuel, and Sandra Polanía-Reyes. 2012. Economic incentives and social preferences: Substitutes or complements? *Journal of Economic Literature* 50 (2): 368–425.

Bradler, Christiane. 2009. Social Preferences under Risk—An Experimental Analysis. Discussion Paper 09, Zentrum für Europäische Wirtschaftsforschung.

Brennan, Geoffrey, Luis G. González, Werner Güth, and M. Vittoria Levati. 2008. Attitudes toward private and collective risk in individual and strategic choice situations. *Journal of Economic Behavior and Organization* 67 (1): 253–262.

Brock, J. Michelle, Andreas Lange, and Erkut Y. Ozbay. 2013. Dictating the risk: Experimental evidence on giving in risky environments. *American Economic Review* 103 (1): 415–437.

Camerer, Colin F. 2003. *Behavioral Game Theory: Experiments in Strategic Interaction*. Princeton University Press.

Charness, Gary, and Matthew Rabin. 2002. Understanding social preferences with simple tests. *Quarterly Journal of Economics* 117 (3): 817–869.

Croson, Rachel, and Uri Gneezy. 2009. Gender differences in preferences. *Journal of Economic Literature* 47 (2): 448–474.

Dana, Jason, and Roberto A. Weber. 2007. Exploiting moral wiggle room: Experiments demonstrating an illusory preference. *Economic Theory* 33 (1): 67–80.

Dickinson, David L., and Jill Tiefenthaler. 2002. What is fair? Experimental evidence. *Southern Economic Journal* 69 (2): 414–428.

Dufwenberg, Martin, and Astri Muren. 2006. Gender composition in teams. *Journal of Economic Behavior and Organization* 61 (1): 50–54.

Eckel, Catherine C., and Philip J. Grossman. 2008. Forecasting risk attitudes: An experimental study using actual and forecast gamble choices. *Journal of Economic Behavior and Organization* 68 (1).

Engel, Christoph. 2011. Dictator games: A meta study. *Experimental Economics* 14 (4): 583–610.

Engelmann, Dirk, and Martin Strobel. 2007. Preferences over income distributions: Experimental evidence. *Public Finance Review* 35 (2): 285–310.

Fehr, Ernst, and Klaus M. Schmidt. 1999. A theory of fairness, competition, and cooperation. *Quarterly Journal of Economics* 114 (3): 817–868.

Fernandez, Raquel, and Dani Rodrik. 1991. Resistance to reform: Status quo bias in the presence of individual-specific uncertainty. *American Economic Review* 81 (5): 1146–1155.

Fischbacher, Urs. 2007. z-Tree: Zurich toolbox for ready-made economic experiments. *Experimental Economics* 10 (2): 171–178.

Frey, Bruno S., and Felix Oberholzer-Gee. 1997. The cost of price incentives: An empirical analysis of motivation crowding-out. *American Economic Review* 87 (4): 746–755.

Gneezy, Uri, and Aldo Rustichini. 2000. A fine is a price. *Journal of Legal Studies* 29 (1): 1–17.

Gneezy, Uri, Stephan Meier, and Pedro Rey-Biel. 2011. When and why incentives (don't) work to modify behavior. *Journal of Economic Perspectives* 25 (4).

Greiner, Ben. 2004. The Online Recruitment System ORSEE 2.0—A Guide for the Organization of Experiments in Economics. Working Paper 10, Department of Economics, University of Cologne.

Güth, Werner, Steffen Huck, and Peter Ockenfels. 1996. Two-level ultimatum bargaining with incomplete information: An experimental study. *Economic Journal* 106 (436): 593–604.

Güth, Werner, M. Vittoria Levati, and Matteo Ploner. 2008. On the social dimension of time and risk preferences: An experimental study. *Economic Inquiry* 46 (2): 261–272.

Höchtl, Wolfgang, Rupert Sausgruber, and Jean-Robert Tyran. 2012. Inequality aversion and voting on redistribution. *European Economic Review* 56 (7): 1406–1421.

Holt, Charles A., and Susan K. Laury. 2002. Risk aversion and incentive effects. *American Economic Association* 92 (5): 1644–1655.

Huck, Steffen. 1999. Responder behavior in ultimatum offer games with incomplete information. *Journal of Economic Psychology* 20 (2): 183–206.

Kamas, Linda, and Anne Preston. 2012. Distributive and reciprocal fairness: What can we learn from the heterogeneity of social preferences? *Journal of Economic Psychology* 33 (3): 538–553.

Klempt, Charlotte, and Kerstin Pull. 2009. Generosity, Greed and Gambling: What Difference Does Asymmetric Information in Bargaining Make? Jena Economic Research Papers.

Konow, James. 2000. Fair shares: Accountability and cognitive dissonance in allocation decisions. *American Economic Review* 90 (4): 1072–1091.

Mitzkewitz, Michael, and Rosemarie Nagel. 1993. Experimental results on ultimatum games with incomplete information. *International Journal of Game Theory* 22 (2): 171–198.

Paetzel, Fabian, Rupert Sausgruber, and Stefan Traub. 2014. Social Preferences and Voting on Reform: An Experimental Study. Unpublished.

Powell, Melanie, and David Ansic. 1997. Gender differences in risk behaviour in financial decision-making: An experimental analysis. *Journal of Economic Psychology* 18 (6): 605–628.

Rapoport, Amnon, and James A. Sundali. 1996. Ultimatums in two-person bargaining with one-sided uncertainty: Offer games. *International Journal of Game Theory* 25 (4): 475–494.

Sauermann, Jan, and Andre Kaiser. 2010. Taking others into account: Self-interest and fairness in majority decision making. *American Journal of Political Science* 54 (3): 667–685.

Schubert, Renate, Martin Brown, Matthias Gysler, and Hans Wolfgang Brachinger.1999. Financial decision-making: Are women really more risk-averse? *American Economic Review, American Economic Association* 89 (2): 381–385.

Selten, Reinhard, and Axel Ockenfels. 1998. An experimental solidarity game. *Journal of Economic Behavior and Organization* 34 (4): 517–539.

Tyran, Jean-Robert, and Rupert Sausgruber. 2006. A little fairness may induce a lot of redistribution in democracy. *European Economic Review* 50 (2): 469–485.

3

Who Gains from Competition? The Ultimatum Game in a Labor-Market Setting in Ghana

C78 C72 J23

Elwyn Davies and Marcel Fafchamps

B55 O15

Understanding how labor-market institutions function is crucial for economic development. Developing countries have traditionally relied on other forms of employment than wage employment, such as being an own-account worker or a contributing to the family firm. In these types of work, the profits from labor are not divided, because the worker is either self-employed or a member of the family. Wage employment is different, as this requires an explicit transfer to the worker, who is often outside the household. Furthermore, competition plays a role in the recruitment and contracting of labor: there is competition between workers for a job, but also competition between employers for a specific worker. In this chapter we use experimental methods to assess how the profits from labor are shared by the worker and the employer in a developing country. Furthermore, we look at how competition affects how the profits from labor are shared.

The process of contracting a worker is often close to ultimatum bargaining: the employer specifies a job description and proposes a wage, and the worker accepts or rejects.[1] To examine ultimatum bargaining behavior, we invited students from colleges and universities in Ghana to play a labor-market version of the ultimatum game. In the ultimatum game, proposed by Güth et al. (1983), there are two players: the Proposer and the Responder. To receive a sum of money, they need to agree on the division of this sum. The Proposer proposes a division, which the Responder can accept or reject. If the Responder accepts the proposed division, the players receive their share according to the proposed split. If the Responder rejects the division, both players earn nothing.

Under the assumption that participants are rational and maximize their own payoffs, subgame perfect equilibrium predicts that a Proposer offers the smallest amount possible to the Responder and that the Responder accepts any amount that is larger than zero. However, a wide range of studies, conducted in both developed and developing countries, have shown that a large share of the Proposers propose a payment that is significantly larger than zero and that a large share of Responders reject small but positive payments. (See, e.g., Güth and Tietz 1990; Roth et al. 1991; Cardenas and Carpenter, 2008; Henrich et al. 2006.)

Our labor-market version of the ultimatum game uses different wording (the Proposer is framed as the employer and the Responder as the worker), but the payoffs are equivalent to those in the ultimatum game. The purpose of framing is to trigger heuristics associated with labor-market behavior in the studied country. Instead of making a proposal for the division of the money received, the employer makes a wage offer to the worker, specifying a wage and a level of effort from the worker. The wage and the level of effort in the offer determine the payoffs of both parties if the wage offer is accepted: the employer's payoff is equal to a profit that is increasing with the worker's effort minus the wage, and the worker's payoff is equal to the wage minus a cost that is increasing with the effort. It is common knowledge how the wage and the level of effort translate into the final payoffs of both parties in that period.

The participants in our study are students from universities and colleges in Accra, the capital of Ghana. In Ghana, as in many other developing countries, the labor market is characterized by a large presence of the informal sector and the share of wage employment in total employment is low: in 2012–13, only 20.2 percent of the entire country's working population and 32.5 percent of the working population in urban areas was wage employed (Ghana Statistical Service 2014). The rest of the working population is mostly either an own-account worker (46.4 percent), a contributing family worker (22.3 percent), or an employer (6.2 percent). Even though the share is still low, the share of wage employment in total employment has been growing: in 2005–06 only 16.4 percent of the working population in Ghana was wage employed (Ghana Statistical Service 2008). Urbanization, the growth of the economy, and the growth of the service sector play roles here: the number of jobs in agriculture has declined, while the service sector has become more important. The service sector now accounts for 40.9 percent of employment, whereas in 2005–06 it accounted for only 26.4 percent.

Next, we introduce competition in our ultimatum game. Instead of one employer facing one worker, three employers face three workers at the same time. The workers take turns in accepting or rejecting offers. A worker can accept only one offer, and an employer can have only one offer accepted. We predict that this form of competition increases the offer made by the employers above the bare minimum of what the worker would except, even if employers do not have any fairness considerations. We find empirical evidence for this: the employers make offers that lead to higher workers' payoffs in the treatment with competition and the workers capture a larger share of surplus. This shows that even though the number of employers and workers is equal, this competition structure affects the final outcomes.

The chapter is organized as follows: Section 3.1 presents the experimental design and introduces the competition treatment. Section 3.2 discusses the actual implementation in Accra. Section 3.3 formulates predictions on the basis of economic theories. Section 3.4 presents the results and relates this to the predictions. Section 3.5 concludes the chapter and provides a discussion of the main results.

3.1 Experimental Design

Each participant was randomly assigned the role of a Proposer (employer) or the role of a Responder (worker) for the entire duration of the experiment. Each period consisted of three stages: an offering stage, in which the Proposers made offers to the Responders; an acceptance stage, in which the Responders could choose to accept or reject their offer; and a recontracting stage, in which the Proposer could make an offer for the next period and the Responder could indicate the minimum payment required for acceptance of the offer.

As was mentioned earlier, the experiment is framed in labor-market language. In each period, the Proposers, as the employers, are given the opportunity to offer a contract to the Responders, specifying a wage w and a level of effort e. There are three levels of effort: high, medium, and low. The combination of the wage and the effort level determines the payoff of the Proposer and the Responder if the contract is expected. For the Proposer (employer), the payoff from contracting is given by

$$x_P = \pi(e) - w, \tag{1}$$

where $\pi(e)$ is the benefit that the employer gets from the worker's exerting an effort level e and w is the wage. For the Responder (worker), the payoff from contracting is given by

$$x_R = w - c(e), \tag{2}$$

where $c(e)$ is the worker's cost of effort. Table 3.1 shows the values of $\pi(e)$ and $c(e)$ for the three effort levels. Both $\pi(e)$ and $c(e)$ are increasing in the

Table 3.1
The payoff parameters used in the experiment.

Effort level e	Low (e_L)	Medium (e_M)	High (e_H)
Benefit to Proposer (employer) $\Pi(e)$	5	20	40
Cost to Responder (worker) $c(e)$	0	2	6
Surplus $S(e) = \Pi(e) - c(e)$	5	18	34

The payoff of the Proposer (employer) is equal to $x_p = \Pi(e) - w$ and the payoff of the Responder (worker) is equal to $x_R = w - c(e)$. The surplus is equal to the sum of the payoffs of both parties. One point is equal to 0.05 Ghana cedis (which equals approximately US$0.02 at the time of the experiment).

level of effort: a higher level of effort is more costly to the worker, but also more beneficial to the employer.

The payoff structure is similar to the payoff structures in gift-exchange games (Brown et al. 2004, 2012; Charness and Haruvy 2002; Charness et al. 2004; Davies and Fafchamps 2015a,b), but with the main difference that the workers cannot choose the level of effort: after accepting, they have to exert the effort level demanded by the employer.[2] By specifying the wage and the effort level, the employer exactly determines the payoffs of both parties, provided that the worker accepts the offer. In this way, the experiment is monetarily equivalent to the traditional ultimatum game, with the level of effort e determining the total size of the "pie" and the wage w representing its division.

We have two treatments: treatment (1–1) without competition and treatment (3–3) with competition. In the (1–1) treatment the market consists of one Proposer and one Responder. They face the same contracting partner for five periods. In the (3–3) treatment the market consists of three Proposers and three Responders, who remain in the same market for five periods. Each Proposer can simultaneously make offers to the three Responders in his or her market. Similarly, each Responder can receive offers from three Proposers, but can accept only one. The Responders take turns to either select an offer or reject all available offers. The Responders' choosing order is randomized every period. Each participant can contract only once every period, so if one Responder has accepted an offer from one Proposer, the offers from that Proposer are no longer available to the Responders choosing after that Responder.

In the (3–3) treatment, we show the Proposers what offers were made by the other two Proposers in their market. Next, we offer them a chance to revise their offers before they are sent to the Responders. These revised offers are not shown to the other Proposers.[3] In the (1–1) treatment, no additional information is shown, but Proposers are still allowed to make a revision.

Furthermore, we introduce a rehiring mechanism, to elicit the minimum wage that the Responder requires in order to accept the offer. This mechanism works as follows: after the Responder accepts the offer and the payoffs are realized, the Responder is asked which minimum wage he or she requires in the next round from the Proposer. Similarly, the Proposer is asked to make an offer to this particular Responder. If the offer of the Proposer is higher than the minimum required payment, the Responder automatically accepts the offer of the Proposer in the next period.[4]

3.2   Implementation

The experimental sessions took place in Accra in September 2015. The participants were recruited from local universities and colleges. Most of the participants were social science students, and more than half had at least one parent who was an entrepreneur. Table 3.2 shows some summary statistics on the participants of the project. The experiment was conducted in English, which is the main language of instruction at Ghanaian universities and colleges. The subjects were paid in cash at the end of the experiment, based on the number of points they accumulated over the periods in the game, excluding the practice periods. As an incentive, we handed out a bonus of 10 Ghana cedis to participants who showed up on time. Besides this, we gave the participants an initial allocation of points at the beginning of each game. The average earnings in each session was around 25–30 Ghana cedis (including the bonus for being on time), which is equivalent to about 15 US dollars.

Each participant played two five-period games. The participants played the games in two different sequences of treatments: 28 participants played the (1–1) treatment for two five-period games; the other 120 played the (1–1) treatment in the first game and then the (3–3) treatment in the second game. (See table 3.3.) Between games, Proposers and Responders were randomly rematched.

Both oral and on-screen instructions were given to explain the game. Each participant played the game for two practice periods to increase familiarity. No points could be earned or lost during these practice periods. Making offers was made easy: Proposers had to use a slider to select a wage. Furthermore, we facilitated the calculations of the payoffs by showing the participants bar charts of what they and their contracting

Table 3.2
Characteristics of participants.

	Frequency	Percentage
Gender		
Female	44	29.73
Male	104	70.27
Type of school		
Polytechnic	19	12.84
University	95	64.19
Teacher education	3	2.03
Other	9	6.09
Not enrolled	14	9.46
Not specified	8	5.41
Area of studies		
Economics, business, accounting	44	29.73
Political science	7	4.73
Other social sciences	36	24.32
Computer sciences	12	8.11
Science, engineering and technical degrees	12	8.11
Arts and languages	9	6.09
Other	7	4.73
No subject area	11	7.43
Not given	10	6.76
At least one parent is entrepreneur		
Yes	87	58.78
No	54	36.49
Not specified	7	4.73
Total	148	100.00
Average age (years)	22.2	

Table 3.3
Treatment sequencing and number of participants.

Treatment sequence	Game 1 (five periods)	Game 2 (five periods)	Number of participants
I	(1–1)	(1–1)	28
II	(1–1)	(3–3)	120
Total			148

partner would earn. These bar charts were updated interactively when the participants changed their choices.

3.3 Predictions

In the one-to-one classical ultimatum game, under the assumption that players care only about their own monetary payoffs, subgame perfect equilibrium predicts that the Proposer offers the smallest non-negative amount possible, and that the Proposer accepts any offer in which he or she receives a non-negative amount. However, in practice, many studies of the ultimatum game have shown that a substantial share of Responders reject low positive offers and that a substantial share of Proposers proposes an offer that is significantly higher than zero.

Fehr and Schmidt (1999) suggest that players not only have preferences over their own payoffs, but also over how their own payoffs compare with the payoff of the other players. They introduce an utility function in which there is a disutility from having a payoff higher or lower than that of another agent. In the case of our ultimatum game, the Fehr-Schmidt utility function for the Responder can be expressed as follows:

$$U_R(x_R, x_P) = x_R - \alpha_{R}\max\{x_P - x_R, 0\} - \beta_{R}\max\{x_R - x_P, 0\}. \tag{3}$$

In this equation, x_R is the (monetary) payoff of the Responder and x_P is the (monetary) payoff of the Proposer. The coefficients α_R and β_R represent the degree of inequality aversion: α_R represents the disutility from having a lower payoff than the other player (disadvantageous inequality), and β_R represents the disutility of having a higher payoff than the other player (advantageous inequality).

When α_R is positive, Responders will reject positive low offers if the disutility from receiving less than the other player is larger than the utility from the payoff. Suppose that $x_R < x_P$ (i.e., the Responder's payoff is less than the Proposer's payoff), so the inequality is disadvantageous for the Responder. In the subgame perfect equilibrium, the Responder will accept if and only if the utility of accepting is greater than or equal to the utility of rejecting:

$$x_R - \alpha_R(x_P - x_R) \geq 0. \tag{4}$$

This implies that in order for the Responder to accept it is necessary that

$$\frac{x_R}{x_P - x_R} \geq \alpha_R. \tag{5}$$

The higher the value of α_R, the higher the threshold $x_R/(x_P - x_R)$ is for the Responder to accept the offer.[5] Only when $\alpha_R = 0$, the Responder will accept all positive relatively disadvantageous offers, because the fraction $x_R/(x_P - x_R)$ on the left-hand side of the equation is always larger than zero, so the condition for acceptance is always satisfied. Unless β_R is very large, it is unlikely that a Responder will reject relatively advantageous offers (i.e., when $x_P > x_R$).[6]

In our set-up, $x_R = w - c(e)$ and $x_P = \pi(e) - w$, which implies that a disadvantageous offer will be accepted if

$$\frac{w - c(e)}{\pi(e) - 2w + c(e)} \geq \alpha_R.$$

Here the left-hand side is an increasing function in w as long as $\pi(e) > c(e)$, as is the case with our set of parameters. (See table 3.1). This implies that for the Responder there is a threshold level $\bar{w}_R(e)$ above which the Responder will accept the offer and below which the Responder will reject the offer. Proposers will always demand the highest level of effort, as such offers Pareto dominate offers asking for lower levels of effort: for each low-effort offer that is accepted, the Proposer could come up with a high-effort offer that gives both parties a higher utility, even when taking inequity aversion preferences into account.[7]

The optimal contract for a purely self-interested Proposer is a contract asking for high effort and offering the threshold wage of the Responder. The wage offered could be higher in case the Proposer has strong preferences against inequality (e.g., a high β in the Fehr-Schmidt model). The value of α_R can vary between the various Responders, and therefore threshold wages will vary. Uncertainty about threshold wages could also increase the offers, depending on the Proposer's level of risk aversion.

Competition can increase the threshold wages as well, as Proposers will want to compete for the Responders with a low threshold wage.

Assume that the threshold levels $\overline{w}_R(e)$ are public knowledge. In our treatment with competition the Proposer can make offers to three Responders, who then in a randomly determined sequence can choose to accept or reject the offer. Without competition from other Proposers, a Proposer would offer each Responder their threshold wage. The Proposer achieves the maximum payoff x_{max} if the worker with the lowest threshold wage accepts and the minimum payoff x_{min} if the worker with the highest threshold wage accepts.

The number of offers available to a Responder depends on the Responder's position in the choosing sequence. If all Proposers made offers to all Responders, the first Responder in the sequence will have three offers available, while the last Responder might only have one offer available. As long as the first two Responders in the choosing sequence accepted their offers, the third Responder will face only one offer, and will accept that offer if it is above his threshold wage. In this case, a Proposer can ensure a minimum payoff of x_{min} by offering all workers their threshold wages. The minimum payoff of x_{min} will be achieved if the third Responder is the Responder with the highest threshold wage. Offering a higher wage than the threshold wage to the Responder with the highest threshold wage does not make sense: if this Responder is the third one choosing, he would have accepted a lower offer, and if this Responder is the first or second one choosing, the Proposer is actually better off if the Responder does not accept her offer, but that of another Proposer, so that your offer to the next Responder, with a lower threshold wage, is still available.

However, for the Responders with lower threshold wages the Proposers have an incentive to increase the wage: in this way it is more likely that this Responder accepts their offer, and not the offer of another Proposer. This bidding for these Responders by the Proposers will increase the wage levels up to the threshold wage level of the Responder with the highest threshold wage. In this way, the strategic interaction between Proposers will lead to higher wages (at least if there was heterogeneity in threshold wages) and to wage convergence.

3.4 Results

This section focuses on the proposed division of surplus by the Proposer, the acceptance behavior of the Responder, and the final distribution of the surplus.

Proposals

The first three columns in table 3.4 show the average wage offers and the payoffs for the Responder and the Proposer corresponding to the offered contracts. To facilitate comparisons with results from other ultimatum games, instead of focusing on the wage, we will mainly focus on the Responder's payoff corresponding to the wage and effort level of the proposed contract, x_R, as this parallels the "proposed amount" in the traditional ultimatum game. As was mentioned earlier, the payoffs of the Responders and Proposers depend directly on the wage and the effort level specified in the contract (see equations 1 and 2), and both the Responders and the Proposers are made aware of the corresponding payoffs while making an offer or accepting an offer.

In the (1–1) treatment, the average Responder's payoff corresponding to the proposed wage is 15.9 in game 1 and 14.4 in game 2. In the (3–3) treatment, which is only played as game 2, the average corresponding Responder's payoff is 15.6. Figure 3.1 shows the distribution of the Responder's corresponding payoff in the two treatments. It is clear that in both treatments most Proposers offer a wage that corresponds to a Responder's payoff that is strictly higher than the bare minimum amount predicted by the "classical" subgame perfect equilibrium. In fact, for game 1 of treatment (1–1) and for game 2 of treatment (3–3) the offered contracts correspond to a division of surplus in which the Responder receives more than half of the surplus: the offers correspond to the Responder receiving respectively 69 percent and 64 percent of surplus. In game 2 of treatment (1–1) this share is lower, at 46 percent.

A t-test shows that the average Responder's payoffs corresponding to the offered contracts are not significantly different from each other.[8] Furthermore, the non-parametric Kolmogorov-Smirnov equality-of-distributions test shows that there is no significant difference in the distribution of proposed payoffs for the Responders between the (1–1) treatment in game 1 and the (3–3) treatment in game 2 ($p = 0.116$). However, the difference between the (1–1) treatment in game 2 and the (3–3) treatment in game 2 is significant at a 10 percent level ($p = 0.054$).

Proposers can refrain from making offers, but rarely do so in the (1–1) treatment: this happens in only 3.0 percent of the cases in game 1 and never in game 2. In game 1 the number of non-offers decreases over time: in periods 2–5, there are only one or two Proposers each period not making an offer. In the (3–3) treatment, where Proposers can make separate offers to three Responders, the number of non-offers is considerably higher, at 10.8 percent.[9] However, in practice it is rare for a Responder to

Table 3.4
Average offered wages, corresponding payoffs and surplus, the share of offers accepted and the realized payoffs and surplus.

	Average wage offered	Average corresponding payoffs (share of surplus)		Average corresponding surplus	Share of offers accepted	Average realized payoffs (share of surplus)		Average realized surplus
		Responder	Proposer			Responder	Proposer	
(1–1) Game 1	20.5	15.9 (69%)	12.5 (31%)	28.4	81.3%	13.4 (77%)	8.7 (23%)	22.1
(1–1) Game 2	20.0	14.4 (46%)	17.8 (54%)	32.2	75.7%	10.7 (46%)	13.9 (54%)	24.6
(3–3) Game 2	20.4	15.6 (64%)	13.1 (36%)	28.8	35.9%* (90.3%)**	15.6 (57%)	11.5 (43%)	27.1

Surplus is equal to the sum of the Responder's payoff (x_R) and the Proposer's payoff (x_P), and depends on the effort level demanded (see table 3.1). The percentages in the parentheses show the share of the payoffs as a share of the surplus. The share of offers accepted is reported as a share of all offers made, and does not include cases where the Proposer did not make an offer to a particular worker. In the (1–1) treatment Proposers made offers in almost all periods (in game 1 the offer rate is 97.0% and in game 2 the offer rate is 100.0%), while in treatment (3–3) the offer rate is 89.2%, meaning that some Proposers did not make offers to some Responders. The realized payoffs and surplus figures are averaged over all Proposers and Responders and includes Proposers and Responders without a contract (and therefore a zero payoff). The amounts are reported in "points." One point is equal to 0.05 Ghana cedis (which equals approximately US$0.02 at the time of the experiment).

* Represents the acceptance rate of an offer, given that the offer was presented to the Responder. By construction, when Proposers make multiple offers, this figure cannot be 100%, as Responders that receive multiple offers automatically reject the offers they do not accept.

** Represents the share of Responders accepting one of the offers presented to them, or equivalently, the share of Proposers who have one of their offers accepted.

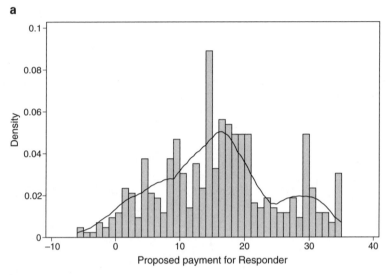

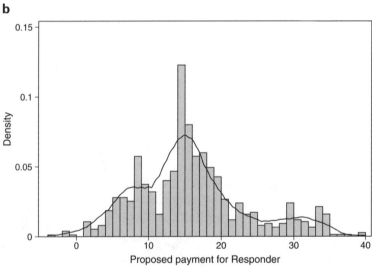

Figure 3.1
The Responder's payoffs corresponding to the proposed offers in the (1–1) treatment (a) and the (3–3) treatment (b). Figure a includes data from all periods in both game 1 and 2 (both five-period games); figure b includes only data from all periods in game 2 (the (3–3) treatment was only conducted in game 2). Solid line represents a kernel density estimate using an Epanechnikov kernel function.

not receive a single offer at all during a trading period: this happened in 1.33 percent of the cases.

Table 3.5 shows fixed-effects reduced-form regression estimates of the treatment effect on the proposed payment. Regression 1 shows the treatment effect, without accounting for the sequencing of the treatments. (The (3–3) treatment is only played as the second game; see table 3.3). The estimate is positive but not significantly different from zero ($p = 0.664$).

Regression 2 includes an indicator variable to control for the sequencing of the treatments. The coefficient for the treatment effect is positive and significant at a 5 percent significance level. The coefficient for being in the second game is negative and significant as well. This indicates that, without competition, proposed payments in the second game tend to be lower. However, introducing competition cancels this decrease and is associated with higher proposed payments by the Proposer; on average the proposed contribution is 3.0 points higher. Including indicators for the period of the game, as is done in Regression 3, does not change these coefficients. These indicators are not significantly different from zero, which suggests that there are no strong time trends within the game periods.

Acceptances

The fifth column in table 3.4 shows the share of offers that were accepted in each treatment and game. The acceptance rate in the (1–1) treatments in game 1 and game 2 are respectively 79 percent and 76 percent, which means that 21 percent and 24 percent of the offers are rejected. In the (3–3) treatment, Responders could choose offers from multiple Proposers, and thus the acceptance rate for a particular offer is lower, at 36 percent, as they automatically rejected the offers from Proposers they did not choose. However, the share of Responders that accepted any offer in a given period is higher, at 90 percent, and this figure is significantly higher than in the (1–1) treatments (the p values of the t-test of the difference of the means are 0.0001 and 0.0008 for treatment (1–1) in respectively game 1 and 2). Competition therefore leads to a higher number of contracts.

There is a positive and significant correlation between the Responder's payoff corresponding to the proposed offer and acceptance of the offer. Table 3.6 shows a linear probability model regression of acceptance on the proposed Responder's payoff. From regression 1 we can see that in the (1–1) treatment an increase in the proposed payoff is, on average, associated with an increase in probability of 1.61 percent of accepting the

Table 3.5
Reduced-form estimates of the proposed Responder's Payoff. Dependent variable: x_R (proposed responder's payoff).

	(1)	(2)	(3)
Competition (3–3)	0.241	2.979**	2.977**
	(0.544)	(1.057)	(1.056)
Second game		-2.738**	-2.721**
		(0.944)	(0.938)
Period 2			0.752
			(0.502)
Period 3			0.620
			(0.496)
Period 4			0.574
			(0.495)
Period 5			-0.178
			(0.640)
Constant	15.48*	15.64*	15.28*
	(0.476)	(0.458)	(0.683)
Observations	1176	1176	1176
R^2	0.642	0.645	0.647
Adjusted R^2	0.617	0.621	0.621
Proposer fixed effects	Yes	Yes	Yes

$*\ p < 0.10;\ **\ p < 0.05;\ ***\ p < 0.01$
The dependent variable is the Responder's payoff corresponding to the proposed wage and effort level. "Competition (3-3)" is an indicator variable indicating whether the observation was in the competition treatment (3–3). "Second game" indicates that this observation was from the second game (i.e. the second set of five periods), see also table 3.3. "Period 2-5" indicates the period within the game. The robust standard errors are clustered at the session-game level and are reported in parentheses.

offer. In regression 2 we control for the sequencing of the treatments by including an indicator variable for game 2 as well as the interaction between the proposed payoff and whether the observation is from game 2. In regressions 3 and 4 we also include observations from the (3–3) treatment, but we exclude observations where Responders had to choose from more than one offer.[10] Again, we find a positive correlation between the proposed Responder's payoff and the acceptance of the offer.

Surplus

Who captures the benefits from competition? In principle, both employers and workers could benefit from competition—at least, they can benefit if competition leads more workers to accept offers, which is beneficial to the employers as well.

The rightmost two columns in table 3.4 show the actual realized payoffs and total surplus. We see that the game 2 (3–3) treatment is associated with the highest realized surplus.[11] This is due primarily to a higher rate of offer acceptance by Responders. In game 2, responders fare better in the treatment with competition: in the game 2 (3–3) treatment they receive a higher share of the surplus than in the game 2 (1–1) treatment (57 percent versus 46 percent) and a higher absolute payoff (15.6 versus 10.7).

The absolute and relative earnings of the Proposers are higher in the two game 2 treatments than in game 1 (1–1). The process by which this is achieved differs, however. In the game 2 (11) treatment, Proposers lower their offers and demand higher levels of effort relative to game 1 (1–1). It appears that in the no-competition case Proposers learn to be more demanding, even though this tends to reduce the proportion of accepted offers. In contrast, in game 2 (3–3) offers are kept at the same level as in game 1 (1–1), but we observe an increase in the share of Responders that accept an offer. It therefore appears that Responders respond to increased competition by becoming more accommodating.

Table 3.7 shows the reduced-form estimates of the effects of the treatment on the payoff of the Responder, the payoff of the Proposer, and the total surplus. Responder and Proposer fixed effects are included. The coefficient of the impact of the competition treatment (3–3) on the payoff of the Responder is positive, but only statistically significant at the 10 percent level ($p = 0.066$). For the payoff of the Proposer, this coefficient is negative, but not significant at the 10 percent level ($p = 0.562$). For the total surplus, this coefficient is positive, but not significant at the 10 percent level ($p = 0.533$).

Table 3.6
Linear probability model of acceptance.

Dependent variable: Acceptance of offer by Proposer	Panel A: All offers in treatment (1–1)		Panel B: All offers in treatment (1–1) and sole remaining offers in (3–3)	
	(1)	(2)	(3)	(4)
Proposed payoff	0.0161 ***	0.0192 ***	0.0146 ***	0.0160 ***
	(0.00247)	(0.00207)	(0.00241)	(0.00303)
Proposed payoff × Game 2		-0.0142 *		-0.0117
		(0.00653)		(0.00715)
Proposed payoff × Competition (3–3)				0.0128
				(0.00951)
Competition (3–3)			0.0152	-0.172
			(0.0476)	(0.130)
Game 2	0.0285	0.246 ***	0.0215	0.196 **
	(0.0591)	(0.0622)	(0.0547)	(0.0823)
Constant	0.549 ***	0.498 ***	0.581 ***	0.559 ***
	(0.0495)	(0.0393)	(0.0461)	(0.0535)
Fixed effects	Yes	Yes	Yes	Yes
Observations	427	427	551	551
R^2	0.323	0.333	0.301	0.307
Adjusted R^2	0.178	0.188	0.189	0.193

* $p < 0.10$; ** $p < 0.05$; *** $p < 0.01$
The dependent variable is a binary variable whether the offer is accepted (1 = accepted, 0 = rejected). Panel A includes observations from treatment (1–1) only, while panel B also includes acceptance decisions from treatment (3–3) where only one offer was available to the Responder ("sole remaining offers"). The "proposed payoff" is the Responder's payoff corresponding to the wage and effort level offered in the proposed contract. "Competition" is an indicator variable indicating the (3–3) treatment. "Game 2" is an indicator variable indicating the second set of five periods. The robust standard errors are clustered at the session-game level and are reported in parentheses.

Table 3.7
Reduced-form estimates of the treatment effects on the actual payoff of the
Responder and the Proposer, and the total surplus (the sum of both payoffs).

Dependent variable	(1) Payoff Responder	(2) Payoff Proposer	(3) Total surplus
Competition (3–3)	8.237*	−1.330	2.970
	(4.155)	(2.241)	(4.653)
Game 2	−5.457	4.357**	1.343
	(3.923)	(2.001)	(4.539)
Constant	13.43***	8.697***	22.13***
	(0.578)	(0.267)	(0.681)
Observations	740	740	740
R^2	0.355	0.391	0.264
Adjusted R^2	0.282	0.322	0.181
Fixed effects	Responder	Proposer	Proposer

$* p < 0.10; ** p < 0.05; *** p < 0.01$
"Competition (3-3)" is an indicator variable indicating whether the observation
was in the competition treatment (3–3). "Game 2" indicates that this
observation was from the second game (i.e. the second set of five periods), see
also table 3.3. Standard errors are clustered on the session-game level and are
reported in parentheses.

3.5   Conclusion and Discussion

The institution of wage employment is less prevalent in Ghana than it is
in developed countries: less than a quarter of the working population
in Ghana is wage employed. We therefore expect differences in people's
perceptions of wage employment. By framing our experiment explicitly
in labor-market terms, we encouraged our subjects to think of the ultimatum game in a context of wage employment and to use the heuristics they
considered applicable in such a context.

We confirm the main earlier findings of the ultimatum game: Proposers make offers that are strictly higher than what rational utility maximizing theory would tell us. Earlier findings typically find that Proposer's
propose to the Responders a share of surplus of 40–50 percent (Cardenas
and Carpenter 2008). An earlier ultimatum-game experiment in Accra
conducted by Henrich et al. (2006) with urban workers found a proposed
Responder's share of 44 percent. In our experiment, the offers made

by the Proposers correspond on average to a Responder's share of 69 percent in treatment (1–1) in game 1, of 46 percent in treatment (1–1) in game 2 and of 64 percent in treatment (3–3) in game 2. Apart from the value in treatment (1–1) in game 2, these values are higher than the values found by Henrich et al.

The theory tells us that introducing competition in the ultimatum game increases offers, as Proposes compete for the Responders with lower reservation wages. Besides this, winner's curse can increase offers: just feeling the pressure of competition might lead to overbidding, as participants care more about making sure they edge out their competitors than whether this is rationally the best bid. Auction studies have noted the prevalence of such winner's curses, particularly when competition is increased (Kagel and Levin 1986).

We find some evidence that competition increases offers. This increase tilts the balance even more in favor of the Responders, who are now receiving a larger share of the surplus. However, at the same time, competition leads to acceptance of a higher number of contracts, which increases total surplus. This means that, on an aggregate level, competition is beneficial.[12]

What happens when there are competition effects resulting from excess demand or supply—for example, when the number of Proposers and the number of Responders are not equal—is a separate question. In labor markets, an excess or a shortage of labor supply, depending on the type of position and the required qualifications, is possible. Experiments with gift-exchange games have shown that the market power resulting from excess demand or supply influences the division of surplus in favor of the side of the market with market power, but does not necessarily affect the size of the surplus and the principle of gift exchange (Brown et al. 2012; Brandts and Charness 2004). In this chapter we focus on the competition effects that arise from moving away from bilateral one-to-one interactions to consider multilateral many-to-many interactions. To rule out market-power considerations, we have set the number of Proposers and the number of Responders equal to each other.

We conjecture that the high offers by the employers in our experiment are influenced by our participant's perception of labor relations: for example, employers may feel that they have a responsibility toward the worker, while workers may see employers as in general better-off and may therefore be less concerned about the employers' payoffs.

We find a similar result in a companion experiment in which we let students in Accra play a gift-exchange game instead of an ultimatum game (Davies and Fafchamps 2015b). The gift-exchange game is similar in set-up to our version of the ultimatum game, but it introduces contractual incompleteness on the side of the worker: the worker can now exert a lower effort than what the employer asked for, and the employer cannot enforce the request. As in other gift-exchange games (see, e.g., Fehr et al. 1993, 1998a,b; Brown et al. 2004; Charness and Kuhn 2011), the employers make offers that are above the bare minimum. We find a pattern of conditional reciprocity for a large share of the workers, who reciprocate a high offer with high effort, but a substantial minority of workers do not reciprocate. However, we do not see a pattern of conditional reciprocity for the employers: contrary to earlier gift-exchange games, low-effort workers are not punished by the employers in the next periods. Only a few employers lower the wage in response to low effort. As a result, employers tend to make losses or very small earnings, while workers capture most of the surplus. A follow-up experiment confirms this behavior (Davies and Fafchamps 2015a). This difference in conditional reciprocity between workers and employers is surprising, since assignment was random.

The results from our experiments seem to suggest that identity and framing matter, and that they lead to more generous and forgiving behavior on behalf of the employer. In our ultimatum game we find that a substantial share of employers offer the Responder a share of surplus of more than 50 percent. Furthermore, we find some evidence that competition increases this generosity further. Follow-up experiments are needed to ascertain the respective roles of identity and framing.

Acknowledgments

These experimental sessions are part of a wider study on Ghanaian entrepreneurship. This document is an output from research funding by the UK Department for International Development (DFID) as part of the iiG, a research program to study how to improve institutions for pro-poor growth in Africa and in South Asia. The views expressed are not necessarily those of DFID. Funding from the Economic and Social Research Council (ESRC) and the Oxford Social Sciences Doctoral Training Centre is gratefully acknowledged. Many thanks to Václav Těhle for excellent research assistance, and also thanks to Andrew Kerr and Denise Gray for their assistance during trial sessions of this experiment. Furthermore, we would like to thank Moses Awoonor-Williams for his role in helping out with the logistical matters, as well as our local team in the field, in particular Eric Agyekum and Bismark Owusu Tetteh Nortey. We would like to thank the participants of the CESifo Conference on Social Economics (Munich) and members of the Oxford Firms & Development Research Group for helpful comments.

Notes

1. Depending on the profession and the labor-market situation, some bargaining over the wage or the job description might take place. The ultimatum game does not allow for this type of negotiation. Often, the resulting bargain is not drastically different from the initial wage offer made by the employer.

2. Some of these papers include a treatment where workers or responders have no effort choice, such as the (C) treatment in Brown et al. 2004 and Brown et al. 2012 and the (1C) treatment in Davies and Fafchamps 2015b and Davies and Fafchamps 2015a.

3. Note that if Proposers do not want to share their offers with the other Proposers, they can wait with making their offers until they are offered to revise their offers.

4. This provides a way for Proposers and Responders to develop a bilateral relationship, even in the (3–3) treatment. In the (1–1) treatment, this rehiring mechanism leads to a contract in 13.6% of the Proposer-Responder pairs. In the (3–3) treatment, this leads to a contract for 11.7% of Proposers.

5. Note that if $x_R < x_P$ and $x_P > 0$ this function is increasing in x_R, since

$$\frac{d}{dx} \frac{x_R}{x_P - x_R} = \frac{x_P}{(x_R - x_P)^2} > 0.$$

6. If the Responder rejects the offer, this means that the Responder cares so much about the inequality that is to the disadvantage of the Proposer that he is are willing to reject the division proposed by the Proposer, such that both of them receive a payoff of zero and they achieve full equality. For example, for a sufficient high value of β_R, the Responder would reject a division of 39 points to the Responder and 1 to the Proposer, because of the inequality in payoffs. This is not very likely. Rejection of offers like these is not widely documented. Charness and Haruvy (2002) note that in the ultimatum game only a meaningful estimation of α can be achieved. In the Fehr-Schmidt model β is bounded at 1, which rules out rejection of such offers as long as both payoffs are positive.

7. Suppose that a Responder accepts an offer asking for medium effort, with payoffs $\tilde{x}_P$ and $\tilde{x}_R$. This means that $\tilde{x}_R / (\tilde{x}_P - \tilde{x}_R) > \alpha_R$ in order for the Responder to have accepted this offer. (See equation 5.) The total surplus of this transaction was $\tilde{x}_P + \tilde{x}_R = 18$ points. If the Proposer demanded high effort (with a surplus of 34 points) instead of medium effort, and divided the difference in surplus of 16 points equally between the Responder and Proposer (such that $x_P = \tilde{x}_P + 8$ and $x_R = \tilde{x}_R + 8$, the Responder would have accepted this offer as well, since

$$\frac{\tilde{x}_R + 8}{(\tilde{x}_P + 8) - (\tilde{x}_R + 8)} = \frac{\tilde{x}_R + 8}{\tilde{x}_P - \tilde{x}_R} > \frac{\tilde{x}_R}{\tilde{x}_P - \tilde{x}_R} \geq \alpha_R.$$

This high-effort offer Pareto dominates the corresponding medium-effort offer.

8. The p value of the difference between (1–1) in game 1 and (3–3) in game 2 is 0.603 and the p value of the difference between (1–1) in game 2 and (3–3) in game 2 is 0.209.

9. Every instance in which a Proposer could have made an offer to a particular Responder, but did not do so, is counted as a non-offer.

10. In the case that the Responder has more than one offer, the offer(s) that the Responder did not choose are rejected automatically, as the Responder can choose only one offer. To ensure comparability with treatment (1–1), we excluded these cases.

11. Note that even though 90.3% of the Proposers have one of their offers accepted, the total surplus does not equal $0.903 \times 34 \approx 30.7$, with 34 the surplus associated with high effort. The main reason for this is that not all Proposers demand the highest level of effort.

12. Competition should not be confused with market imbalance, which is a common occurrence in labor markets (e.g., too many or too few qualified applicants for the available positions). Our experiment is not designed to investigate the effect of market imbalance; gift-exchange experiments have already examined this issue. Excess demand or excess supply has indeed been shown to affect the division of surplus in favor of the short side of the market (Brown et al. 2012; Brandts and Charness 2004). Existing experiments, however, have not sought to disentangle the effect of competition from that of market imbalance. In this chapter we focus on the competition effects that arise as a result of moving from a bilateral to a multilateral interaction. To isolate this effect from that of market imbalance, we have deliberately set the number of Proposers and the number of Responders equal to each other.

References

Brandts, J. and Charness, G. 2004. Do labour market conditions affect gift exchange? Some experimental evidence. *Economic Journal* 114 (1999): 684–708.

Brown, M., A. Falk, and E. Fehr. 2004. Relational contracts and the nature of market interactions. *Econometrica* 72 (3): 747–780.

Brown, M., A. Falk, and E. Fehr. 2012. Competition and relational contracts: The role of unemployment as a disciplinary device. *Journal of the European Economic Association* 10 (4): 887–907.

Cardenas, J. C., and J. Carpenter. 2008. Behavioural development economics: Lessons from field labs in the developing world. *Journal of Development Studies* 44 (3): 311–338.

Charness, G., G. R. Frechette, and J. H. Kagel. 2004. How robust is laboratory gift exchange? *Experimental Economics* 7 (2): 189–205.

Charness, G., and E. Haruvy. 2002. Altruism, equity, and reciprocity in a gift-exchange experiment: An encompassing approach. *Games and Economic Behavior* 40 (2): 203–231.

Charness, G., and P. Kuhn. 2011. *Lab Labor: What Can Labor Economists Learn from the Lab?* Volume 4. Elsevier.

Davies, E., and M. Fafchamps. 2015a. Pledging, Praising, Shaming: Experimental Labour Markets in Ghana. CSAE Working Paper.

Davies, E., and M. Fafchamps. 2015b. When No Bad Deed Goes Punished: A Relational Contracting Experiment in Ghana. CSAE Working Paper.

Fehr, E., E. Kirchler, A. Weichbold, and S. Gächter. 1998a. When social norms overpower competition: Gift exchange in experimental labor markets. *Journal of Labor Economics* 16 (2): 324–351.

Fehr, E., G. Kirchsteiger, and A. Riedl. 1993. Does fairness prevent market clearing? An experimental investigation. *Quarterly Journal of Economics* 108 (2): 437–459.

Fehr, E., G. Kirchsteiger, and A. Riedl. 1998b. Gift exchange and reciprocity in competitive experimental markets. *European Economic Review* 42: 1–34.

Fehr, E., and K. M. Schmidt. 1999. A theory of fairness, competition, and cooperation. *Quarterly Journal of Economics* 114 (3): 817–868.

Ghana Statistical Service. 2008. Ghana Living Standards Survey Report of the Fifth Round (GLSS 5).

Ghana Statistical Service. 2014. Ghana Living Standards Survey Round 6 (GLSS 6). Labour Force Report.

Güth, W., R. Schmittberger, and B. Schwarze. 1983. An experimental analysis of ultimatum bargaining. *Journal of Economic Behavior and Organization* 3: 367–388.

Güth, W., and R. Tietz. 1990. Ultimatum bargaining behaviour: A survey and comparison of experimental results. *Journal of Economic Psychology* 11: 417–449.

Henrich, J., R. McElreath, A. Barr, J. Ensminger, C. Barrett, A. Bolyanatz, J. C. Cardenas, et al. 2006. Costly punishment across human societies. *Science* 312 (5781): 1767–1770.

Kagel, J. H., and D. Levin. 1986. The winner's curse and public information in common value auctions. *American Economic Review* 76 (5): 894–920.

Roth, A. E., V. Prasnikar, M. Okuno-Fujiwara, and S. Zamir. 1991. Bargaining and market behavior in Jerusalem, Ljubljana, Pittsburgh, and Tokyo: An experimental study. *American Economic Review* 81 (5): 1068–1095.

4

(US)

Why Give Away Your Wealth? An Analysis of the Billionaires' View

Jana Sadeh, Mirco Tonin, and Michael Vlassopoulos   D14 D64

B55 D91

Philanthropic giving by the extremely wealthy is and has been historically an important phenomenon.[1] The philanthropic activities of extremely rich individuals, such as Andrew Carnegie and John D. Rockefeller, have not only benefitted many people and causes but have also inspired new generations of philanthropists. Moreover, because of the well-documented tendency in recent years for income to become more concentrated in the United States and other countries (Alvaredo et al. 2013), one would expect that the charitable sector will become increasingly reliant on the contributions of those in the upper tail of the income distribution to sustain its activities. Despite their importance, not much is known about the motivations for giving of the extremely wealthy, largely because of the paucity of data (typically surveys do not cover them).

In this chapter we attempt to shed some light on the characteristics and motivations of the very rich philanthropists. We focus on the Giving Pledge, a recent large-scale philanthropic initiative by billionaires that has received a lot of media attention because of the celebrity status of the founders and some of the contributors. (See, e.g., *Economist* 2012; Loomis 2010.) The Giving Pledge is a philanthropic venture, launched in June 2010 by Warren Buffet and by Bill and Melinda Gates, that encourages billionaires, from the US initially and worldwide later, to donate at least half of their wealth to charitable causes of the pledger's choice. As of May 2014, 127 families and individuals from twelve countries with an estimated net worth of $600 billion have signed the Giving Pledge.[2] There are a few unique features of the Giving Pledge that are worth emphasizing: The pledge is just a moral commitment, and there is no legal obligation deriving from it. Pledgers are invited to state publicly their motivations for taking the pledge. The publicness of the action indicates that the intention of those who started the initiative is for it to carry symbolic value and to act as an example for others to follow. What is important about the Giving Pledge for our purposes is that pledgers have left written testimonies for what inspires their philanthropy. This fact offers us a unique window into the philanthropic motivations of the extremely rich.

In recent years, a large body of literature in economics and other social sciences has identified a set of factors that lie behind philanthropic behavior. (See, e.g., Andreoni 2006; Vesterlund 2006.) These factors include altruism and warm glow (Andreoni 1990; Ribar and Wilhelm 2002; Tonin and Vlassopoulos 2014), social recognition (Andreoni and Bernheim 2009; Ariely et al. 2009), and self-image (Tonin and Vlassopoulos 2013).[3] But billionaires may have separate reasons for giving not shared by the rest of society. For example, a billionaire has the means to individually make a significant impact on an existing philanthropic cause or even carve a niche for a new one. Another distinct motivation for philanthropy, given the extreme level of wealth accumulated by this group of people, is that they may have reached the point where all their material needs have already been satisfied and so further spending on themselves (or their family) may not add to their happiness (Kahneman and Deaton 2010). In some cases it can even be argued that extreme wealth may have a negative effect on well-being—for instance, because inheriting it might spoil their heirs. Feelings of moral obligation to share their wealth can also be particularly strong, especially if wealth is not just the outcome of hard work but can also be attributed to other factors beyond an individual's control, be it sheer luck or some more spiritual blessing (Benabou and Tirole 2006).

The motivations just mentioned are not, of course, the only motivations that may spur giving by the wealthy. One can think also of self-serving reasons. For instance, philanthropic giving in the US and elsewhere is associated with preferential tax treatment, and some of the giving by the rich may be at least partly driven by such motivators (Auten et al. 2000). There may also be reputational/social recognition benefits of giving that are unique to this group, such as the desire to leave a lasting legacy. Also, one gains a certain social status and opportunities to enter prestigious social networks from being a recognizable philanthropist, which may also have positive spillover effects on the main professional activity. Such types of private returns may also drive some of the observed philanthropic activity of the wealthy. Some of these motivations are indeed mentioned in the pledge letters, but whether the letters fully reflect their true relevance is of course questionable. What we can analyze is what billionaires mention in their public letters as motivating their philanthropic activity. Given the importance of this specific group of people for the promotion of charitable causes and the paucity of data available, we believe this is an important aspect to analyze.

In this chapter we first investigate what personal characteristics of billionaires are good predictors for becoming a Pledger. Next, we undertake a textual analysis of the pledgers' letters and classify the expressed motivations for giving into ten categories. We then correlate these motivations with various personal characteristics of the pledgers. The main insight obtained from our analysis is that pledgers are more likely to be self-made billionaires than to have inherited their fortunes, and that their philanthropy is impact-driven.

Previous attempts to understand the philanthropic motivations of the rich and the extremely rich (Ostrower 1997; Schervish 2008; Page et al. 2011; Harvey et al. 2011; Center on Philanthropy 2012; Acs 2013) involve primarily case studies, interviews, and a few small surveys. We are aware of only one study in economics that has analyzed Giving Pledge signatories (Coupe and Monteiro 2013), and it focuses entirely on whether the nature of an individual's wealth—self-made or inherited—mattered for the decision to take the Pledge. Coupe and Monteiro used data on the characteristics of billionaires from the *Forbes* list of billionaires. Consistent with our results, they find, after controlling for various factors, that self-made billionaires are significantly more likely than those who inherited their fortunes to take the Giving Pledge.

The chapter is organized as follows: Section 4.1 provides more details about the Giving Pledge. Section 4.2 analyzes the likelihood of becoming a pledger. Section 4.3 investigates pledgers' motivations. Section 4.4 concludes the chapter.

4.1   What Is the Giving Pledge?

The Giving Pledge is a movement that encourages the wealthiest people in the world to commit to giving more than half their wealth to philanthropic causes during their life, or at the time of their death. The Pledge, the brainchild of Warren Buffett and Bill and Melinda Gates, was launched in June 2010. There were two motivations behind the Pledge: to encourage billionaire philanthropists to be an inspiration for giving by serving as role models to other billionaires and to create a group of Pledgers to serve as a forum for the dissemination of best practice among philanthropists (Giving Pledge 2014). The Pledge does not influence where these philanthropic efforts are to be directed; it requires only a public commitment to give away more than half of an individual's or a family's wealth. It began by focusing on billionaires based in the United States, but in 2013, after interest was expressed from outside the US, the Pledge expanded to include billionaires from all over the world.

The launch of the Pledge coincided with the aftermath of the 2008–09 economic downturn. The impact of the downturn was felt by philanthropic organizations, donations falling by 3.6 percent in the US in 2009 (Banjo 2010). The Pledge started out with 40 pledgers (some individuals, some families) in August 2010. By the end of that year the number of pledgers had grown to 57. In 2011 there were 60 pledgers, and in 2012 there were 81. The year 2013 saw the addition of pledgers from outside the US and the largest annual increase in the number of pledgers, the number reaching 122 by December 2013 and including pledgers from twelve more countries. In 2014 the number of pledgers reached 127.[4]

While the general response of the media has been supportive of the Pledge, it is not without its critics. Concerns have been raised about whether the initiative is sufficiently addressing the urgent needs of today, insofar as many of the pledgers are putting their money into foundations that may not disburse the funds for many years. Others are concerned that the Pledge might just be a public-relations exercise (Lewis 2014). There has been no effort to identify the actual benefit of the money that is being spent, and there has been no follow up to confirm whether the pledgers are keeping their word. Moreover, the number of pledgers is still less than a tenth of the total of the world's billionaires (ibid).

4.2   Who Becomes a Pledger?

In this section, we assess which personal characteristics of billionaires affect the likelihood of joining the Giving Pledge. To this end, we use the Hurun Global Rich List, a list of the world's US-dollar billionaires compiled by the Hurun Report, a Chinese publishing group.[5] The list specifies each billionaire's net worth, age, gender, and country and city of residence, the names of the industry and the company that are the primary source of his or her fortune, and whether the billionaire is self-made or inherited his or her wealth.

The Hurun Global Rich List contains 1,867 entries. Insofar as the Giving Pledge has until recently aimed at recruiting only American billionaires, we select from the list those with US residence, leaving us with 481 entries. In most cases, these entries represent individuals. There are, however, some cases in which an entry is a name followed by "and family" (e.g., "Laurene Powell Jobs and family") and cases in which an entry is a couple (e.g., "Tom and Judy Love"). In the "and family" entries, personal data such as gender and age refer to the individual named; in the entries for couples, data for both members of the couple are listed.

In the population we study here, the average (and median) age is 67. The youngest billionaire, Evan Spiegel of Snapchat, is 23; the oldest, David Rockefeller of Standard Oil, is 99. Ages are missing for eight entries, mostly involving couples, while two different ages are provided for an entry involving a couple. As a result, the final number of entries in our sample is 472. Of these 472 entries, only 52 (11 percent) represent females. The average net worth is $4.6 billion (median: $2.5 billion); the largest, $68 billion, is held by Bill Gates of Microsoft; the lowest is, by definition, $1 billion. Seventy-two percent of the entries are classified as self-made, and 28 percent as having inherited their wealth.

When we matched our list of billionaires with the list of pledgers using personal names, we found that 76 (16 percent) of the 472 had signed the pledge. (As was mentioned earlier, in 2013, when we conducted the analysis, the Giving Pledge had 122 signatories and that, of these, 88 were US residents. The discrepancy with the 76 pledgers found in the list of billionaires is due to the fact that four of the pledgers are deceased and that many pledgers are no longer billionaires, in many cases because they have already given away most of their wealth.)

Regression Analysis

Using the matched data described above, we can investigate which among the personal characteristics of billionaires in our dataset—wealth (both in US dollars and in terms of its origin), age, gender—are good predictors of the decision to join the pledge. What to expect in terms of sign of the effect of these factors is not clear *a priori*. For instance, having more resources, wealthier people may be more likely to give away money and thus more likely to sign the pledge; but, insofar as the pledge requires signers to give away at least half of their accumulated wealth, it is more "expensive" for wealthier people to join, so the overall effect is unclear.

In table 4.1 we report some regression results. For ease of interpretation, we use ordinary least-squares regressions. We first look at the effect of each of the four explanatory variables on the likelihood of joining the pledge separately. Being a self-made billionaire (column 1) and being richer (column 4) increase the probability of pledging. In particular, the probability increases by 19 percentage points for self-made billionaires,

Table 4.1
Who becomes a pledger.

	(1)	(2)	(3)	(4)	(5)	(6)
Self-made	0.190***				0.186***	0.183***
	[0.026]				[0.026]	[0.026]
Female		−0.138***			−0.041	−0.039
		[0.033]			[0.034]	[0.033]
Age			0.001		0.001	0.000
			[0.001]		[0.001]	[0.001]
Net worth (billions of US dollars)				0.007***	0.008***	
				[0.003]	[0.002]	
Net worth 2q						0.000
						[0.046]
Net worth 3q						0.004
						[0.046]
Net worth 4q						0.077
						[0.051]
Constant	0.023*	0.176***	0.127	0.127***	−0.042	−0.021
	[0.013]	[0.019]	[0.088]	[0.020]	[0.082]	[0.087]
Observations	472	472	472	472	472	472
R^2	0.054	0.014	0.000	0.02	0.079	0.063

Dependent variable: Pledge (=1 if Yes). OLS regression. "net worth xq" are dummy variables indicating whether net worth is in x quartile. Robust standard errors in brackets. ***, **, and * denote significance at 1%, 5%, and 10% level, respectively.

while it increases by 7 percentage points for every $10 billion of extra wealth. Age (column 3) does not appear to have an effect, whereas being a female (column 2) has a negative effect. In column 5 we report the results of the multivariate regression in which we include all the explanatory variables. The coefficients for being self-made and for net worth are very similar as in the univariate regressions; however, there is no gender effect. This is because females are significantly more likely than males to have inherited their wealth; thus, if the dummy for self-made is omitted, gender picks up part of its effect. In column 6 we replace net worth with a series of dummies indicating the quartile of the wealth distribution to which each billionaire belongs. The coefficient for the richest among billionaires (i.e., those belonging to the fourth quartile in the wealth distribution) is positive and large, indicating that they are more likely to sign the pledge, but it is not statistically significant at conventional levels ($p = 0.13$).

Thus, all in all, we find evidence that self-made billionaires are more likely to join the pledge, and that there is some indication that the richer among billionaires are also more likely to join. It should be noted that signing the Giving Pledge in itself has a direct effect on wealth. Indeed, as has been mentioned, some of the pledgers no longer are billionaires, as they have given away most of their wealth. If pledging is positively correlated with giving away a vast proportion of one's wealth during one's lifetime, this would induce a negative bias between the likelihood of pledging and wealth.

4.3 What Motivates the Pledgers?

We now turn to the analysis of the motivation for taking the Giving Pledge. In this section, we consider all pledgers, regardless of their country of residence. We first discuss how we compile the data on the motivation of the pledgers, then provide some descriptives and analysis.

Data
The information we have on the pledgers includes basic demographics (age, gender, marital status, country of residence, ethnicity, education, number of children, religion, political views), plus information on net worth, industry and source of wealth (self-made or inherited), whether a charitable foundation has been established and whether the spouse is involved in the foundation. These data have been provided by Wealth-X,

a consultancy firm specialized in ultra-high-net-worth individuals,[6] but for several categories we have many missing values.

We combine this information with a textual analysis of pledge letters. Note that not all pledgers have written a letter yet. In particular, out of 122 pledgers, we have a letter for 96 (79 percent) of them. For each letter, we classified each sentence into a list of categories (to be discussed below). In particular, we conducted two independent classifications, one by one of the authors and the other by a research assistant. In this chapter, we consider all sentences that were categorized consistently in both classifications.

The ten categories we use are meant to capture the main possible motivations behind giving by billionaires (outlined in the introduction). Below we provide a list that includes the name of the category, a short description, and an example of a sentence belonging to it.

No need Mention the fact that even after giving away wealth, resources are enough to cover needs. Example: "The approach of my wife, Susie, and I to philanthropy is very simple. We do not believe that spending any more money on ourselves or our family would add anything to our happiness."

No inheritance Mention of disbelief in inherited wealth, of pernicious effects of being wealthy, or desire not to spoil children. Example: "My choice was to ruin my son's life by giving him money or giving 90+ percent to charity. Not much of a choice."

Warm glow Mention that giving brings joy or gives meaning to life, talk about passion for giving. Example: "Over the years, the emotional and psychological returns I have earned from charitable giving have been enormous. The more I do for others, the happier I am."

Impact Mention that giving is meant to address an issue or produce some change. Example: "As a philanthropist, I've also had the opportunity to see the impact private donations can have in other countries—and just how far each dollar can go. For instance, with private funding, we can prevent tens of millions of premature deaths caused by tobacco-related diseases and traffic accidents—just two areas where my foundation has been active."

Legacy Mention importance of leaving a bequest or legacy or of name being remembered. Example: "Giving also allows you to leave a legacy that many others will remember. Rockefeller, Carnegie, Frick, Vanderbilt, Stanford, Duke—we remember them more for the long-term effects of their philanthropy than for the companies they founded, or for their descendants."

Received example Mention that giving has been influenced by role models or by experiences of other givers. Example: "My earliest memories include my father's exhortations about how important it is to give back. These early teachings were ingrained in me, and a portion of the first dollars I earned, I gave away."

Provide example Mention that giving or pledging is done to encourage others to do the same. Example: "We hope to extend this legacy of giving not only within our family, but also to all of society."

Values Mention moral values or responsibility to give back. Example: "We are pleased to lend our names and philanthropic commitment to The Giving Pledge campaign. We have been extraordinarily blessed in life, and like the others who are participating in this effort, believe very strongly in giving back to the country, communities and causes that have been vital to shaping our lives and success."

Luck Recognize the role of good luck/fortune in generating wealth. Example: "My wealth has come from a combination of living in America, some lucky genes, and compound interest. Both my children and I won what I call the ovarian lottery."

Blessing Mention that wealth is a blessing or explicitly mention god, religion or afterlife. Example: "Coming from a relatively poor family and without the benefit of a formal tertiary education, I have been blessed with material success beyond my wildest imagination. Yes, I have worked hard and smart, but there are many who undoubtedly have worked harder and who are far smarter than I and yet have not achieved the same level of material success. My success could not have been possible without divine blessings."

This list is not exhaustive, in that other motivations are mentioned in the letters. For instance, one pledger mentions that giving is good for business,[7] and several emphasize the benefits of signing the Giving Pledge as a way "to share lessons, perspectives and best practices," or even its social aspect.[8] We believe, however, that the ten categories listed above capture the most important motivations for giving mentioned in the letters. Also, some of the sentences belong to more than one category. For instance, the sentence "Making a difference in people's lives—and seeing it with your own eyes—is perhaps the most satisfying thing you'll ever do. If you want to fully enjoy life—give" belongs to both the *Warm glow* category and the *Impact* category

Who Are the Pledgers?

Only about half of the pledges for which we have a letter are made on behalf of an individual (50 out of 96 cases); the rest are split between pledges done on behalf of a couple (35 cases) and pledges done on behalf of a family (11 cases). In the latter cases, the demographic data refer just to one person, usually the one who had the primary role in wealth accumulation.

The average age of pledgers is 69 years (median: 70). The oldest pledger is also the oldest American billionaire according to the list analyzed in the previous section (David Rockefeller); the youngest are Mark Zuckerberg and Dustin Moskovitz, both 30 and both with their fortune related to Facebook. Only four pledgers are female, although (as was mentioned above) in many cases the pledge is made on behalf of a couple or a whole family. Melinda Gates, for instance, is one of the initial promoters of the pledge, but the pledge is attributed to her husband, Bill Gates, who is the one who accumulated wealth through Microsoft. In terms of wealth, the average is $4.6 billion. The pledger with the highest net worth is also the richest US billionaire according to the list analyzed in the previous section, Bill Gates; the pledger with the lowest net worth is Charles Francis Feeney, whose net worth, after he gave away most of his fortune, is estimated at $5 million. In terms of the origin of wealth, the data source used here distinguishes between self-made (101 out of the 116 for whom we have data, 87 percent), inherited (eight cases, 7 percent), and a combination of the two (seven cases, 6 percent).

In terms of the commitment made through the pledge, one fourth of the letters contain a specific reference. In only one case is an absolute amount specified ($1 billion); the others indicate the share of the fortune to be given away. In most cases the committed amount is at least 90 percent of the estate, but several cases involve 100 percent. In three fourths of the cases the timing of the donation is mentioned, the vast majority indicating that donations will take place during the pledger's lifetime rather than after their death). Finally, in the majority of cases the pledge letter mentions the specific causes to which donations will be directed and the existence of a foundation to manage these philanthropic activities.

Motivations for Philanthropy
To summarize the relative importance of the different types of motivation discussed above, in figure 4.1 we display the fraction of pledgers that have mentioned each of the motivational categories in their letter. What we see is that "impact" features in 80 percent of the cases and is by far the most popular category. The next most popular category is "values," invoked by 40 percent of pledgers. "Warm glow" is mentioned in 35 percent of the cases. The rest of the categories appear in less than one-third of the letters.

To go beyond a simple mention and gain some insight into the weight pledgers put on each category in their letters, in figure 4.2 we plot the average share of classified text belonging to each category. In particular, for each letter we sum the number of characters devoted to each of the ten categories and then divide for the number of characters devoted to any of these categories in the letter. We then take the average across individuals. In this way we give equal weight to each letter, regardless of its total length. The sum across the ten categories is then, by construction, 1. Notice that for two of the letters we could not classify any part of the text in any of the ten categories, and therefore they are not considered in this section.[9]

In figure 4.2 one can see that at 43 percent, the category "Impact" is clearly dominant; the second, "Values," comes in at 12 percent. Perhaps not surprisingly, billionaires, when writing about their motivation for giving large amounts of money to charity, talk mostly about what kind

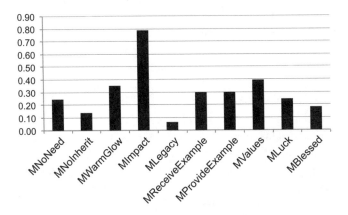

Figure 4.1
Fraction of pledgers mentioning each motivational category.

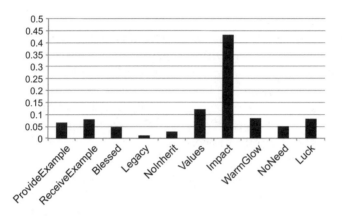

Figure 4.2
Motivational shares.

of changes they want to achieve. The joy of giving and the recognition that luck has played a role in the accumulation of wealth are also quite important, both at 8 percent. The desire to leave a legacy is rather marginal, perhaps because mentioning it may make one appear to be too self-serving.

In line with what we did in the previous section, we investigate here whether origin of wealth, amount of wealth, and age affect the stated motivations for giving. Because of the small number of women among pledgers, we cannot investigate the role of gender. We include in the "self-made" category only those classified as self-made, excluding those whose wealth is partly inherited and partly self-made.

Table 4.2 investigates whether mentioning in the letter a motivation belonging to one of the ten categories outlined above is related to the aforementioned variables. Again, for ease of interpretation, we estimate OLS regressions. What emerges is that being self-made is associated with a higher likelihood of mentioning the desire not to leave a large inheritance and the fact that luck has played a role in generating wealth as motivations for giving. This seems reasonable, insofar as people who inherited wealth are probably less likely to see this as an issue for the next generation and also may be less likely to experience at first hand the importance of luck in accumulating great fortunes (unless, of course, one considers "the ovarian lottery," as Warren Buffett does in his pledge letter). Age is related to a lower likelihood of mentioning values and to a higher likelihood of mentioning the joy of giving, although in this case

Table 4.2
Mentioning motivations.

Dependent variable	(1) No need	(2) No inherit	(3) Warm glow	(4) Impact	(5) Legacy	(6) Receive example	(7) Provide example	(8) Values	(9) Luck	(10) Blessed
Self-made	0.058	0.161***	0.048	-0.161	-0.032	-0.22	0.132	-0.181	0.223**	-0.102
	[0.123]	[0.045]	[0.147]	[0.104]	[0.083]	[0.157]	[0.124]	[0.157]	[0.105]	[0.135]
Age	-0.001	-0.002	0.007*	0.000	-0.001	0.001	-0.004	-0.009**	0.005	-0.003
	[0.004]	[0.003]	[0.003]	[0.003]	[0.002]	[0.004]	[0.003]	[0.004]	[0.003]	[0.003]
Net worth	0.002	-0.004**	0.005	0.004**	0.001	0.000	0.001	-0.001	0.000	0.003
(billions of US dollars)	[0.005]	[0.002]	[0.004]	[0.002]	[0.002]	[0.005]	[0.004]	[0.004]	[0.004]	[0.004]
Constant	0.246	0.145	-0.205	0.878***	0.177	0.425	0.463*	1.191***	-0.285	0.474
	[0.300]	[0.211]	[0.281]	[0.293]	[0.172]	[0.325]	[0.273]	[0.320]	[0.266]	[0.288]
Observations	92	92	92	92	92	92	92	92	92	92
R^2	0.008	0.044	0.049	0.027	0.009	0.028	0.026	0.068	0.044	0.025

Dependent variables: =1 if mentioned. OLS regression. Robust standard errors in brackets. ***, **, and * denote significance at 1%, 5%, and 10% level, respectively.

the coefficient is only marginally significant. Finally, higher-net-worth individuals are more likely to mention impact and less likely to mention the desire not to leave inheritance. Again, it seems reasonable that the focus on impact increases with the ability to have one—that is, with wealth.

Table 4.3 considers also the intensive margin, as the dependent variable in each regression is the share of classified text belonging to a given category. It confirms that self-made individuals write more, in relative terms, about the desire not to leave an inheritance and about the role of luck as motivations. They also write more about the desire to provide an example. Age is associated with less talk about values, net worth with less talk about the desire not to pass over excessive wealth to the next generation.[10]

4.4   Concluding Remarks

Our analysis indicates that an important consideration for the decision to pledge is the impact that the philanthropic activities will have. In fact, a businesslike attitude is often used in the pledge letters when pledgers describe their approach to philanthropy. For example, Eli and Edythe Broad state "[w]e view our grants as investments, and we expect a return—in the form of improved student achievement for our education reform work … ," Charles F. Feeney writes "[w]hile my approach to philanthropy has surely developed and matured through experience, fundamental guides for me have always been the same methods of working and values that served me well in my business career," and Bernard Marcus states "I must say that just because we were involved with charity we didn't lose our fundamental business acumen. Our staff insists on outcomes for every grant we make." From the point of view of a fundraiser, this would then suggest that an essential tool when approaching this type of potential donors is a detailed "business plan" clearly pointing out the objectives of the philanthropic activity and the necessary means to achieve them.

What also emerges from our analysis is that self-made billionaires are more likely than billionaires who inherited their fortunes to sign the Giving Pledge, and that their decision to do so it motivated somewhat differently. This finding raises some interesting questions regarding the future of philanthropic initiatives by the super-wealthy. Recently a great debate was sparked by the publication of Thomas Piketty's book *Capital in the Twenty-First Century* (2014). Piketty's book is about the increasing

Table 4.3
Intensity of motivations.

Dependent variable	(1) No need	(2) No inherit	(3) Warm glow	(4) Impact	(5) Legacy	(6) Receive example	(7) Provide example	(8) Values	(9) Luck	(10) Blessed
Self-made	0.02	0.032***	0.04	−0.12	−0.011	−0.074	0.047**	−0.046	0.097***	0.015
	[0.023]	[0.012]	[0.033]	[0.093]	[0.018]	[0.058]	[0.019]	[0.062]	[0.036]	[0.036]
Aage	0.000	0.000	0.002	0.000	0.000	0.001	−0.001	−0.003**	0.002	0.000
	[0.001]	[0.001]	[0.001]	[0.003]	[0.001]	[0.001]	[0.001]	[0.002]	[0.002]	[0.001]
Net worth	0.002	−0.001**	0.000	0.000	0.000	−0.001	0.002	−0.001	0.000	−0.001
(billions of US dollars)	[0.002]	[0.000]	[0.001]	[0.002]	[0.000]	[0.001]	[0.003]	[0.001]	[0.001]	[0.001]
Constant	0.011	0.028	−0.072	0.568**	0.055	0.064	0.097	0.399***	−0.165	0.016
	[0.069]	[0.056]	[0.090]	[0.226]	[0.040]	[0.119]	[0.067]	[0.144]	[0.137]	[0.079]
Observations	92	92	92	92	92	92	92	92	92	92
R^2	0.064	0.021	0.031	0.017	0.022	0.044	0.053	0.047	0.039	0.007

Dependent variables: share of category. OLS regression. Robust standard errors in brackets. ***, **, and * denote significance at 1%, 5%, and 10% level, respectively.

concentration of wealth and the return to a "Gilded Age" of patrimonial capitalism, with wealth passed from generation to generation. As Paul Krugman wrote in a *New York Times* opinion piece, "so far, the rise of America's 1 percent has mainly been driven by executive salaries and bonuses rather than income from investments, let alone inherited wealth," but "[Piketty] makes a powerful case that we're on the way back to 'patrimonial capitalism' in which the commanding heights of the economy are dominated not just by wealth, but also by inherited wealth, in which birth matters more than effort and talent." If this is indeed the case, and if signing the Giving Pledge can be considered an indication of increased willingness to donate to charitable causes, then we might expect a decline in donations from the very wealthy as the current generation of self-made billionaire entrepreneurs is slowly replaced by their heirs. Of course, the Giving Pledge, with its focus on giving away accumulated wealth, may counteract such a tendency. Whether it will be successful in persuading more and more of the extremely rich to follow this path remains on open question.

Acknowledgments

We thank Jaimie Ellis and Juan Pinto del Rio for research assistance. This work has received financial support from Social Sciences, University of Southampton. We would like to acknowledge CESifo support and to thank WealthX for providing data.

Notes

1. According to the Wealth-X and UBS Billionaire Census 2013, it is estimated that in the period 2011–2013 billionaires donated $69 billion (p. 24). By comparison, the annual report *Giving USA* estimates that total annual giving in the US in 2012 was $316 billion.

2. Source: Giving Pledge press release (http://givingpledge.org/press/ PressRelease_5_9_2014.pdf).

3. These psychological factors are considered in addition to the standard factors studied by economists, such as income and the incentives that the tax system creates.

4. These figures are drawn from the Giving Pledge website (http://givingpledge.org).

5. For more information, see www.hurun.net.

6. For more information, see www.wealthx.com.

7. "While my motivations for giving are not driven by a profit motive, I am quite sure that I have earned financial returns from giving money away. Not

directly by any means, but rather as a result of the people I have met, the ideas I have been exposed to, and the experiences I have had as a result of giving money away."

8. "When we began giving we were looking to receive nothing in return—but we have seen an important and unexpected 'fringe benefit.' We have come to know a number of wonderful people we would not otherwise have met. It happens when you go in this direction: you meet interesting and inspiring people who are out there trying to make this a better world. These are some of the best people you will ever know. We look forward to meeting more such people in the Giving Pledge group."

9. One letter, by John and Ginger Sall, is a brief, matter-of-fact statement about joining the pledge. The other letter, by Paul Singer, mainly concerns the role of government vs. private initiative.

10. Using a Tobit instead of an OLS regression broadly confirms these results. Being a self-made billionaire has a significant positive effect on "no inherit," whereas the effect on "provide example" and "luck" is positive but insignificant (in the latter case with a p value of 0.12). Age is negatively associated with value, but also with "no inheritance," and is positively associated with "warm glow." Net worth is negatively associated with "no inheritance."

References

Acs, Z. J. 2013. *Why Philanthropy Matters: How the Wealthy Give, and What It Means for Our Economic Well-Being.* Princeton University Press.

Alvaredo, F., A. B. Atkinson, T. Piketty, and E. Saez. 2013. The top 1 percent in international and historical perspective. *Journal of Economic Perspectives* 27 (3): 3–20.

Andreoni, J. 1990. Impure altruism and donations to public goods: A theory of warm-glow giving. *Economic Journal* 100 (401): 464–477.

Andreoni, J. 2006. Philanthropy. In *Handbook of the Economics of Giving, Altruism and Reciprocity,* ed. S.-C. Kolm and J. Mercier Ythier. Elsevier.

Andreoni, J., and B. D. Bernheim. 2009. Social image and the 50–50 norm: A theoretical and experimental analysis of audience effects. *Econometrica* 77 (5): 1607–1636.

Ariely, D., A. Bracha, and S. Meier. 2009. Doing good or doing well? Image motivation and monetary incentives in behaving prosocially. *American Economic Review* 99 (1): 544–555.

Auten, G. E., C. T. Clotfelter, and R. L. Schmalbeck. 2000. Taxes and Philanthropy among the Wealthy. In *Does Atlas Shrug? The Economic Consequences of Taxing the Rich,* ed. J. Slemrod. Russell Sage Foundation.

Banjo, S. 2010. U.S. super rich to share wealth. *Wall Street Journal,* August 3.

Benabou, R., and J. Tirole. 2006. Belief in a just world and redistributive politics. *Quarterly Journal of Economics* 121 (2): 699–746.

Center on Philanthropy at Indiana University. 2012. Bank of America Study of High Net Worth Philanthropy (http://www.philanthropy.iupui.edu/files/research/2012_bank_of_america_study_of_high_net_worth_philanthropy.pdf).

Coupe, T., and C. Monteiro. 2013. The Charity of the Extremely Wealthy. Discussion Paper 51, Kyiv School of Economics.

Economist. 2012. Spreading gospels of wealth America's billionaire Giving Pledgers are forming a movement. The Economist, May 19.

Giving Pledge. 2014. Frequently Asked Questions (http://givingpledge.org/faq.aspx#faq1).

Harvey, C., M. Maclean, J. Gordon, and E. Shaw. 2011. Andrew Carnegie and the foundations of contemporary entrepreneurial philanthropy. Business History 53 (3): 425–450.

Kahneman, D., and A. Deaton. 2010. High income improves evaluation of life but not emotional well-being. Proceedings of the National Academy of Sciences 107 (38): 16489–16493.

Krugman, P. 2014. Wealth over work. New York Times, March 23.

Lewis, N. 2014. Giving Pledge signers gave big in 2013 but not much for today's needs. Chronicle of Philanthropy, February 9 (http://philanthropy.com/article/Signers-of-the-Giving-Pledge/144567/%).

Loomis, C. 2010. The $600 billion challenge. Forbes, June 16 (http://fortune.com/2010/06/16/the-600-billion-challenge/).

Ostrower, F. 1997. Why the Wealthy Give: The Culture of Elite Philanthropy. Princeton University Press.

Page, B. I., F. Lomax Cook, and R. L. Moskowitz. 2011. Wealthy Americans, Philanthropy, and the Common Good. Working Paper WP-11-13, Institute for Policy Research, Northwestern University.

Piketty, T. 2014. Capital in the Twenty-First Century. Harvard University Press.

Ribar, D. C., and M. O. Wilhelm. 2002. Altruistic and joy of giving motivations in charitable behavior. Journal of Political Economy 110 (2): 425–457.

Schervish, P. G. 2008. Why the wealthy give. In The Routledge Companion to Nonprofit Marketing, ed. A. Sargeant and W. Wymer. Routledge.

Tonin, M., and M. Vlassopoulos. 2013. Experimental evidence of self-image concerns as motivation for giving. Journal of Economic Behavior and Organization 90: 19–27.

Tonin, M., and M. Vlassopoulos. 2014. An experimental investigation of intrinsic motivations for giving. Theory and Decision 76 (1): 47–67.

Vesterlund, L. 2006. Why do people give? In The Nonprofit Sector: A Research Handbook, second edition, ed. R. Steinberg and W. Powell. Yale University Press.

5

Altruism and Egoism/Warm Glow in Economics and Psychology: Building a Bridge Between Different Experimental Approaches D64 C91

Mark Ottoni-Wilhelm
D91 B55

The standard theory in the economics of charitable giving is a dual-motive theory that combines altruism and warm glow. Altruism is defined as a desire for "improve[ment in] the general well-being of recipients" (Becker 1974). This definition leads to altruism being modeled as a public good: a donor's utility increases if her gift improves the well-being of recipients, but her utility increases exactly in the same way if someone else's gift improves the well-being of recipients. In contrast, warm glow is modeled as a private good (Andreoni 1989). The donor obtains utility from warm glow only if she herself makes the gift.

A warm glow/private good component in utility is intended to model a person giving to a charitable organization because, in addition to altruism, she desires the internal self-satisfaction at having done her duty, a good feeling that comes from the act of giving, social approbation, and/or the avoidance of shame (Andreoni 1989; Steinberg 1987). Economists have long recognized that such motives can explain giving. Becker (1974) recognized the desires to avoid shame (scorn) and receive approbation (acclaim), as of course did Smith (1759/1997). Arrow (1972) discussed avoiding shame ("a response to personal social pressures") and duty. Sugden (1982) emphasized moral principles and duty.

There is much interest among economists in these warm-glow motives because it is well known that altruism on its own is not sufficient to explain charitable giving. A single-motive pure-altruism model cannot explain the stylized facts about giving in a large economy (Andreoni 1988). The dual-motive theory predicts, under fairly weak conditions, that the motive operative on the margin when many donors are giving to the same charitable organization is not altruism, but rather warm glow (Ribar and Wilhelm 2002; Yilidrim 2014). Pure altruism's prediction of complete crowd-out (Warr 1982)—essentially a prediction that a donor's giving responds strongly to changes in the recipient's net need—has been rejected by most experiments and econometric studies (Vesterlund, forthcoming; Ribar and Wilhelm 2002). Dictator games that provide participants with decision options that plausibly provide a way to avoid guilt even if the participant chooses not to give (e.g., an option to take money from the recipient, an option that the participant can refuse) result in much lower levels of giving to recipients (Bardsley 2008; Dana, Weber, and Kuang 2007; List 2007). The importance of social pressure in giving situations (DellaVigna, List, and Malmendier 2012) is consistent with motives of approbation and/or avoidance of shame.

The same warm-glow motives that are of interest to economists have been investigated extensively by social psychologists (Batson 2011; Dovidio, Piliavin, Schroeder, and Penner 2006). That literature is relevant to economists for several reasons. First, the standard theory in the social psychology of helping behavior is the same dual-motive theory used in economics. The definition of altruism is identical: "altruistically motivated helping is directed toward the end-state goal of increasing the other's welfare" (Batson and Coke 1981, p. 173). The motives that economists call "warm glow" psychologists call "egotistic." In the paper that coined the term "warm glow," Andreoni (1989) used "warm glow" and "egoism" interchangeably, noting "We could call such [warm glow] preferences 'egoistic.'" Second, psychologists have thought a lot about specific types of warm glow, and their work provides a theoretical foundation that economists can use to build further research on warm glow. Third, a frequently used experimental design in this literature provides economists with an approach that we also can use to investigate dual-motive altruism and warm glow. Finally, a main aim of the psychology literature has been to test the empathy-altruism hypothesis that empathic emotion evokes altruistic motivation (Batson 2011). This is relevant because there is increasing interest among economists in the relationship between empathy and charitable giving. (See, e.g., Andreoni and Rao 2011.)

The literature of empathy and altruism is not entirely unknown to economists (see, e.g., Andreoni and Rao 2011; Konow 2010), but neither is it widely known. This is because the literature is large (there have been more than two dozen empathy-altruism experiments) and it is not immediately clear how to think systematically about the experiments using an economic framework. The objective of this chapter is to provide that framework. We do this by extending Cornes and Sandler's (1984) characteristics model of dual-motive giving to include a second way, in addition to giving, by which warm-glow utility can be obtained. In short, in this framework the frequently used 2 × 2 design in the empathy-altruism experiments is understood to be a manipulation of the price of the second way to obtain warm-glow utility while manipulating empathy. We then use the framework to provide a concise summary of 27 empathy-altruism experiments.

Although our primary audience is economists working with the ` dual-motive altruism and warm-glow model, the chapter also leads to an insight important for psychologists. Describing the 2 × 2 empathy-altruism design in an economic framework allows the design to be compared straightforwardly with the crowd-out design often used in economics experiments. This comparison makes it easy to see how the crowd-out design addresses two persistent criticisms of the empathy-altruism design: the sequential test and residuum criticisms (Cialdini 1991).

We begin with an overview of impure altruism, as the dual-motive theory is called in economics. Following Ottoni-Wilhelm, Vesterlund, and Xie (2014), we emphasize that the predictions focused on in crowd-out experiments are income effects. We then briefly discuss the dual-motive theory as described in the psychology literature. Next we extend Cornes and Sandler's (1984) characteristics model of dual-motive giving. This leads to a discussion of the experimental investigations of specific types of warm glow in the empathy-altruism literature, and to the sequential test and residuum criticisms.

5.1   Dual-Motive Altruism and Warm Glow in Economics

Dual-Motive Theory in Economics

In economics the initial theory to explain voluntary giving was that donors are motivated by altruism.[1] However, a single-motive, pure-altruism model produces surprising predictions. For example, the giving of purely altruistic donors will be completely crowded out by the giving of others (Warr 1982), and very few people, and only the richest, will be observed giving at all (Andreoni 1988). These predictions are at odds with the evidence about giving. The incompatibility between single-motive altruism and the evidence led Andreoni (1989) to propose a dual-motive theory in which donors also are motivated by warm glow. (Also see Cornes and Sandler 1984; Steinberg 1987.)

In dual-motive altruism and warm glow, individual i derives utility $U(c_i, G, g_i)$ from consumption goods c_i, from the charity's output G that is used to improve the well-being of recipients (altruism), and the size of the gift g_i the individual herself puts into the charity. From the size of her own gift is the warm-glow benefit derived. The sum of the charitable gifts by all donors is

$$G = \sum_{i=1}^{n} g_i.$$

G is a public good because i's welfare is improved if other donors give to the charity: giving by others,

$$G_{-i} = \sum_{j \neq i} g_j,$$

improves the well-being of recipients that is of concern to i.

Utility derived from g_i is egoistic/warm glow because it motivates the donor to give over and above her desire to see an improvement in the well-being of recipients. For example, if in a situation where the well-being of recipients already is being improved by a large amount of giving by others G_{-i}, a donor should she choose $g_i = 0$ may nevertheless feel guilty because she would not have done her part. Therefore she would give $g_i > 0$ to avoid guilt. As another example, if social approbation matters to her, she will not receive it if she chooses $g_i = 0$. She can satisfy such desires—avoid guilt or to receive social approbation—only by exercising agency in making her own private gift to the charity. Hence, g_i is a private good.

Individual i chooses her optimal gift in the context of her budget constraint $c_i + g_i \leq y_i$, in which, to simplify the discussion, the price of giving is set to $p_g = 1$. The budget constraint can be rewritten in terms of the public good G by adding G_{-i} to both sides: $c_i + G \leq y_i + G_{-i}$, where the right-hand side, $y_i + G_{-i} \triangleq Z_i$, is called i's "social income." With the usual assumptions about utility (continuous, strictly quasi-concave), and assuming that i's optimal gift g_i^* is greater than zero, the first-order condition determining g_i^* is

$$U_A(c_i, G, G - G_{-i}) + U_e(c_i, G, G - G_{-i}) = U_c(c_i, G, G - G_{-i}), \tag{1}$$

where $U_A \equiv \partial U / \partial G$ is the partial with respect to the second component of utility (altruism) and $U_e \equiv \partial U / \partial g_i$ is the partial with respect to the third component of utility (warm glow). The left-hand side is the marginal benefit of giving, and it has two components: the marginal benefit due to altruism (U_A) and the marginal benefit due to egoism/warm glow (U_e). The marginal benefit to i of giving one more dollar to the charity is the marginal benefit that dollar generates in terms of improving the well-being of recipients plus the marginal benefit that dollar generates in terms of, say, avoiding guilt, taking guilt avoidance as a specific type of warm glow in order to fix ideas. U_c is the marginal cost, in terms of sacrificed consumption, of i's giving that one more dollar.

Equation 1 is solved for i's optimal gift g_i^* in terms of $G^* = g_i^* + G_{-i}$:

$$G^* = q(y_i + G_{-i}, G_{-i}),   \text{(2)}$$

which implies

$$g_i^* = -G_{-i} + q(y_i + G_{-i}, G_{-i}).   \text{(3)}$$

The function $q(., .)$ is an Engel curve for the public good and has two income components: social income $y_i + G_{-i}$ and giving by others G_{-i}.

The second income component is due to the warm-glow motive. To see why, consider the following thought experiment. Start with income $y_i =$ \$375 and giving by others $G_{-i} =$ \$500. Imagine that, faced with this budget, i chooses $g_i^* =$ \$25 and $c_i^* =$ \$350. This would raise total giving G to the charity to $G^* =$ \$525. In terms of equation 1, i would be saying that by giving $g_i^* =$ \$25, when this is combined with the giving by others so that G is raised to $G^* =$ \$525, the well-being of the recipients is being improved enough, and at the same time $g_i^* =$ \$25 is large enough for i to avoid guilt, so that raising g_i to \$26 would not improve the well-being of recipients enough and would not increase i's satisfaction at avoiding guilt enough so that it to be worthwhile to i to sacrifice one more dollar of consumption.

Now imagine that we tax i one dollar and, for the moment, that she reduces her giving by one dollar to $g_i =$ \$24 and keeps her consumption at $c_i^* =$ \$350. Also, imagine that we take the taxed dollar and give it to the charity so that $G_{-i} =$ \$501; note that with g_i at \$24 we still have $G =$ \$525. If i should decide to raise her giving above $g_i =$ \$24, it must be because $g_i =$ \$24 is *not* large enough to satisfy i that guilt has been avoided. Why? Because G is still at \$525 and before we taxed i that was enough to have improved the well-being of the recipients so that i was not willing to sacrifice any more consumption in order to further improve the well-being of the recipients. So after paying the tax, if she sacrifices more consumption (chooses a new $c_i^* <$ \$350) to increase her new (after-tax) giving g_i^* above \$24, it must be because $g_i =$ \$24 is not enough to avoid guilt. In terms of equation 2, the one dollar "tax and increase G_{-i}" policy leaves the first income component (social income $Z_i = y_i + G_{-i}$)

unchanged. This leaves the second income component (giving by others G_{-i}, which has increased by one dollar) to account for the guilt-avoiding, warm-glow increase in giving above \$24.

The thought experiment in the two previous paragraphs held social income Z_i constant while raising giving by others G_{-i}. In terms of equation 2 this is

$$\left.\frac{\partial G^*}{\partial G_{-i}}\right|_{\Delta Z_i=0} \triangleq q_2. \tag{4}$$

This is the income effect from the second component in equation 2, and the thought experiment implies that this is due to the warm-glow motive. From equations 3 and 4,

$$\left.\frac{\partial g^*}{\partial G_{-i}}\right|_{\Delta Z_i=0} = -1 + q_2. \tag{5}$$

This is the degree to which an increase in giving by others that is "balanced-budget" in the sense that the increase is funded by a reduction in i's own income (i.e., $\Delta Z_i = 0$) "crowds out" individual i's giving.

Although the income effect in equation 4 and crowding out in equation 5 embody the same description of behavior, just as equations 2 and 3 do, it is easier to see the thought experiment in terms of the crowding out (equation 5). In the thought experiment, if i reduces her giving to $g_i^* = \$24$ (after being taxed one dollar and giving one dollar to the charity), that corresponds to

$$\left.\frac{\partial g^*}{\partial G_{-i}}\right|_{\Delta Z_i=0} = -1$$

in equation 5. If she raises her giving above \$24, that corresponds to

$$\left.\frac{\partial g^*}{\partial G_{-i}}\right|_{\Delta Z_i=0} = --1 = -1 + q_2$$

in equation 5, where $-1 + q_2$ is between -1 and 0, and the only motivation to do that is warm glow. Why? Because the net need of the charity, defined to be the exogenous need that occasioned the giving in the first place minus giving by others, has not changed because the one dollar tax was given to the charity. Note that the dual-motive altruism and warm-glow model reduces to a single-motive pure-altruism model if $q_2 = 0$.

The usual own income effect is just the income effect of the first component in equation 2:

$$\frac{dG^*}{dy_i} \overset{\triangle}{=} q_1. \tag{6}$$

The change in i's giving in response to a change in giving by others (holding own income y_i constant, but not holding social income Z_i constant) is both income effects combined:

$$\frac{dG^*}{dG_{-i}} \overset{\triangle}{=} q_1 + q_2. \tag{7}$$

This implies, from equation 3,

$$\frac{dg^*}{dG_{-i}} = -1 + q_1 + q_2. \tag{8}$$

Equation 8 is the degree to which a change in giving by others that is "unfunded," in the sense that the change in giving by others is not funded by changing i's own income, changes individual i's giving. If giving by others G_{-i} gets smaller, then the well-being of the recipients (served by the charity) falls because recipients' net need has become greater (assuming that their exogenous need remains at the same level). If i does not increase her gift at all when giving by others G_{-i} gets smaller—when the net need of the recipients becomes greater—then it must be that i's giving, at the margin, is motivated only by warm glow. This situation corresponds to

$$\frac{dg_i^*}{dG_{-i}} = 0,$$

which from equation 8 implies $q_1 + q_2 = 1$; hence, in this case the dual-motive altruism and warm-glow model reduces to a single-motive pure-warm-glow model if $q_1 + q_2 = 1$. If $q_1 + q_2 < 1$, $q_1 > 0$, and $q_2 > 0$, then at the margin both altruism and warm glow motivate giving. These elegant results using the derivatives of equations 2 and 3 to explain how the model nests single-motive pure altruism, single-motive pure warm glow, and dual-motive altruism and warm glow were derived by Andreoni (1989).

Understanding how these results connect to an everyday understanding of altruism is straightforward. To the extent that a donor increases her giving in response to an increase in the net need of the recipient, her giving is motivated by altruism (equation 8), but if she does not increase her giving at all when the net need of the recipient increases then her giving is motivated by pure warm glow (equation 8 with $q_1 + q_2 = 1$). If a donor gives more even though the net need of the recipient has not increased, her giving is motivated by warm glow (equation 5), but if she does not give more in this case her giving is motivated by single-motive pure altruism (equation 5 with $q_2 = 0$).

An Experimental Design in Economics Based on Income Effects

A frequently used experimental design in economics investigates dual-motive altruism and warm glow by implementing the thought experiment described above. The design estimates the degree of balanced-budget crowd-out presented in equation 5, equivalently the income effect presented in equation 4. For example, Bolton and Katok (1998) investigate a dictator game in which one participant can give to another (anonymous) participant, use a between-subjects design, and compare giving decisions when the donor-participant's income is $y_i = \$18$ and giving by others to the anonymous recipient is $G_{-i} = \$2$ to when $y_i = \$15$ and $G_{-i} = \$5$. The main result is that balanced-budget crowd-out $-1 + q_2$ (from equation 5) is 0.74. This implies $q_2 = 0.26 > 0$, and a null hypothesis of pure altruism ($q_2 = 0$) can be rejected. A variety of similar experiments have been conducted, for instance replacing the dictator game with a public goods game or replacing the in-lab recipient in the dictator game with a real-world charitable organization, and most though not all, have found $q_2 > 0$ and rejected pure altruism (Vesterlund, forthcoming).

Note that the crowd-out/income-effects design positions pure altruism as the null hypothesis to be tested. Although the experiments are motivated by the prediction from the dual-motive theory that

$$\left. \frac{\partial g^*}{\partial G_{-i}} \right|_{\Delta z_i = 0} \neq -1$$

(equivalently, $q_2 > 0$), the existence of warm glow is not directly tested. Rather, the existence of warm glow is inferred from the rejection of single-motive pure altruism. We point this out because the most frequently used design in psychology takes a different approach that positions egoism/warm glow as the null.

Ottoni-Wilhelm et al. (2014) have developed the crowd-out/income-effects design so that it can position dual-motive altruism and warm glow as the null. In this way, the dual-motive theory itself can be directly tested.

Their approach also allows for single-motive pure warm glow to be positioned as the null, and for the relative strengths in altruism and warm glow to be measured. This latter advantage is important because it allows hypotheses about altruism and/or warm glow to be directly tested.

5.2 Dual-Motive Altruism and Egoism (Warm Glow) in Psychology

Dual-Motive Theory in Psychology: The Empathy-Altruism Hypothesis

In psychology the initial theoretical perspective was that helping behavior is motivated by egoism: "the doctrinaire view in psychology has been that altruism can ultimately be explained in terms of egoistic, self-serving motives" (Hoffman 1975). Batson and Coke (1981) characterized the prevailing view as that "theories of motivation based on behaviorism or psychoanalysis were sufficiently sophisticated to provide an egoistic account of any behavior that might appear to be altruistically motivated," and Batson, Darley, and Coke (1978) remarked that "modern psychology's devotion to egoistic models of motivation is breathtakingly extreme."

An early egoistic theory of helping behavior was aversive-arousal reduction (Piliavin and Piliavin 1973, cited in Piliavin et al. 1982). The theory is that seeing another in need raises one's own internal distress, and one way to reduce one's own distress is to help the other in need. The other in need receives help, but this is just a joint product of an action taken to reduce one's own internal distress. The ultimate goal is to reduce one's own distress, and helping is an instrument to do so. Hence, aversive-arousal reduction is a specific type of egoism.

Predictions of single-motive pure altruism that were both theoretically surprising and empirically contradicted led economists to consider egoistic motives. What led some psychologists to step away from a single-motive pure egoism theory of helping behavior to consider altruism? There seem to have been three factors. First, if experimentally validated, a challenge to the dominant view of egoism could lead to an important paradigm shift in psychology (Batson et al. 1978). Second, despite the preeminent role egoism theory was playing in explaining helping behavior, it had not been experimentally tested (Krebs 1975; Hoffman 1975). Third, if helping behavior is in part motivated by altruism, then the socialization of helping behavior should move beyond the suppression of egoistic tendencies to be selfish to include encouragement of tendencies to be altruistic (Batson and Coke 1981).

As was noted in the introduction to this chapter, the definition of altruism in the psychology literature is the same as that used in economics. Altruistically motivated behavior is "directed toward the end-state goal of reducing another's pain or increasing another's pleasure," or quoting the dictionary definition "'unselfish concern for the welfare of others'" (Batson et al. 1978, pp. 123–124). While psychology and economics share the same definition of altruism, what is unique to the psychology literature is the hypothesis that empathic emotion evokes altruistic motivation to help—the empathy-altruism hypothesis (Aronfreed 1970; Hoffman 1975; Krebs 1975; Batson et al. 1978).[2]

The flip side of the empathy-altruism hypothesis is that empathic emotion does not evoke egoistic motivation to help. Of course, this claim cannot be accepted without evidence. For example, a strong empathic reaction to seeing another in need could raise one's desire to mitigate the awful situation in order to alleviate one's own personal distress from seeing the awful situation—the aversive-arousal-reduction hypothesis. Alleviating personal distress can be achieved by giving help to the other in need, but it can also be achieved by removing oneself from the awful situation. Giving help and escaping from the situation are substitute goods in satisfying this egoistic motive. Presented with two alternative goods to satisfy this egoistic motive, the participant will choose more of the alternative that has the lower price.

A Characteristics Model of the Empathy-Altruism Experimental Design in Psychology: Empathy and Price Effects

To generate evidence that empathic emotion does not evoke egoistic motives to help, the majority of experiments in psychology use a design in which empathy is manipulated to be either low or high while the price of an alternative way to satisfy the egoism motive is manipulated. For example, if the specific egoistic motive being investigated is aversive-arousal reduction, the idea is to lower the price of relieving the participant's own distress by allowing the participant an easy way to escape the experiment and remove herself from witnessing the other in need. If manipulating empathy to the high level evokes the desire to reduce own personal distress, then when the experiment manipulates the price of escape to be very low the participant will choose to escape rather than help: "the likelihood that the egoistically motivated bystander will *help* should be ... a direct function of the cost of escaping" (Batson and Coke 1981, p. 176). But if, when empathy is manipulated high at the same time the price of escape is manipulated to be very low, the participant nevertheless chooses to help, then the motivation of that help could not have been to reduce her own personal distress. If it had been, she would have taken the easy escape. This design, introduced by Batson and Coke (1981), can be straightforwardly described in a household production framework by extending Cornes and Sandler's (1984) characteristics model of dual-motive giving so that it includes a second good that can substitute for giving help in the production of egoistic/warm-glow utility. In the household production framework, utility is derived from the characteristics that goods generate (altruism and egoism) rather than from the goods themselves (giving and escaping). Utility is $U(c_i, A, e_i)$, the altruism characteristic is $A \equiv \alpha(G_{-i} + g_i)$, and the egoism characteristic is $e_i \equiv \beta f(g_i, x_i)$, where x_i is the second good (e.g., escaping the situation) that can substitute for g_i in producing the egoism characteristic (e.g., aversive-arousal reduction), $f(g_i, x_i)$ is the production function of the egoistic characteristic (for example, one's own distress that can be reduced either by giving or escaping, and α and β are scalar parameters indicating the strengths of altruism and egoism respectively. In general, the production function for A would not have to be linear; it is linear here only to allow the discussion to focus on $f(g_i, x_i)$.

The budget constraint is now $c_i + p_g\, g_i + p_x\, x_i \leq y_i$, where p_x is the price of x_i. The first-order conditions include

$$\frac{\alpha U_A + \beta f_g U_e}{U_c} = p_g, \tag{9}$$

which corresponds to equation 1 and which still describes the tradeoff between giving more to charity and devoting more resources toward one's own consumption. There is now a second first-order condition:

$$\frac{\alpha U_A + \beta f_g U_e}{\beta f_x U_e} = \frac{p_g}{p_x}, \tag{10}$$

which describes the tradeoff between giving more to charity and devoting more resources toward escaping the situation.[3] Equation 10 can be rewritten as

$$\frac{\alpha U_A}{\beta f_x U_e} = \frac{p_g}{p_x} - \frac{f_g}{f_x}. \tag{11}$$

The empathy-altruism hypothesis is that the strength of altruism, α, is a positive function of empathic emotion. If empathic emotion is denoted

m, then $\alpha(m)$ should be rewritten with $\alpha' > 0$. The frequently used 2×2 experimental design in psychology is to manipulate m (e.g., low and high) and manipulate p_x (e.g., $p_x \approx 0$ and $p_x > 0$). If the empathy-altruism hypothesis is true, then in the high-empathy treatment the marginal benefit due to altruism that comes from giving will have been raised relative to both own consumption (equation 9) and escape (equation 11). In contrast, the aversive-arousal-reduction hypothesis is that β is a positive function $\beta(m)$ of empathic emotion. Hence, if one observes more giving in the high-empathy treatment it could be because of higher α or higher β in equation 9.

The p_x manipulation can tell you whether the high-empathy treatment has produced higher α or higher β. If the aversive-arousal-reduction hypothesis is true, meaning that in the high-empathy treatment $\beta(m_{High})$ is large and α is unchanged, then when $p_x \approx 0$ escape has become a much cheaper way (relative to giving) to produce egoistic utility, so that initially equation 11 becomes

$$\frac{\alpha U_A}{\beta(m_{High})f_x U_e} < \frac{p_g}{p_x} - \frac{f_g}{f_x} \tag{12}$$

(where p_x is small enough to make the right-hand side positive). Then the participant would lower g_i and raise x_i until the left-hand side of equation 12 is increased and the equality in equation 11 re-established. In contrast, if the empathy-altruism hypothesis is true—in the high-empathy treatment $\alpha(m_{High})$ is large and β is unchanged—then, even though $p_x \approx 0$ makes escape a very cheap way (compared to giving) to produce egoistic utility, the inequality in equation 12 is reversed:

$$\frac{\alpha(m_{High})U_A}{\beta f_x U_e} > \frac{p_g}{p_x} - \frac{f_g}{f_x}. \tag{13}$$

In this case, the participant will raise g_i and lower x_i until the left-hand side of equation 13 is reduced and the equality in equation 11 is re-established.

In summary, if the empathy-altruism hypothesis is true, then when $p_x \approx 0$ the high-empathy treatment is predicted to give help even though escape from the situation is easy/cheap, but the low-empathy control is predicted to escape. If the aversive-arousal-reduction hypothesis is true, then more escape and less giving is predicted in both high-empathy and low-empathy manipulations when $p_x \approx 0$. What is tested is the null hypothesis that giving is equal in these two conditions. This positions aversive-arousal reduction as the null, and that null has been rejected in ten experiments. (See, e.g., Batson et al. 1981; Toi and Batson 1982; Batson et al. 1983.) Note that this design, when applied to the specific type of egoism that is the aversive-arousal-reduction hypothesis, directly tests an aversive-arousal-reduction null. Support for the empathy-altruism hypothesis is inferred indirectly from the inability of aversive-arousal-reduction theory to explain why people whose empathy has been raised give help even though an easy escape is available.[4]

The characteristics model has been presented in terms of aversive-arousal reduction as the specific type of egoism/warm glow that is competing with the empathy-altruism hypothesis. There are five other specific types of egoism that have been that have been investigated in the psychology literature. Specific types of egoism differ on two dimensions: internal versus social group orientation (for example, your own self-evaluation versus your social group's evaluation of you) and reducing or avoiding a negative cost (punishment) versus seeking a positive benefit (reward).

Table 5.1 lists the specific types of egoism/warm-glow motivation that have been proposed in the psychology literature by their formal names in psychology and by the labels that we will use in the remainder of this chapter. Internally oriented types of egoism include giving to charity to avoid a negative self-evaluation of one's own identity should one not give—that is, to avoid guilt. Alternatively, upon being made aware of a need, a person may feel sad and may give simply to improve her mood, to feel better; this negative-state-relief hypothesis comes closest to what economists often have in mind when thinking about "warm glow." A third type of internally oriented egoism is to seek a positive self-evaluation of one's own identity, such as living up to one's moral principles or duty. Seeking a positive self-evaluation of identity and avoiding guilt are positive and negative sides of the same coin. Aversive-arousal reduction is, of course, internally oriented. Two social-group-oriented types of egoism are giving to avoid the shame that would come from the disapproval of one's social group if one did not give and giving to gain the approbation of one's social group. Avoiding shame and seeking approbation are negative and positive sides of the same coin.[5]

In terms of the characteristics model developed above, the egoistic motivations in table 5.1 represent six characteristics that potentially enter the utility function: $e_i^t \equiv \beta f^t(g_i, x_i^t), t = 1, 2, \ldots, 6$, where x_i^t represents a second good that can substitute for g_i in producing the tth type of egoistic characteristic. Table 5.1 also lists these six characteristics and the

Table 5.1
Six types of egoistic/warm-glow motivation.

Egoistic/warm-glow motivation	Keyword	Characteristic being sought	Good that can substitute for giving help in producing the characteristic
Internal orientation			
1. Empathy-Specific—Punishment	Guilt	Avoiding guilt, self-censure, negative self-evaluation.	Justification for not helping.
2. Empathy-Specific—Reward: Negative state relief	Negative mood	Feeling sad and seeking to do something to improve one' emotional mood. Seeking to feel better. Seeking to gain a general feeling of happiness.	Any good that can improve mood: e.g., money, praise.
3. Empathy-Specific—Reward	Identity	Seeking to fulfill duty, obligation, live in line with moral principles, follow a personal norm, enhance one's self esteem.	An experiment using a substitute good has not been conducted.
4. Aversive-arousal reduction	Personal distress	Eliminate one's own emotional (reflexive) distress at seeing another in need.	Easy escape from the situation.
Social group orientation			
5. Empathy-Specific—Punishment	Shame	Avoiding disapproval, censure, transgression of a social norm.	Anonymity
6. Empathy-Specific—Reward	Approbation	Seeking recognition, praise, to follow a social norm.	An experiment using a substitute good has not been conducted.

respective goods that can substitute for giving help in producing each characteristic. Each empathy-altruism experiment conducted in the psychology literature picks one of these specific egoistic characteristics to focus on, one egoistic characteristic at a time. The majority of the experiments manipulate the price of the second substitute good to be low or high, or keep that price low.[6]

For example, if t = Guilt then a second good x_i^t that can substitute for g_i to produce guilt avoidance is having a reasonable justification that explains why it is all right not to give help in this situation. To lower the price of having a reasonable justification means to provide the participant an easy-for-her-to-accept justification for not giving help. For example, Batson, Dyck, et al. (1988, study 3) conducted an experiment in which a participant was required choose to do either task A or task B. If task A was chosen, points earned by performing the task benefitted the participant herself and could later be exchanged for raffle tickets. If task B was chosen, points earned benefited another participant, for example by reducing the number of mild electric shocks he would otherwise receive. Hence, choosing task B was the measure of giving help. The tasks were easy. One was to read a page of random numbers and circle each "13" and each "47." A second version used random letters instead of numbers, and the task was to circle each "AB" and each "JX." To provide a reasonable justification explaining why it is all right for a participant to not help (i.e., not to choose task B), treated participants were told: "Some people seem to prefer working on numbers and some seem to prefer letters, although most people seem to prefer numbers. You can, however, work on whichever option you wish." This provided a justification for a participant motivated to help primarily to avoid guilt, a way to not help and still avoid guilt by telling herself "Like most people I just have a preference for working with numbers (the self-benefiting task A being the task with numbers)." The results were that people with high empathy gave help even when they had a reasonable justification not to do so. Support for the empathy-altruism hypothesis is inferred indirectly from the inability of a guilt avoidance theory to explain why people with high empathy give help even when they have a reasonable justification available that would allow them to not help and still avoid guilt. Batson, Dyck, et al. (1988, studies 2 and 4) used different procedures to provide justification for not helping, and obtained similar results.

As a second example, if t = Negative mood, then any x_i^t good that can improve one's mood is a substitute for g_i. For example, Cialdini et al. (1987) set up the aversive-arousal-reduction experiment described above in which high-empathy participants gave help even when escape was easy. However, in their experiment, just before the participants in the high-empathy treatment made their decision about helping or not, some were given a monetary reward (a one-dollar bill), and some were given a "praise" reward (told that they had scored highly on a test of social ability, and that such people are typically well liked by others, interesting, intelligent, good conversationalists, and creative). A third group of participants were given no reward. The results were that the participants receiving rewards helped less, especially those who received the dollar. This is consistent with the negative-state-relief hypothesis and inconsistent with empathy-altruism. Because there were some indications that offering a reward just before the helping decision was made may have reduced helping simply because participants were distracted, Schaller and Cialdini (1988) created a design with a distracted control group and again found results generally supportive of the negative-state-relief hypothesis.[7, 8]

In a third example from the socially oriented egoistic motivations, if t = Shame then a second good x_i^t that can substitute for g_i to produce avoidance of shame is anonymity. To lower the price of anonymity—to make anonymity easily obtainable—is simply to set up the experimental procedure so that the participant truly feels that she can make an anonymous decision, even to the extent that she thinks the experimenters do not even know that she has received a request for help. Fultz et al. (1986, study 2) designed an experiment with this objective. In their experiment, the participant received two notes from a second participant named "Janet Arnold" who was sitting in another room. Janet was not a real person, but the participant did not know that. Janet's notes arrived in a sealed envelope, so that the research assistant administering the experiment with the participant did not know the content of the notes. The participant read the notes in private. The second note revealed that Janet was lonely and suggested getting together "just to talk or spend time together." The participant was told that, although she would have stay to fill out a questionnaire, Janet had completed her part of the experiment and had left; hence, the participant would not run into Janet in the hall. After completing the questionnaire, the participant was given a letter from the professor running the project saying that sometimes the two subjects in the experiment just completed had become interested in participating in a second study about long-term relationships and hade "expressed interest in actually meeting and establishing a relationship with the other person." However, the other participant (Janet) would be contacted "*only* if you want a meeting; if you do not, then we will not contact the communicator [Janet], and he or she will not know that you were ever asked about actually meeting." Ostensibly, the participant believed that the professor did not know about Janet's request for help in the second note. The professor's recruitment letter was not a request for help, but rather an invitation to participate in a second study. Whether or not one thinks that a participant in this experiment truly feels that she can make an anonymous decision about meeting with Janet, there was certainly a stronger sense of anonymity than in the non-anonymous control. In the non-anonymous control, the participant was told that the research assistant would be reading the notes and the participant's completed questionnaire. Nothing was in a sealed envelope. The invitation letter said that the other participant (Janet) had also received an invitation, so the participant knew that Janet would know if she were to decline to participate in the second study. The results showed that people in the high-empathy condition helped even when their anonymity was relatively safe.[9]

In addition to the design that manipulates empathy while manipulating the price of a second substitute good, there have been three alternative designs used to investigate empathy-altruism. The alternative designs can be understood in terms of constructs from the characteristics model described above: (i) measure a within-person change in mood (in terms of the characteristics model: a proxy measure for a change in utility (i.e., $\Delta U(c_i, G, g_i)$)), (ii) use cognitive interference (characteristics model: use reaction times to figure out if the participant is focusing on the altruism-G part of utility or the egoism/warm glow-g_i part), and (iii) try to convince the participant that giving $g_i > 0$ will not improve mood (characteristics model: try to convince participant that $f_g \approx 0$).

Three experiments have measured change in mood as the dependent variable (Batson, Dyck, et al. 1988, study 1; Batson and Weeks 1996, studies 1 and 2). Batson and Weeks (1996) manipulated empathy (low, high), set the experiment up so that any help given by the participant would be ineffective (i.e., would not benefit the recipient), then manipulated the reason the participant's help was ineffective: the participant plausibly could have tried harder to make her help effective in improving the recipient's well-being versus no matter how hard the participant tried it would not have been enough to meet the recipient's need. The empathy-altruism hypothesis predicts that, because a high-empathy participant wants to see an improvement in the recipient's well-being, the participant will register a large drop in mood when she learns the help she gave was ineffective, even if her help would have been ineffective no matter how hard she tried (that is, even when the ineffectiveness was not her fault). In contrast, if what high empathy does is evoke the desire to avoid guilt— an egoism/warm-glow null—the participant will register a small drop in mood, if any, when she learns the help she gave was ineffective, because she successfully avoided guilt by giving the help. She would still get the guilt-avoidance warm glow from $g_i > 0$ in her utility function $U(c_i, G, g_i)$, even though the well-being of the recipient (G) is unchanged. Batson and Weeks (1996) found that high-empathy participants experienced large drops in mood upon learning that their help had been ineffective even when the ineffectiveness was not their fault.

One experiment has been conducted using the cognitive-interference design (Batson, Dyck, et al., 1988, study 5). Cognitive-interference theory implies that if the participant is focused on the well-being of the recipient it will take her longer to name the color in which an altruism-relevant word such as "needy" is printed, and that if the participant is focused on avoiding guilt it will take her longer to name the color in which the word "guilt" is printed. Batson, Dyck, et al. found that high-empathy participants reacted more slowly to the altruism-relevant words, but not to the guilt-relevant words, which indicated that the high-empathy participants were focused on the well-being of the recipient rather than on egoism/warm glow.

In two other experiments Cialdini et al. (1987, study 2) and Schroeder et al. (1988) tried to convince a participant that giving could not improve mood, because a side effect of the drug ostensibly being evaluated in the experiment was "to take whatever mood is present in an individual and prolong it artificially." The negative-state-relief hypothesis predicts that high-empathy participants will give larger amounts of help *only if* they believe so doing will improve their mood; i.e., only those high-empathy participants *not* given the drug with the mood-fixing side effect will give larger amounts of help. The empathy-altruism predicts equal help given by high-empathy participants regardless of whether or not they have been given the drug. The results reject empathy-altruism. However, a replication experiment by Schroeder et al. (1988) produced the opposite result.

Two types of egoistic/warm-glow motivation represented in table 5.1 have not been extensively investigated in the psychology experiments: "identity" (meaning giving help to fulfill one's duty, live in line with moral principles, or follow a personal norm) and "approbation" (meaning giving help to receive recognition or praise or to follow a social norm).

Batson (2011) argues that the results from the three experiments in which change in mood was the dependent variable (Batson, Dyck, et al. 1988, study 1; Batson and Weeks 1996, studies 1 and 2) and from the one cognitive-interference experiment (Batson, Dyck et al. 1988, study 5) that are consistent with the empathy-altruism hypothesis are evidence against the identity and approbation types of egoism. For example, in the cognitive-interference experiment in which high-empathy participants did not react more slowly to the guilt-relevant words (indicating they were not cognitively focused on guilt), neither did they react more slowly to identity-relevant and approbation-relevant words, such as "duty," "proud," "honor," and "praise."[10]

The Sequential-Testing and Residuum Criticisms

Two main criticisms have been made about the experimental designs in psychology. The first is that each experiment focuses on one egoistic/warm-glow motivation at a time. The research program of 27 experiments described in the previous section tests the different types of egoistic motivations sequentially, one at a time (Cialdini 1991). Testing the egoistic motivations sequentially leaves open the possibility that, say, when testing for aversive-arousal reduction and more giving is observed in the high-empathy/$p_x \approx 0$ group than in the low-empathy/$p_x \approx 0$ group, it could be because the high empathy evoked the desire to avoid guilt or live in line with moral principles, egoistic motivations whose prices were not lowered by allowing the participant an easy escape from the situation. Furthermore, in principle the list of possible egoistic motivations to consider is an "open set" (Batson 2011). If in the future a seventh type of egoistic motivation is found to have plausible theoretical justification, the experimental research program must be expanded to include a focus on that seventh type.

The second criticism is that, by testing a specific type of egoistic motivation, each experiment, with few exceptions, positions that egoistic motivation as the null.[11] Each rejection of an egoistic motivation provides direct evidence against that specific egoistic motivation but only indirect evidence of altruism. Although the argument that the overall pattern of evidence across the 27 experiments is consistent with the empathy-altruism hypothesis and the argument that a few of the experiments are able to rule out more than one egoistic motivation (Batson 2011, pp. 131–134) may be compelling, it is nevertheless the case that the evidence for altruism is based on a residuum (Cialdini 1991). To address the problem of sequential testing and the problem of a residuum, Cialdini (ibid.)

calls for evidence from a design that could simultaneously handle all types of egoistic motivations and measure altruism directly.

The crowd-out/income-effects design used in economics does what Cialdini (1991) requested: it simultaneously handles all types of egoistic motivations because it positions single-motive pure altruism as the null. Recall that testing the single-motive pure altruism null is based on an income effect: the balanced-budget crowd-out test. If a participant gives an additional amount even when a lower level of her own giving, in combination with a higher level of giving by others, could leave the net need of the recipient unchanged, her additional giving must be motivated by something other the single-motive pure altruism that would imply that the only construct that matters is the recipient's net need. Egoism/warm glow is now the residuum. The disadvantage of the economics design is that, because egoism/warm glow is a residuum, the experiment does not indicate which specific type or types of egoistic motivation giving is driven by. It could be guilt avoidance, negative mood, identity, and/or personal distress.[12]

A second, subtle disadvantage of the crowd-out/income-effects design is that, although it can detect the existence of egoism/warm-glow motivations, it cannot be used to measure the relative strengths of altruistic and egoism/warm-glow motivations, as Ottoni-Wilhelm et al. (2014) demonstrated. They expanded the design so that it could measure the relative strengths of altruistic and egoism. Although they found evidence supporting the dual-motive theory (i.e., statistically significant evidence that both altruism and egoism drive giving), the majority of giving in their experiment was driven by altruism. This result complements the indirect evidence of the existence of altruism from the psychology research program, while using an entirely different design not subject to the sequential-testing criticism and the "altruism as a residuum" criticism.

5.3   Conclusion

Research on altruism and egoism/warm glow in economics and psychology is built on the same dual-motive theory that both altruism and egoism/warm glow motivate charitable giving and helping behavior. However, economics and psychology have taken different approaches to experimental investigation of the theory. Psychologists have conducted experiments that focus on four specific types of egoism: the desires to reduce one's own personal distress, to avoid guilt, to improve mood, and to avoid shame. Two additional types of egoism—wanting to live in line with moral principles and wanting to receive approbation—have not been investigated as extensively.

The majority of experiments in psychology reject hypotheses that empathic emotion evokes egoistic/warm-glow motivations to give help (Batson 2011). Although this impressive body of evidence is consistent with the empathy-altruism hypothesis that empathic emotion evokes altruistic motivation, the evidence is subject to two criticisms (Cialdini 1991). First, the body of evidence is based on sequentially testing each possible egoistic hypothesis one at a time, meaning that when one specific type of egoism is being tested the other specific types are not under experimental control. Second, the tests that reject a specific egoistic hypothesis provide indirect support for the empathy-altruism hypothesis and, as a corollary, provide indirect support for the existence of altruism.

The crowd-out/income-effects design in economics focuses on the participant's responses to changes in the net need of a recipient. This avoids the problem of sequential testing because *any* of the six types of egoistic motivation will lead to a rejection of a single-motive pure altruism null. In addition, the recent expansion of this design by Ottoni-Wilhelm et al. (2014) enables an experiment to provide direct support for the existence of altruism. Their results support the dual-motive theory—there is statistically significant evidence that both altruism and egoism drive giving. At the same time, their results indicate that the majority of giving in their experiment was driven by altruism.

The bridge between the experimental literature in psychology and that in economics is important for three reasons. First, the experiments in psychology provide a systematic taxonomy of six warm-glow motivations that can form a basis for investigating specific types of warm-glow motives in charitable giving. Second, the psychology experiments suggest designs that economists can use to investigate the specific types of warm glow. Although some aspects of the psychology designs that involve deception would be less useful to economists, other aspects, such as providing an easy escape or a mood-improving reward, would be useful to them. Third, experiments in economics suggest a design that psychologists can use to investigate the empathy-altruism hypothesis that would not be subject to the problem of sequential testing or to the problem of altruism's being indirectly inferred as a residuum.

Acknowledgments

I am grateful to participants of the 2014 CESifo Conference on Social Economics, and to Sara Konrath and Lise Vesterlund for helpful discussions.

Appendix A Historical Note on Empathy-Altruism in the Economics Literature and Crowd-Out in the Psychology Literature

Boulding (1962) described a *quid pro quo* in which in exchange for giving help to a disadvantaged person one receives "a certain *glow* of emotional virtue" (emphasis added), a harbinger of the phrase "warm glow." He recognized approbation ("vanity," "self-aggrandizement") as a motive to give, and distinguished this from "genuine philanthropy," by which he meant altruism. Boulding also stated the empathy-altruism hypothesis, without calling it such: "It is this capacity for empathy—for putting oneself in another's place, for feeling the joys and sorrows of another as one's own—which is the source of the genuine gift" (p. 61)—here again, Boulding meant the source of the altruistic gift.

Batson, Darley, and Coke (1978, p. 123) stated the dual-motive impure altruism model, though not using that term: "Motivation for helping may be a mixture of altruistic and egoistic desires; it need not be solely or even primarily altruistic to have an altruistic component." They stated the basis of the crowd-out design later used in economics that manipulates giving by others to reduce a recipient's net need in order to test for pure altruism: "Reduction of the other's need is both necessary and sufficient to reduce altruistic motivation."

Appendix B Two Additional Motives: Empathic Joy and Exchange

Batson (2011, p. 124ff) lists an additional type of empathy-specific reward called "empathic joy" as an egoistic motive. (See also see Dovidio et al. 2006.) Originally proposed by Smith, Keating, and Stotland (1989), the empathic joy hypothesis is that empathy does not evoke a desire for an increase in the other's welfare (altruism), but rather evokes a desire for vicarious joy that will come from actually seeing the increase in the other's welfare. Actually seeing the increase in the other's welfare requires feedback to the helper about the other's increased welfare, and manipulating whether or not this feedback is received is how the hypothesis is tested.

From the perspective of economists, there is negligible difference between the definition of empathic joy and the definition of altruism. From an economic perspective, actually seeing the increase in the other's welfare would not be necessary to experience empathic joy, because a fundamental assumption in economics is that people are able to anticipate the future results of their actions even if those results are removed in time and space. Although providing feedback information to the helper about the other's increased welfare may make the situation more salient, and increase giving help for that reason, that would not be evidence against altruism. Indeed, Smith et al. (1989) write: "In many situations, the empathic witness need not help in order to expect an experience of empathic joy, and should be equally pleased when others help." This statement is a precise description of the income effect used in economics to test pure altruism.

Another possible egoistic motivation is that what appears to be voluntary giving is actually an exchange of material goods. Because the *quid pro quo* here is observable (in principle the material good being received by the giver can be directly measured), exchange is typically not included in psychological discussions of egoism or economic discussions of warm glow. In theory, the exchange can be either direct (e.g., receiving a coffee mug as thanks for giving to National Public Radio) or "generalized" (I give now expecting that someone else will give back to me later on). See Ekeh 1974 for an exposition of generalized exchange.

Notes

1. See Becker 1974. Exchange in a situation where one person cares about the well-being of another was first analyzed by Edgeworth (1881) and further developed by Boulding (1962). Collard (1978) provided the first textbook treatment. See Fontaine 2007 for an intellectual history of the early work in economics on altruism.

2. An early statement of the empathy-altruism hypothesis in the economics literature can be found in Boulding 1962. See appendix A to the present chapter.

3. A third first-order condition expresses the tradeoff between x_i escaping) and own consumption: $\beta f_x U_e / U_c = p_x$.

4. Our description of the aversive-arousal-reduction experiments and the descriptions of other experiments in the remainder this section are intentionally brief. See Batson 2011 for a more detailed review of the experimental results.

5. See Batson 2011 and Dovidio et al. 2006 for more extensive discussions of the egoistic motivations summarized here in table 5.1.

6. Eighteen experiments manipulated the price of a substitute good to be either high or low while manipulating empathy high or low as described above. Four other experiments kept the price of the second substitute good low while manipulating empathy. Five experiments did not use a second substitute good. In these totals we do not include three experiments conducted to test the "empathic-joy" hypothesis; in appendix B we explain why, from an economics perspective, empathic-joy is indistinguishable from altruism.

7. A complication in the experiment of Schaller and Cialdini (1988) was that the results supportive of the negative-state relief were significant only if the time of semester was controlled. Hence, cost of helping was not completely controlled in the randomization (e.g., at midterm time a participant faced a higher cost of helping). Batson, Batson, et al. (1989) ran a similar experiment but obtained results consistent with the empathy-altruism hypothesis.

8. Like other experiments in the empathy-altruism literature, the experiments of Cialdini et al. (1987) and Schaller and Cialdini (1988) focused on one egoistic motivation: negative-state relief. However, unlike most other empathy-altruism experiments, their experiments positioned the empathy-altruism hypothesis (not the egoistic negative state-relief) as the null. For example, empathy-altruism predicts, in the high-empathy treatment, no difference in help given between participants who receive a low-price, mood-improving substitute good x_i^j (e.g., the dollar or the praise) and those who do not. Dovidio, Allen, and Schroeder (1990) conducted an experiment in which the substitute good (the opportunity to help the same person but with a need that is different from the need for which empathy was manipulated to be high) positioned negative-state relief as the null: negative-state relief predicts the same level of help given even if the need is different because under the null the participant just wants some way, any way, to improve mood. Because more help was given only when the opportunity to help was for the same need for which empathy was high, Dovidio et al. reject the negative-state-relief hypothesis and argue that their result is consistent with empathy-altruism.

9. Similarly, Dana, Cain, and Dawes (2006) developed a dictator game design in which the potential giver could, albeit at a cost, exit the experiment without the recipient's ever knowing that the potential giver exited from an opportunity to give.

10. However, outside the empathy-altruism literature there are experiments in economics about identity (e.g., Tonin and Vlassopoulis 2013) and approbation (e.g., Andreoni and Bernheim 2009; Ariely, Bracha, and Meier, 2009).

11. In addition to the three experiments by Cialdini et al. (1987) and Schaller and Cialdini (1988) mentioned in note 6, the negative-state relief experiment of Schroeder et al. (1988) positions empathy-altruism as the null.

12. Because economic experiments typically are conducted with procedures that guarantee anonymity, the socially oriented types of egoism/warm glow (shame and approbation) often can be ruled out.

References

Andreoni, J. 1988. Privately provided public goods in a large economy: The limits of altruism. *Journal of Public Economics* 35: 57–73.

Andreoni, J. 1989. Giving with impure altruism: Applications to charity and Ricardian equivalence. *Journal of Political Economy* 97: 1447–1458.

Andreoni, J., and B. D. Bernheim. 2009. Social image and the 50–50 norm: A theoretical and experimental analysis of audience effects. *Econometrica* 77: 1607–1636.

Andreoni, J., and J. M. Rao. 2011. The power of asking: How communication affects selfishness, empathy, and altruism. *Journal of Public Economics* 95: 513–520.

Ariely, D., A. Bracha, and S. Meier. 2009. Doing good or doing well? Image motivation and monetary incentives in behaving prosocially. *American Economic Review* 99: 544–555.

Aronfreed, J. 1970. The socialization of altruistic and sympathetic behavior: Some theoretical and experimental analyses. In *Altruism and Helping Behavior: Social Psychological Studies of Some Antecedents and Consequences*, ed. J. Macaulay and L. Berkowitz. Academic Press.

Arrow, K. J. 1972. Gifts and exchanges. *Philosophy and Public Affairs* 1: 343–362.

Bardsley, N. 2008. Dictator game giving: Altruism or artefact? *Experimental Economics* 11: 122–133.

Batson, C. D. 2011. *Altruism in Humans*. Oxford University Press.

Batson, C. D., J. G. Batson, C. A. Griffitt, S. Barrientos, J. R. Brandt, P. Sprengelmeyer, and M. J. Bayly. 1989. Negative-state relief and the empathy-altruism hypothesis. *Journal of Personality and Social Psychology* 56: 922–933.

Batson, C. D., and J. S. Coke. 1981. Empathy: A source of altruistic motivation for helping? In *Altruism and Helping Behavior: Social, Personality, AND Developmental Perspectives*, ed. J. Rushton and R. Sorrentino. Erlbaum.

Batson, C. D., J. M. Darley, and J. S. Coke. 1978. Altruism and human kindness: Internal and external determinants of helping behavior. In *Perspectives in Interactional Psychology*, ed. L. Pervin and M. Lewis. Plenum .

Batson, C. D., B. D. Duncan, P. Ackerman, T. Buckley, and K. Birch. 1981. Is empathic emotion a source of altruistic motivation? *Journal of Personality and Social Psychology* 40: 290–302.

Batson, C. D., J. L. Dyck, J. R. Brandt, J. G. Batson, A. L. Powell, M. R. McMaster, and C. Griffitt. 1988. Five studies testing two new egoistic alternatives to the empathy-altruism hypothesis. *Journal of Personality and Social Psychology* 55: 52–77.

Batson, C. D., K. O'Quin, J. Fultz, M. Vanderplas, and A. Isen. 1983. Self-reported distress and empathy and egoistic versus altruistic motivation for helping. *Journal of Personality and Social Psychology* 45: 706–718.

Batson, C. D., and J. L. Weeks. 1996. Mood effects of unsuccessful helping: Another test of the empathy-altruism hypothesis. *Personality and Social Psychology Bulletin* 22: 148–157.

Becker, G. 1974. A theory of social interactions. *Journal of Political Economy* 82: 1063–1093.

Bolton, G., and E. Katok. 1998. An experimental test of the crowding-out hypothesis: The nature of beneficent behavior. *Journal of Economic Behavior and Organization* 37: 315–331.

Boulding, K. E. 1962. Notes on a theory of philanthropy. In *Philanthropy and Public Policy*, ed. F. Dickinson. North-Holland.

Cialdini, R. B. 1991. Altruism or egoism? That is (still) the question. *Psychological Inquiry* 2: 124–126.

Cialdini, R. B., M. Schaller, D. Houlihan, K. Arps, J. Fultz, and A. L. Beaman. 1987. Empathy-based helping: Is it selflessly or selfishly motivated? *Journal of Personality and Social Psychology* 52: 749–758.

Collard, D. 1978. *Altruism and Economy: A Study in Non-Selfish Economics*. Martin Robertson.

Cornes, R., and T. Sandler. 1984. Easy riders, joint production, and public goods. *Economic Journal* 94: 580–598.

Dana, J., D. M. Cain, and R. Dawes. 2006. What you don't know won't hurt me: Costly (but quiet) exit in dictator games. *Organizational Behavior and Human Decision Processes* 100: 193–201.

Dana, J., R. A. Weber, and J. X. Kuang. 2007. Exploiting moral wiggle room: Experiments demonstrating an illusory preference for fairness. *Economic Theory* 330: 67–80.DellaVigna, S., J. A. List, and U. Malmendier. 2012. Testing for altruism and social pressure in charitable giving. *Quarterly Journal of Economics* 127: 1–56.

Dovidio, J. F., J. L. Allen, and D. A. Schroeder. 1990. Specificity of empathy-induced helping: Evidence for altruistic motivation. *Journal of Personality and Social Psychology* 59: 249–260.

Dovidio, J. F., J. A. Piliavin, D. A. Schroeder, and L. A. Penner. 2006. *The Social Psychology of Prosocial Behavior*. Erlbaum.

Edgeworth, F. Y. 1881. *Mathematical Psychics*. Kegan Paul.

Ekeh, P. P. 1974. *Social Exchange Theory: The Two Traditions*. Harvard University Press.

Fontaine, P. 2007. From philanthropy to altruism: Incorporating unselfish behavior into economics, 1961–1975. *History of Political Economy* 39: 1–46.

Fultz, J., C. D. Batson, V. A. Fortenbach, P. M. McCarthy, and L. L. Varney. 1986. Social evaluation and the empathy-altruism hypothesis. *Journal of Personality and Social Psychology* 50: 761–769.

Hoffman, M. L. 1975. Developmental synthesis of affect and cognition and its implications for altruistic motivation. *Developmental Psychology* 11: 607–622.

Konow, J. 2010. Mixed feelings: Theories of and evidence on giving. *Journal of Public Economics* 94: 279–297.

Krebs, D. 1975. Empathy and altruism. *Journal of Personality and Social Psychology* 32: 2234–1146.

List, J. 2007. On the interpretation of giving in dictator games. *Journal of Political Economy* 115: 482–493.

Ottoni-Wilhelm, M., L. Vesterlund, and H. Xie. 2014. Why do people give? Testing pure and impure altruism. Working Paper 20497, National Bureau of Economic Research.

Piliavin, J. A., J. F. Dovidio, S. L. Gaertner, and R. D. Clark III. 1982. Responsive bystanders: The process of intervention. In *Cooperation and Helping Behavior: Theories and Research*, ed. V. Derlega and J. Grzelak. Academic Press.

Piliavin, J. A., and I. M. Piliavin. 1973. The good Samaritan: Why does he help? Unpublished manuscript.

Ribar, D. C., and M. O. Wilhelm. 2002. Altruistic and joy-of-giving motivations in charitable behavior. *Journal of Political Economy* 110: 425–457.

Schaller, M., and R. B. Cialdini. 1988. The economics of empathic helping: Support for a mood management motive. *Journal of Experimental and Social Psychology* 24: 163–181.

Schroeder, D. A., J. F. Dovidio, M. E. Sibicky, L. L. Matthews, and J. L. Allen. 1988. Empathic concern and helping behavior: Egoism or altruism? *Journal of Experimental Social Psychology* 24: 333–353.

Smith, A. 1997 (1759). *The Theory of Moral Sentiments*. Regency .

Smith, K. D., J. P. Keating, and E. Stotland. 1989. Altruism reconsidered: The effect of denying feedback on a victim's status to empathic witnesses. *Journal of Personality and Social Psychology* 57: 641–650.

Steinberg, R. S. 1987. Voluntary donations and public expenditures in a federalist system. *American Economic Review* 77: 24–36.

Sugden, Robert. 1982. On the economics of philanthropy. *Economic Journal* 92: 341–350.

Toi, M., and C. D. Batson. 1982. More evidence that empathy is a source of altruistic motivation? *Journal of Personality and Social Psychology* 43: 281–292.

Tonin, M., and M. Vlassopoulos. 2013. Self-image concerns as motivation for giving. *Journal of Economic Behavior and Organization* 90: 19–27.

Vesterlund, L. Forthcoming. Using experimental methods to understand why and how we give to charity. In *The Handbook of Experimental Economics*, volume 2, ed. J. Kagel and A. Roth. Princeton University Press.

Warr, P. 1982. Pareto optimal redistribution and private charity. *Journal of Public Economics* 19: 131–138.

Yildirim, H. 2014. Andreoni-McGuire algorithm and the limits of warm-glow giving. *Journal of Public Economics* 114: 101–107.

Culture, Values, and Norms

6

(related countries)

The Microeconomics of Trust

Luigi Guiso

乙13 B55

Besides, the commerce of mankind is not confined to the barter of commodities, but may extend to services and actions, which we may exchange to our mutual interest and advantage. Your corn is ripe to-day; mine will be so tomorrow. It is profitable for us both, that I should labour with you to-day, and that you should aid me to-morrow. I have no kindness for you, and know you have as little for me. I will not, therefore, take any pains upon your account; and should I labour with you upon my own account, in expectation of a return, I know I should be disappointed, and that I should in vain depend upon your gratitude. Here then I leave you to labour alone: You treat me in the same manner. The seasons change; and both of us lose our harvests for want of mutual confidence and security.

David Hume, "A Treatise of Human Nature," book III, part II, section V

Trust is probably among the most researched topics in the social sciences. This comes as no surprise. Trust—the faith and confidence one has that things will turn out as one hopes—enters into nearly all relations and all types of trade, not only in the economic domain but also in social and political domains any time individuals interact with each other. Trust is pervasive, and because of its pervasiveness it has attracted the attention of philosophers, political scientists, psychologists, anthropologists, and sociologists. More recently, biologists and neuroscientists have begun to investigate its biological basis and its neurological foundations (Fehr 2009). Economists, however, have long ignored trust. One reason is that trust is irrelevant if one can write contracts that are enforced by a court. This assumption, made initially more for convenience than for realism, dispenses one from worrying about trust beliefs in bilateral trades. Yet convenient assumptions sometimes tend to become an intrinsic part of the methodology of a discipline to the point that the initial convenience is confused with realism, and this in turn tends to obscure the importance of certain issues. Something of this sort has happened with trust. Trust has come to the fore after the realization that legal contacts usually are

incomplete, costly to write, and difficult to enforce. Indeed, a large literature pioneered by Andrei Shleifer and co-authors (see Djankov et al.
2003) has documented diffuse imperfections in the working of the judi-
cial with lengthy procedures to enforce a contract, with remarkable differences across countries.[1] How can one rely on a court to enforce a debt
contract when it takes 300 days to recoup a bounced check in Argentina
or 650 days in Italy? With imperfect third-party enforcement, and without verifiability of the items of exchange or the conditions that trigger
obligations, many trades could not take place. Whenever this is the case,
as Hume noticed, there is a role for informal promises and for mutual
trust to make those trades possible. Indeed, promises and the trust that
sustains them can be thought as filling in the gaps left by the imperfections of the legal system. In developing countries or for some type of
exchanges these gaps can be substantial and, if not bridged by trust, can
be a serious cause of underdevelopment. Indeed, more than 35 years ago
Kenneth Arrow, recognizing the pervasiveness of trust in commercial and
non-commercial transactions and departing from prevailing economic
thought at the time, went so far as to state that it could be plausibly
argued that much of the economic backwardness in the world could be
explained by the lack of mutual confidence (Arrow 1972, p. 357). Since
then, Arrow's conjecture has received considerable empirical support. A
vast literature investigates the link between aggregate trust and aggregate
economic performance and finds a positive and monotonic relationship.
Trust has been shown to be strongly correlated with GDP per capita and
with GDP growth (Knack and Zak 2001; Knack and Keefer 1996; Guiso
et al. 2004). Though a correlation does not imply a causal role of trust in
fostering GDP levels and growth (the reverse causality from GDP to prevailing levels of trust must first be ruled out), more recent contributions
have been able to sort out strategies that can isolate the casual effect of
trust on economic performance. (See Tabellini 2008b and Algan and
Cahuc 2010.) Furthermore, several papers have documented correlations
that suggest important channels through which trust can influence a
country's economic activity. It has been found that trust is correlated with
the quality of the organization of firms across countries (Bloom et al.
2009) and with their ability to grow large (La Porta et al. 1997), with the
size of a country's stock market and its financial development (Guiso et
al. 2008a), with the quality and extent of regulation (Aghion et al. 2010),
and with cross-country trade patterns in goods and assets (Guiso et al.
2009).

Thus, although the link between trust and aggregate economic performance seems to be relatively well established, much less is known about the microeconomics of trust, how trust differs across individuals and why, how trust evolves, what causes changes in trust beliefs, and whether trust beliefs matter for individual economic achievement. In this chapter we will move the focus from the macroeconomics to the microeconomics of trust and try to shed light on three questions: How is individual trust formed and how it evolves ? Why does trust tend to persist? Are trust beliefs correct, and what do trust mistakes (if there are any) entail? We address the first two questions in section 6.1 and the third in section 6.2. Section 6.3 concludes the chapter.

6.1   Formation and Evolution of Trust

Trust is a belief defining our expectation about the behavior of a specific counterpart in a deal. Saying that I trust person B means that I expect that if I make myself vulnerable to B—e.g., lend money to B, host B in my apartment, or decide to share with B a new idea for a paper—B is not going to take advantage of my vulnerability. That is, B will return the money I lent, will not steal objects from my apartment, and will not steal the idea I shared. Not surprisingly, many decisions—certainly all those that involve an element of time in an exchange—rely upon our beliefs about how much we trust others. Lacking trust, some trades and exchanges will simply not be undertaken, to the detriment of both parties.

Heterogeneity

A large literature, using evidence from different datasets and a variety of countries, has shown that trust tends to persist across generations. (See Algan and Cahuc 2010; Butler, Giuliano, and Guiso 2015b; Dohmen et al. 2012; Guiso, Sapienza, and Zingales 2008a.) Trust beliefs are, however, quite heterogeneous across individuals. Figure 6.1 (taken from Butler et al. 2015b) shows the distribution of trust for each of the countries surveyed in the European Social Survey. Here, trust is the belief about how much a generic person should be trusted, measured on a scale between 0 and 10: 0 means no trust at all; 10 means other people can be fully trusted. The figure indicates systematic differences in the shape of the trust distribution across countries.

In one group, consisting of high-trust North European countries such as Norway, Denmark, Finland, Sweden, Iceland, and the Netherlands,

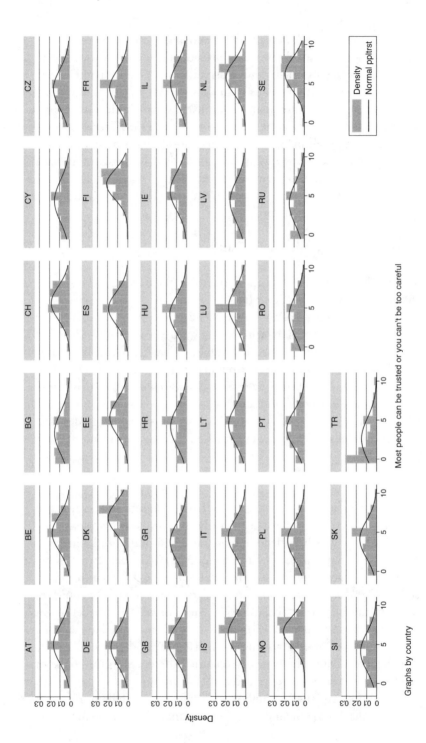

Figure 6.1
Trust beliefs: density functions by country. Source: Butler et al. 2015b, elaborations on ESS data.

the distribution has a fat right tail and the modal level of trust is quite high at around 7. A second group, which includes several Mediterranean and Eastern European countries, features a fat left tail, denoting low average trust. In a third group, consisting of several European countries (e.g., Austria, Germany, France, and the United Kingdom) the distribution is approximately symmetric around modal values of 5. Perhaps more surprisingly, figure 6.1 documents that there is considerable heterogeneity in trust levels *within* each country. Individual opinions differ greatly in each country in the sample, with a non-negligible number of observations at the two tails of the distribution. Individual opinions also vary substantially among countries: in high-trust countries, such as Denmark, the fraction of people reporting 9 or 10 is equal to 12.0 and 6.7 percent of the overall sample respectively, whereas the fraction of people reporting 0 or 1 is equal to 1.0 and 0.9 percent, respectively. At the other extreme is Turkey, where the fraction of people reporting 9 or 10 is equal to 1.0 and 2.3 percent respectively, whereas the fraction of people reporting 0 or 1 is equal to 30.5 and 17.9 percent respectively. Differences within countries are puzzling if people tend to trade and deal with representative samples of people in their country, yet some of this heterogeneity may nevertheless reflect heterogeneity in the pool of people they deal with.

Persistence

To document persistence of trust across generations, one would like to observe the trust beliefs of different generations spaced in time. This would require trust data on the current population of people of certain ages—say, 25–30 years—and data on the population of those aged 25–30 one or two or three generations ago (i.e., 25, 50 or 75 years ago). Unfortunately, data of this type are not available. However, we can compare the distribution of trust beliefs among second-generation immigrants from a certain country currently living in another country against the distribution of trust beliefs in their country of origin. For instance, we can compare the trust of second-generation migrants of Italian origin living in one of the other European countries against the trust of the current Italian population, and we can do the same for second-generation migrants of Spanish, Greek, or Norwegian origin. If trust persists, the trust distribution of the Italian migrants should resemble that of the current Italians. For this we have computed several moments (mean, median, standard deviation, and skewness) of the trust distributions of migrants of various nationalities and correlate them with the corresponding moments of the

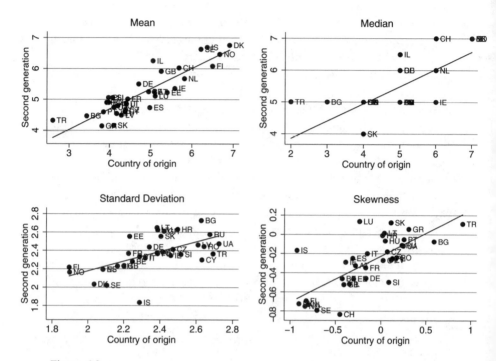

Figure 6.2
Correlations between moments of trust distribution in countries of origin and among second-generation immigrants. Source: Butler et al. 2015b, elaborations on ESS data.

trust distribution in the countries of origin. These correlations are shown in figure 6.2. Inspection of these correlations shows undisputable evidence of a remarkable persistence in the distribution of trust beliefs.

Explaining Heterogeneity and Persistence
But why do trust beliefs differ, and persist or differ, persistently? Persistent heterogeneity in trust beliefs, even among members of the same community, has been explained in the literature in various ways. According to one view, individuals' beliefs are initially acquired through cultural transmission and then slowly updated through experience from one generation to the next. This line of argument has been pursued by Guiso, Sapienza, and Zingales (2008b). They build an overlapping-generations model in which children absorb their trust priors from their parents and then, after experiencing the real world, transmit their (updated) beliefs to their own children. Heterogeneity is the result of family-specific shocks. Within a generation, correlation between current beliefs and received

priors is diluted as people age and learn. Yet this dilution needs not to be complete, and a high degree of persistence may still obtain. Dohmen et al. (2012) provide evidence consistent with this view.

A somewhat slightly different explanation is that parents instill values, such as trustworthiness, rather than beliefs. Focusing on cultural transmission of values of cooperation and trustworthiness, Bisin and Verdier (2000), Bisin, Topa, and Verdier (2004), and Tabellini (2008a) show how norms of behavior are optimally passed down from parents to children and persist from generation to generation. Heterogeneity in parents' preferences and experiences may then result in heterogeneity in instilled trustworthiness. Even if parents do not teach beliefs directly, individuals may extrapolate from their own type when forming beliefs about others' trustworthiness. As Thomas Schelling once wrote, "you can sit in your armchair and try to predict how people behave by asking yourself how you would behave if you had your wits about you. You get free of charge a lot of vicarious empirical behavior" (Schelling 1966, p. 150). Butler, Giuliano, and Guiso (2015a) study this second channel and provide evidence suggesting that false consensus—the tendency of individuals to extrapolate the behavior of others from their own type (Ross, Greene, and House 1977)— may be able to explain the dual patterns of heterogeneity and persistence of trust beliefs. Consistent with Bisin and Verdier (2000), Bisin et al. (2004), and Tabellini (2008a), they are able to document that people trustworthiness differs greatly; through false consensus, this heterogeneity in trustworthiness translates into different prior beliefs. The latter, in turn, evolve as the environment in which the individual trades changes and some learning about the average trustworthiness of the pool people interact with occurs; nevertheless, beliefs tend to be anchored to the trustworthiness of the individual—that is ,they tend to persist, and differences in trust beliefs still reflect the initial type even after several layers of interaction and learning.

False consensus is then a source of initial prior. In the absence of a history of information about the reliability of a pool of people, those interacting with an unknown pool form a prior by asking themselves how they would behave in similar circumstances. Since they would behave differently, they start with different priors. If values (or priors) persist and false consensus does not vanish with learning, then wrong beliefs will also persist. In such a context, false consensus implies that highly trustworthy individuals will tend to think that others are like them and form overly optimistic trust beliefs, while highly untrustworthy people will extrapolate from their own type and form excessively pessimistic beliefs. Both highly trustworthy and highly untrustworthy individuals will tend to systematically form more extreme trust beliefs than are warranted by their experiences. A long history of research on false consensus has indeed shown it to be a persistent phenomenon (Krueger and Clement 1994) that need not drowned out by monetary incentives for accurate predictions (Massey and Thaler 2013).

False Consensus, Own Trustworthiness, and Trust Beliefs: Linked Heterogeneity

To show the importance of false consensus, Butler et al. (2015a) rely on two experiments. In the first they use a repeated version of the standard trust game in the laboratory (Berg, Dickhaut, and McCabe, 1995). From this they obtain a measure of participants' own (initial) trustworthiness—how much they return in the trust game when playing the role of receiver; they also elicit participants' beliefs after each round of game play. Figure 6.3 shows the distribution of the initial trust beliefs (panel a) and of initial trustworthiness (panel b) by the participants in the experiment. Both are highly heterogeneous, which suggests that people's priors differ considerably even when they refer to the average trustworthiness of the same pool. Most interestingly, the two distributions are very highly correlated, which suggests that beliefs are formed by extrapolating from one's own type. Initial trustworthiness can explain about 60 percent of the initial trust beliefs of the experiment participants. To show persistence, they have the trust game repeated for several rounds with the same group. In each round, individuals are randomly assigned the role of sender or receiver. This way they can learn from personal experience about the pool. Interestingly, the correlation between trust beliefs and initial trustworthiness remains strong and significant even after several rounds of game play. After twelve rounds, initial trustworthiness can still explain 30 percent of the cross-sectional heterogeneity in beliefs.

Parental Values and Transmitted Trustworthiness

This leaves us with the question of where is the initial trustworthiness coming from. An interesting conjecture is that young people's trustworthiness is determined by the values that their parents instill as part of the education process. If these values remain stable over age, this would be evidence that trust persists, not only within the lifecycle of an individual, but also across generations as documented in figure 6.2 using the migrants methodology.

a

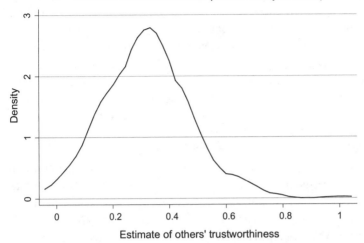

kernel = epanechnikov, bandwidth = 0.0408

b

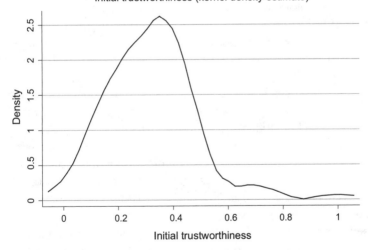

kernel = epanechnikov, bandwidth = 0.0570

Figure 6.3
Heterogeneity in trust beliefs and own trustworthiness. Source: Butler et al. 2015a, elaborations on experimental data.

Butler et al. (2015a) take advantage of participants' recollections of the moral values emphasized by their parents during their upbringing, obtained in a questionnaire that they were asked to fill in. They look at two types of values: how much emphasis an individual's parents placed on always behaving like a good citizen, and how much emphasis parents placed on loyalty to groups or organizations. They average the responses to these questions to get a measure of received cultural values, and they express the indicator on a scale from 0 to 1. Several factors militate against finding any relationship between instilled "good" values (indicator close to 1) and trust beliefs or trustworthiness. First, the measure of received cultural values is a noisy measure of transmitted cultural values, partly because it is retrospective and partly because it is self-reported. Second, participants' own values are likely to reflect not only the values their parents transmitted but also, to varying degrees, values acquired through other channels of socialization, which are not measured. Finally, the identifying variation in receivers' behavior is attenuated by the nature of the pecuniary incentives involved, which pull in only one direction: toward uniformly returning nothing. Despite these factors working against finding a relation, Butler et al. (ibid.) find a significant positive correlation between good values and the trustworthiness and trust beliefs. Most importantly, instilled values have a strong economic effect on trustworthiness: an increase in good values from 0 to 1 (admittedly a large increase) is associated with an increase in initial trustworthiness of more than 50 percent.

In sum, a model in which parents optimally transmit values that shape the trustworthiness of their children (as in Bisin and Verdier 2000, Bisin et al. 2004, and Tabellini 2008a and 2008b), in which these values inform individuals' trust priors when they begin trading in novel environments in which they lack information about the counterpart, and in which individuals extrapolate the trustworthiness of others from their own trustworthiness seems to be a good model of how trust and trustworthiness are formed.

Because parents' values reflect their own experiences and the institutional constraints in the environment in which they anticipate their children will operate, parents will transmit heterogeneous values. Because people rely on their type to form trust priors, trust will be heterogeneous. Hence, the scheme can explain the observed heterogeneity and the correlation between trust and trustworthiness. Needless to say, the correlation will not be perfect, as individuals also receive signals about their counterparts and use them to revise their priors and form their trust beliefs.

Because in this model values are culturally transmitted across generations, trust will persist from generation to generation. But since trust is a belief, it will evolve over the life cycle of the individuals as he learns about the pool of people with whom he interacts. However, every time this pool changes and the individual has to form a new prior, he will rely again on his trustworthiness to make an informed guess. Hence, trust beliefs will always be anchored to the trustworthiness of the individuals and, for the same individual, will show persistence.

6.2   Effects of Trust: Decisions and Performance

As was shown in section 6.1, trust beliefs are remarkably heterogeneous in the cross-section. This is true when one looks at data for individuals within a country (as shown in figure 6.1) and trust refers to the beliefs about the trustworthiness of the country's population, but it is also true when data refer to a pool of people in a lab (as documented in panel a of figure 6.3) and trust is the belief that each participant in the experiment has toward the pool of participants. Because the trust people in a survey express refers to a well-identified group, their beliefs should reflect the average trustworthiness of the group. However, the fact that they express different opinions means either that they all have correct beliefs but they interact with different pools of people that differ in trustworthiness and these differences are correctly anticipated or that, despite the fact that they interact and trade with the same pool, some are able to express a correct guess while others must err, either overstating the trustworthiness of the pool or understating it. The first possibility can be true in the country-level data but can't be true in the experiment. In the lab, all interact with the same pool and thus there is only one true level of trustworthiness: the mean of the group. Thus, those who depart from this level and either exceed in trust or their trust falls short of this mean will make trust mistakes.

Does this matter? What are the consequences for the economic performance of the individual? Because trust beliefs affect behavior in a variety of contexts, miscalibrated beliefs can potentially have serious effects on an individual's performance.

As Butler et al. (2015b) argued, trust mistakes can affect performance through two channels. First, negative mistakes—trust below the rational-expectations level—can lead individuals to make too-conservative decisions and thus to miss important trade opportunities. For instance, a low level of trust may induce people to stay out of the stock market (Guiso et al. 2008a) for fear of being cheated. Yet if the belief understates the true trustworthiness of the participants in the stock market inducing people to wrongly put all the money in bonds, their return on wealth will be much lower than the one they could attain if they had correct beliefs. Because the equity premium is as large as 6 percent, this can result in a significant loss in income. Alternatively, a skeptical investor who assigns to his financial advisor much less trust than is deserved may end up delegating financial decisions much less than he should, giving up useful and profitable information; or—underestimating the trustworthiness of their banker—investors make a run on the bank when it is solid, provoking a collapse and losing all the money deposited. Examples of missed opportunities, easy to find in the domain of financial decisions, are no less extensive in other domains. Among businessmen, many trades, particularly those that require a quick decision before the opportunity is grabbed by a competitor, are concluded by shaking hands. Erroneously mistrusting one's counterpart may lead one to withdraw from a deal and to lose a profitable opportunity. Or one can turn down the offer to participate in a promising research project for fear that the co-author can appropriate the idea, and the fear can be overstated. Second, positive mistakes originating from levels of trust in excess of the true trustworthiness of the counterpart can be equally detrimental, because exceeding in trust exposes one to higher social risk and thus to greater chances of being cheated. Putting one's life savings in the hands of a single portfolio manager on the belief that he deserved to be trusted exposes one to a high risk of losing all of one's capital if the manager turns out to be Bernie Madoff.

Either because trust mistakes cause too little trade and income losses due to missed opportunities, or because they lead to excessive trade and income losses due to cheating, the cumulative losses can be substantial given that, as we have documented, trust beliefs tend to persist and with them the associated mistakes. Butler et al. (2015b) argue that because of these two forces there should be a hump-shaped relationship between an individual's level of income and how much that individual trusts. They show evidence drawn from data from the European Social Survey that this is actually the case. We follow them in exposing the relationship between an individual's income and his or her level of trust, and we illustrate how we can identify and measure the effect of trust beliefs on individual performance.

Modeling the Trust-Income Relationship

Following Butler et al. (2015b), we can represent the hump-shaped relationship between individual trust and income by the following simple model:

$$y_{ic} = y_{\max}(X_c) - a_i(\pi_{ic} - \tau_{ic})^2 + U_i,$$

where y_{ic} is the income of individual i in country c and $y_{\max}(X_{ic})$ is the individual maximum attainable income when trust beliefs are correct. The maximum attainable income depends on a vector of variables (X_{ic}) capturing both features of the country and characteristics of the individual; $L_{ic} = a_i(\pi_{ic} - \tau_{ic})^2$ is a loss incurred by an individual upon failing to correctly anticipate the true trustworthiness of the pool of people with which he or she interacts. The loss L_{ic} depends on the trustworthiness of the pool of people individual i interacts with (π_{ic}), his or her individual level of trust (τ_{ic}) and his or her sensitivity to trust mistakes (a_i). ϵ_i is a random component orthogonal to the explanatory variables. Notice that this specification allows for heterogeneity in both the trustworthiness of the pool of people individuals interact with (π_{ic}) as well as the sensitivity to trust mistakes (a_i). Both sources of heterogeneity may be potentially important and realistic: in large cities and countries, it is reasonable that people face different pools of partners in trades. Some of these differences reflect geographic heterogeneity in the trustworthiness of local populations reflecting long-lasting differences in historical trajectories and influences, as for instance between the North and the South of Italy. Alternatively, they may reflect people sorting into groups of partners in trades that differ in trustworthiness. Similarly, a trust mistake of a given size need not have the same consequences. For some individuals—e.g., for an entrepreneur—a wrong assessment of the trustworthiness of the counterpart in a trade may have very large income costs. To capture these features, Butler et al. model π_{ic} as having two components: an observed heterogeneity component common to all individuals in the same country, π_i, which they assume depends linearly on the average trust in the country (x_c), so that $\pi_c = m + bx_c$, where m and b are parameters, and an unobserved individual-specific component η_i of the trustworthiness of i's pool, so that $\pi_c = m + bx_c + \eta_i$. They also assume that $a_i = a + u_i$, where u_i is a zero mean individual specific component of the income sensitivity to trust mistakes.

Making some reasonable assumption about the relationship between the stochastic components η_i, u_i, and $\eta_{i'}$, they are able to estimate the income trust relationship allowing for heterogeneity in the pool of people trade with and in their sensitivity to mistakes in trust belief. The estimates allow to identify the parameters a, b, and m and to compute for each individuals the level of trust that maximizes his or her income—that is, the level that sets the loss $L_i = 0$. Because the current level of trust of each individual is observed, it is possible to compute each individual's income loss function.

Interestingly, Butler et al. (2015b) find that both sources of heterogeneity—heterogeneity in the sensitivity to trust mistakes and in the pool of people individuals face—are present. Since the level of trust consistent with ϵ_i (which Butler et al. call the right amount of trust) is a function of the average trust in a country, the estimates generate a different right level of trust for each country and also for each individual. Interestingly, Butler et al. find that this right level of trust always exceeds the trust of the average person in the country. Put differently, the average person trusts *less* than the level that would maximize his or her income. That is, people have, on average, too-conservative beliefs. If their objective were to maximize income, they would gain by trusting more.

Panels a–c in figure 6.4 show the cross-sectional distributions of the right amount of trust, trust mistakes, and income losses induced by trust mistakes. For a country with an average trust level of 5, in the cross-section the income-maximizing level of trust ranges from 7 to 6.28 when the individual component of the trustworthiness of the pool faced by the individual ($L_i = 0$, which Butler et al. estimate) ranges between the 5th and the 95th percentile of its distribution. In the overall sample, which includes all countries, the mean value of the right amount of trust is 6.54, with a standard deviation of 0.81. This is shown in panel a of figure 6.4; the sample variation reflects both variation in the average trust across countries as well as heterogeneity in the pool of people faced by each individual. Interestingly, 90 percent of the observations are bounded between 5.5 and 8. Furthermore, most of the variation in the cross-sectional distribution of the right amount of trust is due to variation in average trust across countries rather than in the pool individuals face. This suggests that most people tend to face representative samples of the populations in their country.

Panel b in figure 6.4 shows the cross-sectional distribution of trust mistakes computed as the difference between the income-maximizing trust level and actual trust. Because on average the right amount of trust exceeds the trust of the average person in the country, mistakes are not symmetric around zero but tend to be positive. The mean mistake is 1.65

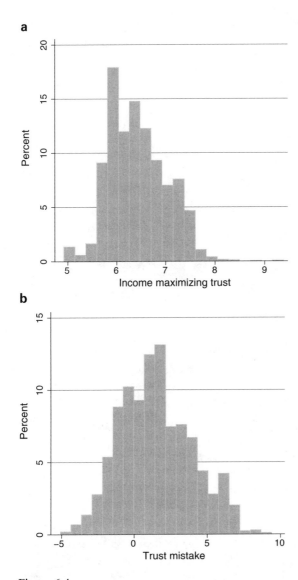

Figure 6.4
Income-maximizing trust, trust mistakes, and income cost of trust mistakes. Source: Butler et al. 2015b.

c

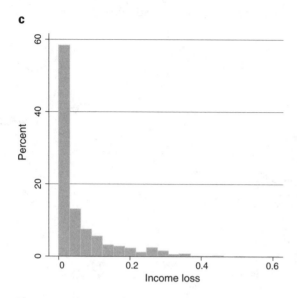

Figure 6.4 (continued)

(median 1.55) with considerable variation as documented by a high standard deviation (2.4). Though a majority of individuals has well-calibrated beliefs (55 percent have an absolute mistake not greater than 1.68), a full 10 percent of the people in the sample make trust mistakes exceeding 4.9. These are typically individuals with very low levels of trust interacting with relatively trustworthy groups. Panel c in figure 6.4 shows the cross-sectional distribution of the income loss implied by estimated trust mistakes computed using 0.005 as the estimated average cost of a mistake. Consistent with the fact that most people have trust beliefs close to the trustworthiness of their pool, the distribution is highly skewed to the right. For around half of the sample the income cost of trust mistakes is less than 1.6 percent of what they would earn if they had correct beliefs, and for three fourths of the sample it is less than 6.4 percent. However, for about 10 percent of the sample the cost exceeds 13 percent of potential income, and for half of these individuals the cost is larger than 17 percent. These figures imply that the economic effect of miscalibrated trust belief can be as large as that of the returns to education. Finally, panel d in figure 6.4 shows the relationship between income loss and the level of individual trust implied by our estimates country by country. Because the trust-income relationship is hump-shaped in all countries, the income loss is u-shaped in trust, with a minimum at the right amount.

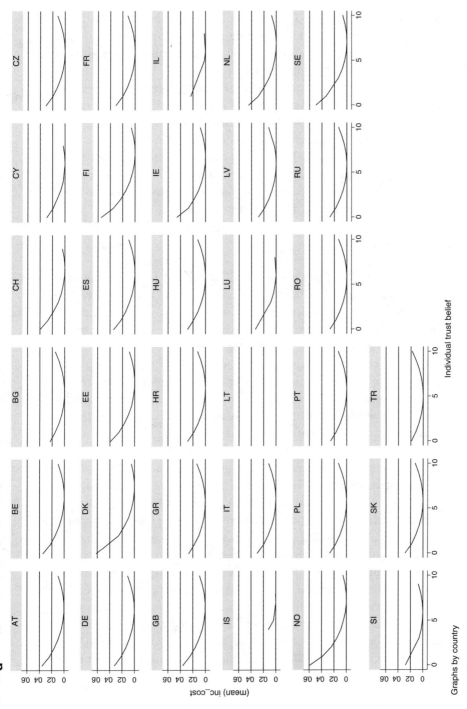

Graphs by country

Figure 6.4 (continued)

The point to take away from this figure is that in all countries in the European Union it is generally true that trusting very little—that is, exposing oneself to the risk of giving up profit opportunities—is more costly than trusting a lot and facing a higher risk of being cheated. The first type of loss is particularly large in high-trust countries such as Denmark and Norway, while in lower-trust countries (e.g., Greece and Turkey) the cost of the two types of mistakes is of comparable size. We can conclude that accounting for systematic differences in trustworthiness across countries, unobserved heterogeneity in the trustworthiness of the pool each individual faces within a country, and unobserved heterogeneity in the sensitivity to trust mistakes still results in a humped-shaped relationship between income and trust beliefs.

6.3   Conclusion

In this chapter we have documented substantial heterogeneity in trust beliefs among individuals within a country. This heterogeneity is only partially a reflection of heterogeneity in the trustworthiness in the group of people one interacts with. In fact, when this heterogeneity is estimated, it seems to be limited. In addition, when people play a trust game and their trust beliefs are elicited, these show as much heterogeneity as that measured in surveys, despite they all play the game with partners drawn from the same pool. Diversity of trust opinions reflects departures from rational-expectations beliefs. What is most important, these departures tend to be persistent, both across generations but also within the same generation. Part of this persistence reflects a tendency of individuals to extrapolate their beliefs about the trustworthiness of others from their own trustworthiness, which seems to be equally heterogeneous. If trustworthiness is a trait of the person and changes only slowly, it may represent the reference point to which trust beliefs tend to converge after they deviate in response to individual experiences. How trust beliefs adjust, how fast, and in response to what type of events are still an underexplored questions. For instance, we know little about how beliefs about a particular group (e.g., bankers or grocers) are affected by the (mis)-behavior of a member of the group and (more interestingly) by the (mis-)behavior of a member of an unrelated group (e.g., a mechanic or a plumber). The available evidence from movers and migrants suggests that people adjust their beliefs to the new environment but that trust has a slow-moving component that persists across generations.

Yet understanding how fast people learn and what inhibits or speeds up learning about the trustworthiness of others is critical because trust mistakes can be, as we have documented, quite costly both when individuals mistrust and when they grant too much confidence.

Note

1. Hume (1738) was already aware of the role and the limitations of formal laws when he wrote: "The invention of the law of nature, concerning the stability of possession, has already rendered men tolerable to each other; that of the transference of property and possession by consent has begun to render them mutually advantageous: But still these laws of nature, however strictly observed, are not sufficient to render them so serviceable to each other, as by nature they are fitted to become."

References

Aghion, Philippe, Yann Algan, Pierre Cahuc, and Andrei Shleifer. 2010. Regulation and distrust. *Quarterly Journal of Economics* 125 (3): 1015–1049.

Algan, Yann, and Pierre Cahuc. 2010. Inherited trust and growth. *American Economic Review* 100 (5): 2060–2092.

Arrow, Kenneth. 1972. Gifts and exchanges. *Philosophy & Public Affairs* 1 (4): 343–362.

Berg, J., J. Dickhaut, and K. McCabe. 1995. Trust, reciprocity and social history. *Games and Economic Behavior* 10: 122–142.

Bisin, Alberto, Giorgio Topa, and Thierry Verdier. 2004. Cooperation as a transmitted cultural trait. *Rationality and Society* 16 (4): 477–507.

Bisin, Alberto, and Thierry Verdier. 2000. Beyond the Melting Pot: Cultural Transmission, Marriage, and the Evolution of Ethnic and Religious Trait. *Quarterly Journal of Economics* 115 (3): 955–988.

Bloom, Nicholas, Raffaella Sadun, and John Van Reenen. 2009. The Organization of Firms across Countries. Discussion Paper 937, Centre for Economic Policy Research.

Butler, Jeffrey V., Paola Giuliano, and Luigi Guiso. 2015a. Trust, values and false consensus. *International Economic Review* 56 (3): 889–915.

Butler, Jeffrey V., Paola Giuliano, and Luigi Guiso. 2015b. Forthcoming. The Right Amount of Trust. *Journal of the European Economic Association*.

Djankov, Simeon, Rafael LaPorta, Florencio Lopez-de-Silanes, and Andrei Shleifer. 2003. Courts. *Quarterly Journal of Economics* 118 (2): 453–517.

Dohmen, Thomas, Armin Falk, David Huffman, and Uwe Sunde. 2012. The intergenerational transmission of risk and trust attitudes. *Review of Economic Studies* 79 (2): 645–677.

Fehr, Ernst. 2009. On the economics and biology of trust. *Journal of the European Economic Association* 7 (2–3): 235–266.

Guiso, Luigi, Paola Sapienza, and Luigi Zingales. 2004. The role of social capital in financial development. *American Economic Review* 94:526–556.

Guiso, Luigi, Paola Sapienza, and Luigi Zingales. 2008a. Trusting the stock market. *Journal of Finance* 63 (6): 2557–2600.

Guiso, Luigi, Paola Sapienza and Luigi Zingales. 2008b. Social Capital as Good Culture. *Journal of the European Economic Association* 6 (2.3): 295–320.

Guiso, Luigi, Paola Sapienza, and Luigi Zingales. 2009. Cultural biases in economic exchange? *Quarterly Journal of Economics* 124 (3): 1095–1131.

Hume, David. 1738. A Treatise of Human Nature (https://www.gutenberg.org/files/4705/4705-h/4705-h.htm#link2H_4_0075).

Knack, Stephen, and Philip Keefer. 1996. Does social capital have an economic payoff? A cross-country investigation. *Quarterly Journal of Economics* 112 (4): 1251–1288.

Knack, Stephen, and Paul Zak. 2001. Trust and growth. *Economic Journal* 111: 295–321.

Krueger, Joachim, and Russel W. Clement. 1994. The truly false consensus effect. *Journal of Personality and Social Psychology* 67 (4): 596–610.

La Porta, Rafael, Florencio Lopez de Silanes, Andrea Shleifer, and Robert Vishny. 1997. Trust in large organizations. *American Economic Review* 87 (2): 333–338.

Massey, Cade, and Richard H. Thaler. 2013. The loser's curse: Decision making and market efficiency in the National Football League draft. *Management Science* 59 (7): 1479–1495.

Ross, Lee, Greene, D., and House, P. 1977. The false consensus phenomenon: An attributional bias in self-perception and social perception processes. *Journal of Experimental Social Psychology* 13 (3): 279–301.

Schelling, T. C. 1966. *Strategic Interaction and Conflict.* Ed. K. Archibald. University of California Press. [Comments.]

Tabellini, Guido. 2008a. The scope of cooperation: Values and incentives. *Quarterly Journal of Economics* 123 (3): 905–950.

Tabellini, Guido. 2008b. Institutions and culture. *Journal of the European Economic Association* 6 (2–3): 255–294.

7

Measuring Value Diversity within Countries

Sjoerd Beugelsdijk and Mariko J. Klasing

High diversity is often associated with poor socioeconomic outcomes, especially in developing countries. For example, slow growth (Easterly and Levine 1997; Glaeser et al. 1995), poor provision of public goods (Alesina et al. 1999, 2003), low quality of institutions (La Porta et al. 1999), a lack of trust (Alesina and La Ferrara 2002; Glaeser et al. 2000), a low willingness to share (Andreoni et al. 2011; Dahlberg et al. 2012), and higher prevalence of civil wars (Montalvo and Reynal-Querol 2005) are all outcomes that have, in the literature, been associated with high diversity within societies.

We argue that researchers, however insightful, have largely ignored a particular dimension of diversity as a result of a lack of data, That dimension is the degree to which members of the same society share common values and have similar attitudes, beliefs, and preferences. The literature has emphasized ethnic, linguistic, religious, and genetic diversity (Alesina et al. 2003; Ashraf and Galor 2013). Although these dimensions can certainly capture some elements of value diversity, it is easy to imagine two societies that have similar levels of genetic or ethno-linguistic diversity, but in which the values and beliefs expressed by the groups in one society are quite similar but very diverse in the other. Thus, value diversity can differ from the previously discussed dimensions of diversity, and it is therefore important to account for it.

In this chapter we develop a novel measure of value diversity and compare it with other existing measures of diversity. In contrast to more commonly used indices reflecting the degree of fractionalization in societies, our index incorporates not only information on the relative size of groups in society but also the distance between these groups. We identify 27 questions in the World Values Survey (WVS) and in the European Values Study (EVS) that can be used to measure value diversity. After an elaborate statistical analysis of these questions and their psychometric properties, we end up with one measure of value diversity that is based on six of the 27 questions. Combined in one index of value diversity, these questions inform us about the average level of value diversity in a country at a certain time. We have data for 111 countries and for six different periods corresponding to the waves of the WVS and EVS, starting in 1981 and ending in 2014.

Analyzing our newly developed measure of value diversity, we find that the variation in value diversity is mostly cross-sectional and that there is only limited variation over time. The top three countries that are most homogeneous in values are the Netherlands, Thailand, and Japan. The three countries that score highest on value diversity are El Salvador, India, and Tanzania. When comparing our measure of value diversity with ethno-linguistic, religious, and genetic diversity, we find that the correlation between our indicator of value diversity and these existing dimensions of diversity is rather weak. We attribute this to the fact that existing diversity measures do not take into account differences between groups. If between-group differences are small, even an ethnically diverse society can be quite homogeneous in the values its citizens hold. On the other hand, a society with a low degree of ethnic diversity can display quite a high degree of value diversity if the underlying values expressed by different groups in society differ strongly from one another.

We show that our newly developed measure of value diversity is related to a variety of indicators of socioeconomic performance, such as institutional quality, educational attainment, and provision of public goods. Hence, our measure of value diversity relates to socioeconomic outcomes that have been studied in previous work (e.g., Alesina et al. 2003). Although qualitatively the correlations between such outcomes and value diversity and ethno-linguistic diversity tend to go in the same direction, we find that in most cases the correlation with value diversity is stronger than that with ethnic diversity. This finding, in combination with the above-mentioned weak correlation between value diversity and ethno-linguistic diversity, suggests that our indicator of value diversity measures aspects of diversity not previously captured and that it may have important implications for socioeconomic development. Future research may, therefore, consider value diversity when studying the role of diversity.

In section 7.1 we discuss different measures that can be used to quantify value diversity. In section 7.2 we describe the nature of the data available. In section 7.3 we apply the different measures to the available survey questions and discuss how the psychometric properties of the questions lead us to develop one single measure of value diversity. In section 7.4 we compare our measure of value diversity with other existing measures of diversity and discuss how it correlates with different indicators of socio-economic performance. Section 7.5 concludes the chapter.

7.1 Measures to Quantify Value Diversity

Fractionalization

The most commonly employed diversity measure is fractionalization, defined as the probability that two randomly selected individuals belong to different groups. In the context of value diversity, fractionalization would reflect the probability that two individuals selected at random from the population of a country hold different values. For example, if there are n different values observed in a country and if we denote by $p_1, p_2, ..., p_n$ the population shares holding each respective value, the level of value fractionalization is

$$F = 1 - \sum_{i=1}^{n} p_i^2.$$

Fractionalization measures are widely employed in the broader social science literature. For example, Alesina et al. (2003) constructed data for ethnic, religious, and linguistic fractionalization in more than 200 countries by aggregating information on the different ethnic and religious groups present in and the languages spoken in these countries. Fractionalization as a measure of diversity is also commonly used by population geneticists to measure the extent of genetic variation across individuals within a given population. Applying this idea, Ashraf and Galor have constructed data on the extent of genetic diversity in 145 countries.[1]

Polarization Index

Although the fractionalization index looks at the overall distribution of values and the relative sizes of different groups in society, thereby capturing one aspect of diversity, it fails to take into account value differences between groups. One measure that does take differences between groups into account is the polarization measure proposed by Esteban and Ray (1994), which was generalized further by Duclos, Esteban, and Ray (2004) and which is based, according to Knack and Keefer (2002), on the most rigorous definition of polarization. Esteban and Ray's measure satisfies certain axioms that describe desirable features a polarization measure should have, which are related to the Dalton axioms in the measurement of inequality. In a nutshell, these axioms maintain that polarization is greatest if a society consists of two equally sized groups that are very different from one another.

Esteban and Ray's (1994) measure of polarization is formally expressed as

$$P(\mu, p) = \sum_{i=1}^{n} \sum_{j=1}^{n} p_i^{1+\alpha} p_j \left| \mu_i - \mu_j \right|,$$

where μ_i and p_i, respectively, denote the conditional mean of the attribute of interest in group i and the share of the population holding it (and correspondingly for group j), and n denotes the number of different groups in the population; α captures the degree of polarization sensitivity or the extent of deviation from a more standard Gini-type inequality measure, which would imply an α equal to 0. The fractionalization measure discussed above, a special case of this more general polarization function, arises if we let $\alpha = 0$ and assume that all groups are equally different from one another ($\left| \mu_i - \mu_j \right| = 1$). Esteban and Ray (1994) show that in order for the polarization measure to have certain desirable properties α must be nonnegative. Duclos et al. (2004) argue further that α should not exceed 1.

With survey questions, we can use the different answer categories available for each question to identify cultural groups and to quantify the distance between them as the difference between answer categories. If we encounter, for example, a question of the form "To what extent do you agree with … ?" with 10 available response categories (1 = "I don't agree at all," and 10 = "I fully agree"), we have ten groups, the distance between which, $\left| \mu_i - \mu_j \right|$, varies between 1 and 9. The corresponding relative size of each cultural group, p_i is given by the share of the sampled population that falls in each category response mentioned above. Determining p_i and μ_i this way, we can calculate the degree of polarization on a specific cultural dimension corresponding to the particular survey question considered.

Table 7.1 shows seven hypothetical distributions of answers on such a survey question with ten answer categories. The bottom rows indicate the levels of polarization corresponding to each distribution. Case 1 shows the hypothetical situation in which all respondents choose answer category 5. In this case, this population is homogeneous and the polarization score is 0. The other extreme scenario is displayed in case 7, in which

Table 7.1
Polarization example.

Answer categories	Case 1	Case 2	Case 3	Case 4	Case 5	Case 6	Case 7
1	0.000	0.000	0.000	0.100	0.250	0.333	0.500
2	0.000	0.000	0.000	0.100	0.000	0.000	0.000
3	0.000	0.000	0.000	0.100	0.000	0.000	0.000
4	0.000	0.500	0.333	0.100	0.250	0.000	0.000
5	1.000	0.500	0.333	0.100	0.000	0.333	0.000
6	0.000	0.000	0.333	0.100	0.000	0.000	0.000
7	0.000	0.000	0.000	0.100	0.250	0.000	0.000
8	0.000	0.000	0.000	0.100	0.000	0.000	0.000
9	0.000	0.000	0.000	0.100	0.000	0.000	0.000
10	0.000	0.000	0.000	0.100	0.250	0.333	0.500
Polarization, $\alpha = 0$	0	0.50	0.89	3.30	3.75	4.00	4.50
Polarization, $\alpha = 0.5$	0	0.35	0.51	1.04	1.88	2.31	3.18
Polarization, $\alpha = 1$	0	0.25	0.30	0.33	0.94	1.33	2.25
Fractionalization	0	0.50	0.77	0.90	0.75	0.77	0.50

50 percent of the respondents choose answer category 1 and the other 50 percent choose category 10. This results in the highest possible polarization score. All columns in between reflect alternative hypothetical distributions of respondents' choices of answer categories with intermediate levels of polarization. Depending on the value of α chosen (between 0 and 1), the maximum score of the polarization index is 4.50 when α is set to 0, 3.18 when $\alpha = 0.5$, or 2.25 when $\alpha = 1$. Irrespective of the level of α, the polarization score increases as the distribution becomes more extreme.

For comparability, we also report the level of fractionalization corresponding to each of the seven distributions. The key difference between the fractionalization index and the polarization index is that the fractionalization index does not take differences between the groups into account.

This becomes particularly obvious when comparing case 2 and case 7. In both cases, the population falls equally into two answer categories, yet the distance between the two subgroups is fundamentally different, something which is not reflected in the fractionalization index. The polarization index, on the other hand, increases when the distance between groups increases even if the relative sizes of groups remain constant.

Because the polarization index is the only measure that takes into consideration the distances between groups, and hence is richer in content than the fractionalization index, we use the polarization index as our preferred measure of value diversity. In the remainder of the analysis, we use as a base-line value in the calculation of the polarization index an α of 0.5.

7.2   Data and Sample

Data

To compute the degree of value diversity, we need information about the distribution of individual values within countries. Among the many well-known cultural databases, including Hofstede 1980, Hofstede 2001, GLOBE (House et al. 2004), Schwartz 1994, the World Values Survey (WVS) (Inglehart 1997), and the European Values Study (EVS), the underlying individual-level data are publicly available only for WVS and EVS. In all other cases, we have access to the country-level mean scores only, so those databases are not suitable for our analysis. Therefore, we use combined WVS and EVS data in our analysis.[2]

The starting point for our data set was the "Official WVS five wave 1981–2008 v20090901" survey file, which is the most comprehensive database and which is publicly available on the WVS website. However, this database is incomplete—it excludes many European countries, which are traditionally covered in EVS. A comparison with WVS's online tool, which includes data from both WVS and EVS but covers only the first four waves of WVS, with the downloadable five-wave file indicated that we were missing 14 European countries in the first wave, 25 European countries in the second, and 30 European countries in the fourth. We consequently retrieved the corresponding information for these countries from WVS's online tool and added it to our database.

The latest EVS survey data from 2008 (which corresponds to WVS's fifth wave) are not accessible via the WVS website. We therefore added them separately. By including information from the 2008 EVS wave, accessible via the GESIS Data Archive for Social Sciences, we were able to add 47 countries, 20 of which were also covered in WVS's fifth wave. Thus, this integration of EVS 2008 allowed us to add information from 27 additional countries for 2007–2008. In case a question was answered by the respondents of a given country in both types of surveys (20 countries), we kept both observations because the EVS and WVS interviews were never conducted in the same year in the same country. Since for most of our cross-country analyses we use the across-wave averages of the polarization scores in each country, retaining the alternative scores from EVS 2008 in addition to the ones retrieved from wave 5 of WVS does not affect our results other than that this method provides us with more scores for each country and thus reduces potential measurement error in the calculated across-wave-average scores.

After combining the first five WVS waves with the latest (fifth) EVS wave, we added the sixth WVS wave, which became available in July 2014. This added another 52 countries to our sample, of which 42 were already covered in previous waves and 10 were not. In total, this leaves us with 111 unique countries, a substantial number of which are included in multiple waves.[3] A detailed overview of the countries and the waves can be found in the appendix to this chapter.

Selection of Questions
Our selection of WVS/EVS survey questions is based on the ambition to measure value diversity. For this, it is necessary that we have questions that allow for a multitude of ordinal answers. A careful screening of all WVS/EVS questions revealed that the majority of questions allow for binominal answers and three or four answer categories only, making these questions unsuitable for the purpose of the present analysis. In addition to having overall too little variation in the responses, many three-point and four-point questions use also nominal rather than ordinal scales. Beyond those questions with two to four answer categories, the WVS and EVS questionnaires include only questions with ten answer categories, and, in waves five and six, also a selection of six-point questions related to the value framework of Schwartz (1994). This limits our analysis to questions with ten-point and six-point answer scales.

In addition to paying attention to the response scales, we need to ensure that the questions used were asked in a large number of countries. Of the 21 questions with ten-point answer scales, four were asked in only a limited number of countries and thus had to be dropped from the analysis. These limitations resulted in the 27 questions with ten-point and six-point answer scales we list in table 7.2.[4]

Table 7.2
Questions with ten-point and six-point answer scales.

Question	Official code	Question text	Answer categories
1	A173	Some people feel they have completely free choice and control over their lives, while other people feel that what they do has no real effect on what happens to them. Please indicate how much freedom of choice and control you feel you have over the way your life turns out.	1 = none at all, … 10 = a great deal
2	E033	In political matters, people talk of "the left" and "the right." How would you place your views on this scale, generally speaking?	1 = left, … 10 = right
3	E035	Incomes should be made more equal *vs.* We need larger income differences as incentives.	1 = more equal, … 10 = need larger income differences
4	E036	Private ownership of business should be increased *vs.* Government ownership of business should be increased.	1 = private ownership, … 10 = government ownership
5	E037	People should take more responsibility to provide for themselves *vs.* The government should take more responsibility to ensure that everyone is provided for.	1 = people, … 10 = government
6	E039	Competition is good. It stimulates people to work hard and develop new ideas *vs.* Competition is harmful. It brings the worst in people.	1 = competition is good, … 10 = competition is harmful

Table 7.2 (continued)

Question	Official code	Question text	Answer categories
7	F063	How important is God in your life?	1 = not at all important, …. 10 = very important
8	F114	Justifiable: Claiming government benefits to which you are not entitled	1 = never justifiable, … 10 = always justifiable
9	F115	Justifiable: Avoiding a fare on public transport	1 = never justifiable, …. , 10 = always justifiable
10	F116	Justifiable: Cheating on taxes if you have a chance	1 = never justifiable, …. , 10 = always justifiable
11	F117	Justifiable: Someone accepting a bribe in the course of their duties	1 = never justifiable, …. , 10 = always justifiable
12	F118	Justifiable: Homosexuality	1 = never justifiable, … , 10 = always justifiable
13	F119	Justifiable: Prostitution	1 = never justifiable, …. , 10 = always justifiable
14	F120	Justifiable: Abortion	1 = never justifiable, …. , 10 = always justifiable

Table 7.2 (continued)

Question	Official code	Question text	Answer categories
15	F121	Justifiable: Divorce	1 = never justifiable, … , 10 = always justifiable
16	F122	Justifiable: Euthanasia ending the life of the incurably sick	1 = never justifiable, … , 10 = always justifiable
17	F123	Justifiable: Suicide	1 = never justifiable, … , 10 = always justifiable
18	A189	It is important to this person to think of new ideas and be creative; to do things one's own way	1 = very much like me, […], 6 = not at all like me
19	A190	It is important to this person to be rich; to have a lot of money and expensive things	1 = very much like me, […], 6 = not at all like me
20	A191	Living in secure surroundings is important to this person; to avoid anything that might be dangerous	1 = very much like me, […], 6 = not at all like me
21	A192	It is important to this person to have a good time; to "spoil" oneself	1 = very much like me, […], 6 = not at all like me

Table 7.2 (continued)

Question	Official code	Question text	Answer categories
22	A193	It is important to this person to help people nearby; to care for their well-being *Wave 6: "it is important for this person to do something for the good of society"*	1 = very much like me, [...], 6 = not at all like me
23	A194	Being very successful is important to this person; to have people recognize one's achievements	1 = very much like me, [...], 6 = not at all like me
24	A195	Adventure and taking risks are important to this person; to have an exciting life	1 = very much like me, [...], 6 = not at all like me
25	A196	It is important to this person to always behave properly; to avoid doing anything people would say is wrong	1 = very much like me, [...], 6 = not at all like me
26	A197	Looking after the environment is important to this person; to care for nature *"and safe life resources" (wave 6)*	1 = very much like me, [...], 6 = not at all like me
27	A198	Tradition is important to this person; to follow the customs handed down by one's religion or family	1 = very much like me, [...], 6 = not at all like me

Source: World Values Survey, www.worldvaluessurvey.org/

These 27 questions are not included in WVS/EVS without a reason, and some have a long history in value surveys. In fact, many of these questions originate from well-known values surveys that preceded the WVS and EVS, such as the Rokeach value survey from the 1970s (Rokeach 1973). In what follows, we discuss the theoretical constructs these questions are related to. Each of the questions except 1 and 7 has a theoretical "origin."

Morally debatable behavior scale   The questions involving the justifiability of certain types of behavior (the Fxxx questions in table 7.2) fit the so-called morally debatable behavior (MDB) scale, originally developed by Crissman (1942) and updated by Harding and Phillips (1986). Katz, Santman, and Lonero (1994) revised the scale. Nowadays it encompasses two dimensions. The first dimension relates to legal and illegal aspects of human behavior as proscribed by law. This dimension is commonly measured by questions similar to questions 8–11 in table 7.2. The second dimension of the MDB scale involves matters of life and death and sexual relations and is commonly measured by questions 12–17 in our table. Although this was not part of the original surveys, the question on the importance of God (F063), which capturing religiosity, is closely related to the questions on moral behavior, especially those on abortion, prostitution, and divorce.

Political ideology   Values related to political ideology have a long tradition in social sciences, going back to Tomkins (1963). In two recent overview articles, Jost and colleagues (Jost, Nosek, and Gosling 2008; Jost, Frederico, and Napier 2009) assess the history of this dimension, defined as the set of beliefs about the proper order of society and how this order can be achieved. They conclude that "the left-right model of ideological structure has parsimony on its side and has fared surprisingly well in terms of theoretical utility and empirical validity" (Jost et al. 2009, p. 312). Questions 2–6 are all related to political ideology and capture different aspects of it. The whole set of questions 3–6 has been used by Lindqvist and Östling (2010) to measure political ideology, and some of the individual questions have been used by other authors to measure particular aspects of political ideological values—e.g., questions 4 and 6 by Aghion et al. (2010) and questions 3, 4, and 6 by Guiso et al. (2003). Question 2 is more difficult to interpret, as the meanings of "left" and "right" may not be the same across countries. Since we are ultimately interested in the dispersion of values within countries, we nevertheless decided to include this question. Although the first question on freedom of choice and control in one's life is not part of the questions traditionally used to measure political ideology, one may expect it to be related. This question captures one's locus of control, which is likely to be related to one's values regarding the role of the state, as people with an internal locus of control are more likely to say that people are responsible to provide for themselves.

Schwartz's cultural dimensions   Starting from a theoretically derived set of cultural aspects, the psychologist Shalom Schwartz discovered 56 individual values that could be further reduced to 45 that have identical meaning across cultures (Beugelsdijk and Maseland 2010). Using a survey on school teachers and college students from 67 countries from 1988 to 1998, he acquired information on values and value differences and later extended his framework to 73 countries. Schwartz defined three basic issues that confront all societies and derived three corresponding value dimensions. In the fifth wave of the WVS and EVS, a set of ten questions was added to capture these dimensions. Although not based on the same set of questions as used by Schwartz, the general idea is that these questions capture aspects of the cultural dimensions developed by him. Since we are not interested in the mean scores on these questions but only in the response distribution within countries, we refrain from a detailed discussion of the meaning of these dimensions and the way the ten questions are related to Schwartz's original dimensions. The interested reader is referred to Schwartz' work (Schwartz 1994, 1999, 2004, 2006).

To conclude our discussion of the selection of questions, we emphasize that most, if not all, of the 27 questions we employ have theoretical roots, have been part of existing value dimensions, and have been used before. Yet they have been employed only to capture average cultural attitudes in societies, and not to measure diversity, which is the focus of the present study.

Sample

For details regarding the sampling procedure of WVS and EVS, we refer to the corresponding survey websites (www.worldvaluessurvey.org and www.europeanvaluesstudy.eu). In a nutshell, both WVS and EVS survey data come from representative samples of the population and the sampling procedures followed by both are very similar. Samples are drawn from the entire population of people 18 years of age and older. In most countries, no upper age limit is imposed and some form of stratified random sampling is used to obtain representative national samples. A random selection of sampling points is made on the basis of statistical regions, districts, census units, election sections, electoral registers or voting stations, and central population registers. In most countries, the population size and/or the degree of urbanization of these so-called Primary Sampling Units are taken into account. In some countries, individuals are drawn from national registers. During the actual interview stage, the selected persons are interviewed during a limited time frame using uniformly structured questionnaires. The survey is carried out by professional organizations using face-to-face interviews or phone interviews. At least 1,000 respondents in each country are surveyed this way and included in the final database. This final number may be smaller for some very small countries, such as Luxembourg. Table 7.A2 in the appendix shows the ultimate number of individual observations used to calculate value diversity for each of the 27 questions.

The number of countries included in the WVS and EVS databases increases, ultimately leading to a coverage of 111 countries for the questions we selected. Assuming that samples in these countries are indeed representative, it implies that these 111 countries cover 90 percent of the world population. Put differently, we are able to calculate value diversity scores for the vast majority of societies in the world. Naturally, the number of people sampled varies by question. For example, the Schwartz questions have been asked only in the fifth and sixth waves, yet are still based on more than 140,000 individuals. For most of the other questions, we have more than 400,000 observations. A detailed overview of the minimum and maximum number of observations per country and wave can be found in table 7.A3.

7.3   Developing One Indicator of Value Diversity

Although all 27 polarization variables are in principle of interest and relevance to researchers, the more interesting question is whether the within-country variation in polarization across the 27 questions can be also captured reasonably well by a smaller subset of polarization scores. Insofar as the degree of value diversity varies across questions and diversity on one particular question may go hand in hand with diversity on another question, it would be good to know if there is a subset of polarization variables that can capture most of the underlying variation in value diversity within countries. Finding such a suitable subset of polarization scores would significantly improve the applicability of our data on value diversity, as with fewer raw data required, the sample size across countries and time probably will be higher. The only way to test for the presence of such underlying patterns is by factor analysis.

To assess whether a subset of polarization scores exists that captures well the within-country variation in the 27 polarization variables, we pool the data for all countries and waves and run factor analyses over the 27 polarization variables to test for common latent factors. We subsequently eliminate redundant items. Having reduced the number of relevant polarization variables this way, we proceed to analyze if there are biases driving the distribution of individual responses. Finally, we test to what extent the level of value diversity present in countries is correlated with the average values present in these countries. High variability or diversity in a variable often goes hand in hand with an increase in the tails of the distribution, leading to a correlation between the degree of diversity observed for a particular variable and its respective mean. Variables that have such properties make it empirically difficult to isolate the effect of diversity.

We then describe in detail how we eliminate items from our list of 27 polarization variables on the basis of factor analyses. We then proceed to discuss how we assess the presence of potential response-style biases and describe the correlation between value diversity and the corresponding mean value scores.

Factor Analyses of the Value Diversity Scores

To assess whether the 27 polarization variables reflect few common underlying factors, we pool all country and wave observations and run a factor analysis over the polarization scores for the up to 351 country-year observations.

We start with a factor analysis of the full set of 27 polarization variables. To identify common factors and the less relevant variables that can be eliminated, we proceed as follows: First, following the standard practice, we keep factors with an eigenvalue greater than 1. Second, we identify the variables that do not belong to these underlying factors. This is done on the basis of two statistics, the communality score and the Kaiser-Meyer-Olkin statistic. The communality score reflects the variance in each variable accounted for by all the latent factors and may be interpreted as the reliability of the variable. Following MacCallum, Widaman, Zhang, and Hong (1999), we apply the rule that the commonality score should exceed 0.6.

The KMO statistic compares for each variable the simple correlations between this variable and any other variable included in the factor analysis with the corresponding partial correlations that result after eliminating the influence of all the other variables. It reaches values between 0 and 1. If the partial correlation is 0 while the simple correlation is nonzero, the variables are measuring a common factor and the KMO statistic equals 1. If the simple correlation is 0, the variables do not share any common factors and the KMO statistic is 0. KMO values above 0.8 are considered very good and KMO values below 0.7 are considered acceptable (Kaiser 1974). We therefore apply the criterion that the KMO value for a variable should exceed 0.7.

For a variable to be retained, it has to meet both the commonality criterion (> 0.6) and the KMO criterion (> 0.7). Any variable that does not meet both criteria is eliminated from the list of variables. The rationale is that we want to retain only variables that clearly belong to a latent factor. Variables that are uncorrelated with other variables and whose variation cannot be well captured by the latent factors are hence removed. Having reduced the set of potential variables this way, we proceed to run a new factor analysis over the remaining set of polarization variables and eliminate further variables on the basis of the same criteria. We repeat this procedure until we have only variables that satisfy both the communality criterion and the KMO criterion.

Table 7.A4 shows the detailed results of the first round in our iterative factor analysis, which resulted in four factors with eigenvalues above 1. According to the communality and KMO criteria, variables A189–A193, A195, A197, A198, F063, and F116 should be eliminated. A new factor analysis over the remaining variables already leaves us with only three retained factors, leading to the elimination of three more variables (A194, A196, and F117). Proceeding this way, we end up after six rounds with six variables that together form one latent factor and meet both selection criteria. These variables (all of which relate to attitudes capturing political ideology), their factor loadings, and their communality and KMO scores are displayed in table 7.3.[5]

Note that the same six variables form a unique factor and meet the communality and KMO criterion even if we let $\alpha = 1$. In the case of $\alpha = 0$, only E035, E036, and E037 meet both selection criteria; the remaining three variables meet only the KMO criterion. When using at the corresponding six fractionalization variables instead, we find that only two variables (e037 and e039) meet both the communality and the KMO criterion and that a173 meets neither criterion. Given that a

Table 7.3
Factor analysis of polarization variables: final results.

Variable	Factor loadings	Communality	KMO
A173	0.794	0.6304	0.9369
E033	0.779	0.6069	0.9657
E035	0.9168	0.8404	0.9281
E036	0.9551	0.9122	0.8555
E037	0.9332	0.8709	0.8555
E039	0.8236	0.6784	0.9121

fractionalization index ignores the distance between groups and $\alpha = 0$ implies that the polarization measure is very insensitive to changes in distance for given relative group sizes, we conclude that the overall statistical fit of the one-factor measure of value diversity improves when the distance between groups is allowed to play a larger role.

Correlations between Mean and Diversity Scores
Having identified the six polarization variables that together form the main latent factor underlying response diversity on the 27 questions, we now document whether and to what extent these six polarization variables are correlated with the respective means on these six questions. If the diversity score for a survey question is highly correlated with the mean score on that same question, it becomes difficult to ascertain if variation in the measured level of diversity truly captures variation in diversity in the responses or variation in the average response. A high correlation between mean and diversity occurs when the responses are relatively extreme so that an increase (reduction) in the mean coincides with increased observations in the right (left) tail of the distribution. Table 7.4 shows the correlations between the mean scores and the four types of diversity scores for each of the six questions we identified above.

The correlations between diversity and the mean scores depend on the diversity measure used. For example, the mean responses to question E039 correlate at 0.52 with the corresponding polarization scores when α is set to 0 and at −0.63 with the corresponding fractionalization index. On the other hand, there is little or no correlation with the polarization scores when using larger values for α. Following the rule of thumb that

Table 7.4
Correlations between mean and diversity scores.

Question	Polarization, $\alpha = 0.5$	Polarization, $\alpha = 1$	Polarization, $\alpha = 0$	Fractionalization
A173	0.32	−0.005	−0.54	0.51
E033	0.19	0.23	0.11	0.10
E035	−0.04	0.07	−0.13	0.21
E036	0.32	0.16	0.44	−0.23
E037	0.11	0.28	−0.10	0.40
E039	0.10	−0.38	0.52	−0.63

correlation coefficients greater than 7 are worrisome because they imply that more than 50 percent of the variance in two variables is shared, we can conclude that none of the questions employed show an important correlation between the mean responses and diversity in these responses, irrespective of how diversity is measured.[6]

Testing for Cultural Response Bias
Because we are interested in the extent to which values are shared within countries, we need to make sure that the measured level of value diversity is not driven by response-style biases. When people complete a survey (especially when paper and pencil are used, but also when face-to-face interviews are used), the assumption is that that their answers are based entirely on the substantive meaning of the items to which they respond (Baumgartner and Steenkamp 2001). That is, however, not always the case, as people's responses are also influenced by their response style. Response-style bias occurs when respondents have a tendency to respond systematically to questionnaire items regardless of their content (ibid). The most common problem concerns the tendency to give extreme responses versus the tendency to select responses lying in the middle of the answer scale (middle response style, abbreviated MRS). In our case, the question arises whether there are any country-specific cultural reasons to do so.

Harzing (2006) found that extreme response styles (ERS) are significantly related to country-level extraversion. She also hypothesized that the higher a country's degree of collectivism (versus individualism), the higher the MRS bias; moreover, the higher the degree of power distance or uncertainty avoidance, the higher the tendency that respondents will "agree" with a given statement (the so-called acquiescence bias). Owing to our explicit interest in the distribution of values within countries, we need to rule out the possibility that our observed levels of value diversity are caused by ERS and MRS biases.

To test for response-style biases, we calculate the percentage of extreme responses (high and low) and the percentage of middle responses for the six questions we identified above. We define low ERS as the fraction of people choosing answers 1 and 2, high ERS as the fraction choosing answers 9 and 10, and MRS as the fraction choosing answers 5 and 6. Following Harzing (2006), we calculate low and high ERS and MRS for each of the six questions and then take averages across the six questions. We then run a set of regressions with country-level extraversion as an independent variable and with low ERS, high ERS, and MRS as dependent variables. In the presence of a response-style bias, we would expect extraversion to be positively correlated with ERS.

To measure extraversion at the country level, we use the scores provided by Van Hemert et al. (2002) and by Lynn and Martin (1995). To assess whether individualism, power distance, or uncertainty avoidance influences the responses people give (as Harzing suggested), we include Hofstede's (1980, 2001) data on power distance, uncertainty avoidance, and individualism versus collectivism. The lower tolerance for ambiguity and diversity in countries with high uncertainty avoidance can be argued to lead to a preference for affirmative answers (acquiescence) over disagreement (disacquiescence) (Harzing 2006). In a similar way, it can be argued that, if there is a response-style bias present, respondents from a collectivistic country with a focus on in-group harmony will be likely to give middle responses, whereas in an individualistic country people may be inclined to give more extreme answers. Finally, high power distance would imply a tendency for respondents to "agree" with a statement because of their natural inclination to not disagree with the investigator.

Because the independent variables are time invariant and we expect the response bias to be country specific, we analyze the across-wave averaged ERS scores. We run separate regressions for the extraversion variable, and for the three Hofstede dimensions combined, because the extraversion variable is available for only 34 countries (versus 66 for Hofstede's variables), and we wish to maximize the number of observations. If we find a consistent and significant effect of either the extraversion variable or the three Hofstede variables, we interpret the finding as

Table 7.5
Analysis of response-style bias.

	Low ERS (1,2)	High ERS (9, 10)	MRS (5,6)
Power distance	0.01 (0.02)	0.02 (0.02)	0.01 (0.02)
Uncertainty avoidance	0.02 (0.01)	.02 (.01)	0.01 (0.01)
Individualism vs.	−0.01 (0.01)	−0.06 (0.02)**	0.04 (0.01)**
collectivism	0.12 (0.19)	0.20 (0.21)	−0.13 (0.18)
Extraversion			

*: Significant at 5% level. **: Significant at 1% level.

evidence for the presence response-style biases. The regression results are shown in table 7.5.

We find that individualism is significantly negatively associated with the fraction of nines and tens in the survey answers (high ERS), and that it is positively correlated with MRS. The presumed positive relationship between individualism and ERS and the negative relationship with MRS, however, is not confirmed. In fact, we find the opposite: collectivistic countries score higher on ERS and lower on MRS. Because this is contrary to what we would expect under a culturally shaped response bias, it is suggestive of a response bias unlikely to be present in our data.

In general, response biases tend to be observed when the anchors of the questions are framed in terms of "agree" and "disagree." Smith (2003) suggested that using a mixture of positive and negative statements (exactly what we have in the six questions we employ) will reduce response bias. The varying structure of the answer scales forces the respondent to focus on the exact meaning of each question and to give more meaningful answers and may explain the absence of a response-style bias. We conclude that our measured degree of value diversity is not the product of some individuals' systematically misreporting their true attitudes, but reflects the true underlying diversity in people's values.

Descriptive Statistics
In what follows, we combine the diversity scores for the six questions discussed above to form one indicator of overall value diversity. Technically, we have two ways to reduce our six items to one overall indicator. The first is to calculate the factor scores using regression weights. The second is to calculate a simple average of the diversity scores on these six questions. The correlation between the two methods is 0.99. Because the number of observations is higher when employing simple averages, as

that method does not require all six diversity scores to be observed in a given country and wave, we choose to calculate overall value diversity by averaging the polarization scores on the six questions.

As was discussed above, we have four different ways of calculating value diversity on the individual survey questions: polarization with $\alpha = 0.5$, $\alpha = 1$, $\alpha = 0$, fractionalization. Hence, we can also construct four measures of overall value diversity corresponding to the six-item average diversity scores generated by each of the four calculation methods. Tables 7.6 and 7.7 give descriptive statistics for each measure of value diversity. Table 7.8 shows the pairwise correlations among the four measures.

We have, in total, 351 observations for value diversity, independent of the calculation method used. The number of countries observed per wave varies substantially and generally increases. Note that in some waves the number of unique countries differs from the numbers of observations. This is due to the fact, as we discussed earlier, that in wave 5 some countries were surveyed under both the WVS and the EVS. Moreover, in waves 2 and 3, for a few countries two separate survey rounds were conducted in different years. If we average the observations across the six waves and calculate average scores per country, we can generate observations for 111 countries.

Table 7.6
Descriptive statistics.

Variable	Obs.	Mean	S.D.	Min	Max
Polarization, $\alpha = 0.5$	351	0.969	0.159	0.726	1.738
Polarization, $\alpha = 1$	351	0.382	0.098	0.284	0.979
Polarization, $\alpha = 0$	351	2.732	0.337	1.734	3.752
Fractionalization	351	0.158	0.037	0.120	0.609

Table 7.7
Observations per wave.

	Wave 1	Wave 2	Wave 3	Wave 4	Wave 5	Wave 6
Obs.	24	46	54	71	104	52
Unique countries	24	43	54	70	83	52

Table 7.8
Correlation between different diversity measures.

	Polarization, $\alpha = 0.5$	Polarization, $\alpha = 1$	Polarization, $\alpha = 0$
Polarization, $\alpha = 1$	0.94	1	
Polarization, $\alpha = 0$	0.89	0.68	1
Fractionalization	0.36	0.65	−0.074

The correlation matrix shown is based on the whole sample of 351 country-year observations. Correlation coefficients based on the average scores per country are very similar.

From table 7.8 we can see that the correlations between the diversity indices employing measures of polarization are high, especially when the values chosen for α do not differ much. On the other hand, the correlations between polarization in values and fractionalization in values are comparably low. Since distances between groups can be substantial on a ten-point answer scale and the fractionalization measure completely ignores these distances, the low correlation is not surprising.

7.4   Patterns of Value Diversity

Value Diversity over Time and Space
The measure of cultural diversity we developed varies both across time and across countries. We have, in total, 111 unique countries and, on average, 2.94 observations per country, and thus a total sample size of 326 unique country-and-wave observations. To assess which share of the total variation in the data is due to cross-sectional variation and which share is due to changes in value diversity over time, we break down the overall variation in value diversity into its between component and its within component. Letting y_{cw} denote the diversity score of country c in wave w, $\bar{y}_c$ the average score in country c, and $\bar{y}$ the overall sample mean, we can decompose the overall variation, T_{yy}, as follows:

$$T_{yy} = \sum_{c=1}^{111}\sum_{w=1}^{W_c}(y_{wc} - \bar{y})^2 = \sum_{c=1}^{111}\sum_{w=1}^{W_c}(y_{wc} - \bar{y}_c)^2 + \sum_{c=1}^{111}\sum_{w=1}^{W_c}(\bar{y}_c - \bar{y})^2.$$

Here W_c denotes the number of observed waves in country c. The first term on the right-hand side is the within variation and the second term is the between (cross-sectional) variation. By dividing the terms by 325 (= sample size − 1), we get the corresponding variances.

Table 7.9
Variance decomposition, with share in overall variance in parentheses.

	Overall	Within	Between
Polarization, α = 0.5	0.0260	0.0069 (0.26)	0.0192 (0.74)
Polarization, α = 1	0.0100	0.0032 (0.32)	0.0069 (0.68)
Polarization, α = 0	0.1156	0.0278 (0.24)	0.0878 (0.76)
Fractionalization	0.0015	0.0006 (0.4)	0.0009 (0.6)

Table 7.9 reports for our four measures of value diversity (which, as discussed above, all reflect diversity regarding political ideological values) the within and between variances and their respective shares in the overall variance in parentheses. The between component makes up 60–76 percent of the overall variance, depending on the measure of value diversity used. This shows that most of the variation in value diversity is cross-sectional and that changes over time are relatively small.

Comparison with Other Measures of Diversity
Focusing on our preferred measure of value diversity (the average level of polarization on the six above-discussed questions with α set to 0.5), and on the average level of diversity per country, we now compare that measure with other measures of diversity. This provides us with a richer picture of the nature of diversity in different countries.

Regarding the ranking of countries by value diversity, we find that the Netherlands is the most homogeneous country and Tanzania the most diverse. Anecdotal evidence suggests that Scandinavian countries and Japan are particularly homogeneous. This is indeed confirmed by our data, as Sweden, Norway, Finland, Denmark, and Japan are all included in the top ten. The average degree of value diversity is 1.01, with a standard deviation of 0.16. The US scores 0.85, placing it in the top 20 percent of the distribution, which suggests that—perhaps contrary to the generally held belief that the US is highly diverse—in terms of political ideological values the US is fairly homogeneous. Alternatively, the distances between the clusters that can be found in the US are small in comparison with the distances in some other countries. The ranking of countries by value diversity is displayed in figure 7.1, which shows the top ten and bottom ten countries and countries, plus some countries around the twentieth percentile and the median of the distribution. The remaining 80 countries in between are omitted to keep the graph compact.

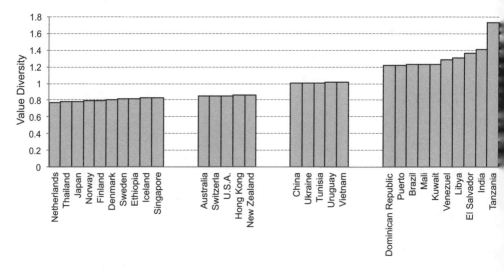

Figure 7.1
Ranking of countries by value diversity.

The concept of social diversity has a long tradition in the social sciences, and several studies have discussed the importance of diversity for socioeconomic outcomes. Among the most widely used indicators of diversity are the data on ethnic, linguistic, and religious diversity introduced by Alesina et al. (2003) and the data on genetic diversity provided by Ashraf and Galor (2011). All four measures of diversity reflect fractionalization in society and ignore differences between groups within a country. Linguistic diversity captures the number of different languages spoken as mother tongues and religious diversity the number of different religious groups in society. Ethnic diversity focuses on the presence of different ethnic groups in society—in some countries these ethnic groups reflect mostly racial characteristics, whereas in other countries they are based largely on languages. Genetic diversity, as the name suggests, reflects diversity in genetic makeup within countries. To what extent does value diversity correlate with these dimensions of diversity?

As the correlation plots in figure 7.2 indicate, there is little correlation between value diversity and ethnic, linguistic, religious, or genetic diversity. The only significant correlations are found with ethnic diversity and linguistic diversity, but even those relationships are weak (0.37 for ethnic and 0.18 for linguistic diversity). For religious and genetic diversity, the correlation is essentially zero. We see, however, a clearly positive relationship for larger value of genetic diversity.

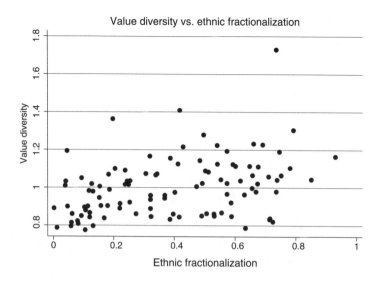

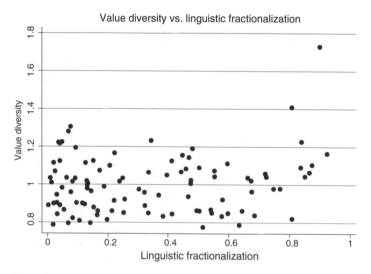

Figure 7.2
Correlation between value diversity and other dimensions of diversity.

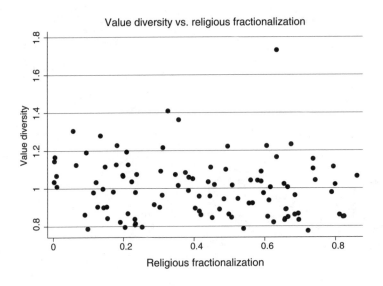

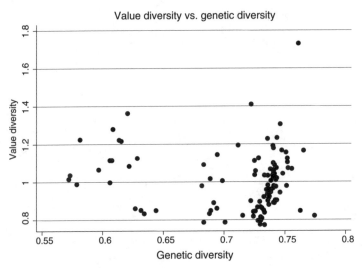

Figure 7.2 (continued)

At a first glance, it may be surprising to see that there is so little correlation between our indicator of value diversity and other commonly used measures of diversity. One would expect an ethnically or linguistically fractionalized society to also display strong value diversity. However, this pattern makes sense if we remember that the alternative dimensions of diversity we are looking at here all capture the presence of different groups in society but do not take into account the degrees of similarity or the distances between groups.

As our example in table 7.1 hinted, the same level of fractionalization can be associated with very different levels of polarization, and even an increase in fractionalization will not necessarily imply an increase in polarization. It all depends on how much the groups we are comparing differ from one another. In the context of our analysis, this implies that even if different ethno-linguistic groups or groups with different genetic makeup hold different values, this does not necessarily imply a strong correlation between value diversity and ethic/linguistic/genetic fractionalization, as distances between groups may greatly differ across countries. This interpretation is visible in figure 7.3, which displays the correlation between linguistic diversity and value polarization for European and Central Asian countries only. Western European countries

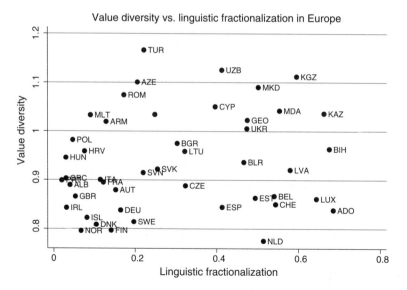

Figure 7.3
Value diversity vs. linguistic diversity in Europe.

have low levels of value polarization, whereas Central and Eastern European countries display high levels of value diversity. In terms of linguistic fractionalization, though, the two country groups are very similar and include both highly fractionalized countries, such as Switzerland or Kyrgyzstan, and countries with very little linguistic diversity, such as Sweden or Turkey.

Relating Value Diversity to Socioeconomic Outcomes

Our indicator of value diversity reflects a dimensions of diversity not previously assessed. Existing diversity measures, most importantly ethnic diversity, have been shown to be correlated with a variety of socioeconomic outcomes. Our previous finding that the correlation between value diversity and ethnic diversity is weak thus naturally raises the question of whether and to what extent value diversity is related to such outcomes. To assess the relevance of value diversity for explaining variation in socioeconomic outcomes, we correlate value diversity with a the large set of indicators of socioeconomic development explored by Alesina et al. (2003).

In table 7.10 we report results of a set of regressions along the lines of Alesina et al. 2003. Each dependent variable listed is regressed on value diversity in addition to the log of population in 1960 (as a measure of country size) and regional dummies for Sub-Saharan Africa, Latin America and the Caribbean, and East and Southeast Asia. To make comparisons with other commonly used indicators of diversity, we repeat the same set of regressions with the measure of ethnic fractionalization used by Alesina et al. (2003) rather than our value diversity index.[7] Columns 1 and 2 in table 7.10 present the estimated standardized β coefficients of value diversity and ethnic diversity respectively, with their significance levels and the number of observations for each regression indicated.

Table 7.10 shows results from regressions of each of the left-hand side variables on either value diversity (column 1) or ethnic fractionalization (column 2). The reported values are the standardized β coefficients. All regressions include the log of population in 1960 and regional dummies (Sub-Saharan Africa, Latin America and the Caribbean, East and Southeast Asia).

The left-hand-side variables cover a broad range of indicators of socioeconomic development, starting with per capita GDP in the first row, and also covering dimensions such as the quality of institutions (broadly

Table 7.10
Value diversity, ethnic diversity, and socio-economic outcomes.

Dependent variable	Observations	Value diversity	Ethnic diversity
Log of per capita GDP	95	–0.458***	–0.138
Business climate			
Property Rights Index	90	–0.423***	–0.112
Business Regulation Index	90	–0.381***	–0.155
Corruption and bureaucratic quality			
Corruption	79	–0.584***	–0.284**
Bureaucratic delays	55	–0.657***	–0.323**
Taxation			
Tax compliance	47	–0.472***	0.00729
Top marginal tax rate	61	–0.151	–0.259**
Size of public sector			
SOEs in economy	69	–0.383***	–0.134
Public-sector employment /Total population	80	–0.279***	–0.160
Size of government			
Government consumption/GDP	69	–0.180	–0.0117
Transfers and subsidies/GDP	63	–0.378***	–0.306***
Public goods provision			
Infrastructure quality	55	–0.610***	–0.276*
Log infant mortality	97	0.525***	0.310***

Table 7.10 (continued)

Dependent variable	Observations	Value diversity	Ethnic diversity
Schooling and literacy			
Illiteracy rate	52	0.164	0.172
Log average years of schooling	59	−0.491***	−0.128
Political Rights			
Democracy index	94	−0.442***	−0.237**
Political rights index	98	−0.468***	−0.341***

*Significant at 10% level
**Significant at 5% level
***: Significant at 1% level

speaking), provision of public goods, educational attainment, and size of the public sector. All variables listed were taken from La Porta et al. 1999. The reader is referred to that article for exact definitions of the variables and data sources.

We find that, for all the indicators considered, the correlation with value diversity goes in the expected direction—that is, higher diversity is associated with lower socioeconomic performance. For example, higher diversity is associated with lower per capita incomes, higher infant mortality, lower educational attainment, more corruption and bureaucratic inefficiency, and less income redistribution. Moreover, we find that—with the exception of the top marginal tax rate—the correlations with value diversity are stronger than those with ethnic diversity. This indicates that high levels of value diversity may have strong detrimental effects on socioeconomic development, which probably go beyond what has been previously established on the basis of diversity indicators such as ethnic and linguistic fractionalization. In light of this and the evidence presented above that value diversity shows very little correlation with previously discussed indicators of diversity, it is important for researchers interested in the consequences of social diversity to include value diversity as an additional dimension in their analyses.

7.5   Conclusion

In this chapter we assessed the diversity in values within countries. To measure people's values, we selected 27 questions from the combined data of the World Values Survey and the European Values Study. To measure diversity in people's values, we employed the polarization index proposed by Esteban and Ray (1994) and derived polarization scores on the basis of the individual-level responses to each of the 27 questions. After a careful analysis of the psychometric properties of the polarization scores for these 27 questions, we developed a single indicator of value diversity on the basis of six questions related to political ideology. Our measure can thus best be interpreted as a measure of diversity in political ideological values. This newly developed indicator of value diversity is available for 111 countries with more than 90 percent of the world population and in as many as six time periods. The vast majority of the variation in value diversity is cross-sectional.

Comparing our measure of value diversity with existing indicators of ethnic, linguistic, religious, and genetic diversity, we find very little correlation between value diversity and those commonly used indicators of social diversity. The likely reason for this lack of correlation is that existing measures of diversity take into account the number and relative sizes of different groups in society but not the differences between them. Since between-group differences in values can vary greatly across countries, it is possible that two countries will display the same level of, for example, ethno-linguistic fractionalization but very different levels of polarization in values. It is difficult, if not impossible, to quantify differences between groups on the basis of purely ethnic/racial or language characteristics. We therefore believe that by looking at actual values expressed by people and being able to explicitly quantify how different individuals are in their values, we make an important contribution to the literature and add a new perspective to the understanding of social diversity. In addition, we find strong evidence that value diversity is highly correlated with various indicators of socioeconomic performance and that these correlations are in most cases quantitatively stronger than those with ethno-linguistic diversity. These results suggest that value diversity is an important additional dimension of diversity that warrants further study in diversity research.

Appendix

Table 7A.1
Sample of countries and years of sampling.

Albania	1998, 2002, 2008
Algeria	2002, 2014
Andorra	2005
Argentina	1984, 1991, 1995, 1999, 2006
Armenia	1997, 2008
Armenia	2008, 2011
Australia	1981, 1995, 2005, 2012
Austria	1990, 1999, 2008
Azerbaijan	1997, 2008, 2011
Bangladesh	1996, 2002
Belarus	1990, 1996, 2000, 2008, 2011
Belgium	1981, 1990, 1999, 2008
Bosnia and Herzegovina	1998, 2001, 2008
Brazil	1991, 1997, 2006
Bulgaria	1990, 1997, 1999, 2006, 2008
Burkina Faso	2007
Canada	1982, 1990, 2000, 2006
Chile	1990, 1996, 2000, 2006, 2011
China	1990, 1995, 2001, 2007, 2012
Colombia	1998, 2005, 2012
Croatia	1996, 1999, 2008
Cyprus	2006, 2008, 2011
Czech Republic	1990, 1991, 1998, 1999, 2008
Denmark	1981, 1990, 1999, 2008
Dominican Republic	1996
Ecuador	2013
Egypt	2000, 2008, 2011

Table 7A.1 (continued)

El Salvador	1999
Estonia	1990, 1996, 1999, 2008, 2012
Ethiopia	2007
Finland	1981, 1990, 1996, 2000, 20005, 2008
France	1981, 1990, 1999, 2006, 2008
Georgia	1996, 2008
Germany	1990, 1997, 1999, 2006, 2008, 2013
Germany (West)	1981
Ghana	2007, 2011
Great Britain	1981, 1990, 1998, 1999, 2006, 2008
Greece	1999, 2008
Guatemala	2004
Hong Kong	2005
Hungary	1982, 1991, 1998, 1999, 2008
Iceland	1984, 1990, 1999, 2008
India	1990, 1995, 2001, 2006
Indonesia	2001, 2006
Iran	2000, 2005
Iraq	2004, 2006, 2013
Ireland	1981, 1990, 1999, 2008
Israel	2001
Italy	1981, 1990, 1999, 2005, 2008
Japan	1981, 1990, 1995, 2000, 2005, 2010
Jordan	2001, 2007, 2014
Kazakhstan	2011
Korea (South)	1982, 1990, 1996, 2001, 2005, 2010
Kosovo	2008
Kuwait	2013
Kyrgyzstan	2003, 2011

Table 7A.1 (continued)

Latvia	1990, 1996, 1999, 2008
Lebanon	2013
Lithuania	1990, 1997, 1999, 2008
Luxembourg	1999, 2008
Libya	2013
Macedonia	1998, 2001, 2008
Malaysia	2006, 2011
Mali	2007
Malta	1983, 1991, 1999, 2008
Mexico	1984, 1990, 1996, 2000, 2005, 2012
Moldova	1996, 2002, 2006, 2008
Montenegro	2008
Morocco	2001, 2007, 2011
Netherlands	1981, 1990, 1999, 2006, 2008, 2012
New Zealand	1998, 2004, 2011
Nigeria	1990, 1995, 2000, 2011
North Cyprus	2008
Northern Ireland	1981, 1990, 1999, 2008
Norway	1982, 1990, 1996, 2007, 2008
Pakistan	1997, 2001, 2012
Palestine	2013
Peru	1996, 2001, 2006, 2012
Philippines	1996, 2001, 2012
Poland	1989, 1990, 1997, 1999, 2005, 2008, 2012
Portugal	1990, 1999, 2008
Puerto Rico	1995, 2001
Qatar	2013
Romania	1993, 1998, 1999, 2005, 2008, 2012
Russia	1990, 1995, 1999, 2006, 2008, 2011

Table 7A.1 (continued)

Rwanda	2007, 2012
Saudi Arabia	2003
Serbia	2006, 2008
Serbia and Montenegro	1996, 2001
Singapore	2002, 2012
Slovakia (Slovak Republic)	1990, 1991, 1998, 1999, 2008
Slovenia	1992, 1995, 1999, 2005, 2008, 2011
South Africa	1983, 1990, 1996, 2001, 2007
Spain	1981, 1990, 1995, 1999, 2000, 2007, 2008, 2011
Sweden	1982, 1990, 1996, 1999, 2006, 2008, 2011
Switzerland	1989, 1996, 2007, 2008
Taiwan	1994, 2006, 2012
Tanzania	2001
Thailand	2007
Trinidad and Tobago	2006, 2010
Tunisia	2013
Turkey	1990, 1996, 2001, 2007, 2008, 2011
Uganda	2001
Ukraine	1996, 1999, 2006, 2008, 2011
United States of America	1982, 1990, 1995, 1999, 2006, 2011
Uruguay	1996, 2006, 2011
Uzbekistan	2011
Yemen	2013
Venezuela	1996, 2000
Vietnam	2001, 2006
Zambia	2007
Zimbabwe	2001, 2011

Total $N \times T$ = 351; Total N unique countries = 111

Table 7A.2
Total number of observations by wave and question.

Question	Code	Wave 1 (1981–1984)	Wave 2 (1990–1991)	Wave 3 (1995–1999)	Wave 4 (1999–2004)	Wave 5 (2005–2008)	Wave 6 (2010–2014)	Total N
1	A173	28,173	56,526	68,666	96,565	146,973	72,742	469,645
2	E033	21,841	45,107	57,793	70,230	109,102	54,501	358,574
3	E035	n.a.	56,667	73,015	85,744	143,142	71,707	430,275
4	E036	n.a.	54,315	71,014	76,876	133,958	69,647	405,809
5	E037	n.a.	56,719	72,692	97,851	146,609	72,350	446,221
6	E039	n.a.	55,904	68,411	74,784	141,859	71,592	412,550
7	F063	27,463	53,380	69,740	98,215	146,572	69,403	464,773
8	F114	28,664	58,654	67,758	89,695	141,881	71,811	458,463
9	F115	28,881	54,410	69,242	75,893	140,349	72,511	441,286
10	F116	27,345	57,595	69,825	90,721	142,867	69,056	457,409
11	F117	28,731	59,162	70,555	96,188	146,136	72,520	473,292
12	F118	27,462	57,476	67,132	88,327	133,011	67,524	440,932
13	F119	28,365	58,554	69,040	74,116	137,079	49,483	416,637
14	F120	28,421	57,586	68,521	94,492	140,274	69,901	459,195

Table 7A.2 (continued)

Question	Code	Wave 1 (1981–1984)	Wave 2 (1990–1991)	Wave 3 (1995–1999)	Wave 4 (1999–2004)	Wave 5 (2005–2008)	Wave 6 (2010–2014)	Total N
15	F121	28,473	58,505	70,511	95,055	144,190	71,827	468,561
16	F122	27,992	54,190	64,663	87,179	136,240	31,118	401,382
17	F123	28,181	56,351	68,647	90,737	139,967	71,700	455,583
18	A189	n.a.	n.a.	n.a.	n.a.	70,815	71,686	142,501
19	A190	n.a.	n.a.	n.a.	n.a.	71,317	72,015	143,332
20	A191	n.a.	n.a.	n.a.	n.a.	71,375	72,483	143,858
21	A192	n.a.	n.a.	n.a.	n.a.	71,184	72,147	143,331
22	A193	n.a.	n.a.	n.a.	n.a.	71,549	68,966	140,515
23	A194	n.a.	n.a.	n.a.	n.a.	70,886	71,842	142,728
24	A195	n.a.	n.a.	n.a.	n.a.	70,748	71,612	142,360
25	A196	n.a.	n.a.	n.a.	n.a.	71,251	72,285	143,536
26	A197	n.a.	n.a.	n.a.	n.a.	71,027	72,357	143,384
27	A198	n.a.	n.a.	n.a.	n.a.	71,466	72,520	143,986
No. of countries		24	46	54	71	84	52	111

Table 7A.3
Minimum and maximum observations per country, by wave and question.

	Code	Wave 1 (1981–1984)		Wave 2 (1990–1991)		Wave 3 (1995–1999)		Wave 4 (1999–2004)		Wave 5 (2005–2008)		Wave 6 (2010–2014)	
		Min	Max	Min	Max	Min	Max	Min	Max	Min	Max	Min	Max
1	A173	305	2,287	301	3,370	405	2,996	717	4,593	483	3,045	816	2,386
2	E033	211	2129	171	3,068	400	2,742	246	4,292	326	2,722	209	2,162
3	E035	0	0	298	3,315	412	2,993	716	4,539	485	3,013	784	2,321
4	E036	0	0	293	3,148	345	2,988	700	4,489	419	3,015	705	2,255
5	E037	0	0	299	3,338	415	2,991	712	4,552	489	3,034	800	2,413
6	E039	0	0	299	3,276	415	2,848	707	2,959	479	3,020	805	2,306
7	F063	306	2,304	303	3,348	414	2,996	716	4,589	483	3,049	807	2,219
8	F114	309	2,288	303	3,393	405	2,995	710	2,976	487	3,044	823	2,343
9	F115	309	2,293	303	3,407	406	2,995	698	2,997	485	3,050	818	2,416
10	F116	312	2,289	302	3,380	406	2,995	706	2,983	485	3,044	812	2,381
11	F117	310	2,278	303	3,378	403	2,993	713	2,997	494	3,050	815	2,410
12	F118	289	2,229	298	3,125	402	2,990	700	3,000	469	3,002	654	2,244
13	F119	301	2,275	300	3,220	404	2,993	942	3,000	475	2,997	763	2,320

Table 7A.3 (continued)

	Code	Wave 1 (1981–1984)		Wave 2 (1990–1991)		Wave 3 (1995–1999)		Wave 4 (1999–2004)		Wave 5 (2005–2008)		Wave 6 (2010–2014)	
		Min	Max	Min	Max	Min	Max	Min	Max	Min	Max	Min	Max
14	F120	304	2,277	304	3,168	405	2,990	709	2,992	476	3,011	788	2,254
15	F121	306	2,272	304	3,154	396	2,993	707	2,996	484	3,041	795	2,334
16	F122	296	2,215	297	3,127	398	2,982	712	3,000	452	3,047	715	2,026
17	F123	295	2,263	296	3,157	393	2,988	714	2,998	470	3,049	779	2,359
18	A189	0	0	0	0	0	0	0	0	921	3,023	815	2,199
19	A190	0	0	0	0	0	0	0	0	959	3,037	818	2,197
20	A191	0	0	0	0	0	0	0	0	957	3,046	818	2,196
21	A192	0	0	0	0	0	0	0	0	954	3,043	818	2,194
22	A193	0	0	0	0	0	0	0	0	970	3,045	817	2,184
23	A194	0	0	0	0	0	0	0	0	945	3,032	818	2,196
24	A195	0	0	0	0	0	0	0	0	942	3,026	815	2,189
25	A196	0	0	0	0	0	0	0	0	952	3,050	812	2,185
26	A197	0	0	0	0	0	0	0	0	944	3,044	816	2,193
27	A198	0	0	0	0	0	0	0	0	965	3,049	817	2,195

Table 7A.4
Factor analysis, round 1.

Variable	Factor 1	Factor 2	Factor 3	Factor 4	Communality	KMO
A173	0.8578				0.7775	0.7986
E033	0.8078				0.722	0.742
E035	0.9488				0.9078	0.6489
E036	0.9516				0.9395	0.6245
E037	0.933				0.8985	0.8171
E039	0.805				0.8031	0.6157
F063		0.6359			0.7444	0.751
F114	0.6378				0.608	0.6687
F115	0.5268	0.6233			0.8396	0.755
F116		0.513			0.6013	0.5852
F117		0.4131			0.8345	0.5813
F118		0.9289			0.8863	0.7963
F119		0.9628			0.952	0.8067
F120		0.8579			0.7677	0.8545
F121	0.6552	0.4484		0.4004	0.8226	0.7834
F122		0.8702			0.8398	0.8858
F123		0.8957			0.904	0.6937
A189				0.475	0.4914	0.8531
A190	0.4284				0.7647	0.876
A191			0.7136		0.6753	0.827
A192	0.4017			0.4636	0.6097	0.8555
A193			0.870		0.7806	0.7972
A194				0.7673	0.7542	0.7886
A195				0.7356	0.7787	0.8262
A196		0.4362	0.5671	0.4449	0.7534	0.8344
A197			0.8229		0.7926	0.8282
A198		0.4319	0.468		0.6182	0.8575

The first four columns display the rotated factors loading of the variables listed on the left. Factor loadings below 0.4 are omitted to facilitate reading.

Notes

1. To be precise, the authors provide data on the level of genetic diversity predicted by migratory distance from Ethiopia, the point of origin of modern humans. Actually observed genetic diversity data are available for only a very limited sample of 21 countries. However, there is a strong negative relationship between migratory distance from East Africa and genetic diversity, which is what the authors utilize to make out-of-sample predictions for other countries.

2. Interestingly, the latest two waves of the WVS have included a set of questions aiming to operationalize Schwartz's (1994) cultural dimensions. Indirectly this allows us to measure the diversity in values as developed by Schwartz.

3. When merging the responses from the different waves, we carefully checked the way the survey questions were framed. This is important because, for reasons that are not clear, the anchors of the response categories are not always the same in all waves. For example, the question on government ownership versus private ownership of firms (e037) has reversed anchors in the sixth wave from their order in the previous waves.

4. Note that in the sixth wave question 22 was phrased slightly differently in all countries, except Morocco and Spain, than in the fifth wave. Because of the close resemblance and similar meaning of the question text, we decided to use both versions interchangeably. In 18 countries, both versions of the question were asked and there we see a correlation of 0.93 between the polarization scores for the two versions. This suggests that although the wording is slightly different, the response distribution is more or less the same. For a similar reason we decided to keep question 26 in our database, even though a few words were added to the question text in wave six.

5. Ignoring the polarization scores on Schwartz's ten value questions for which sample sizes are much smaller and which, as is visible from table 7A.4, have very little in common with one another and with the remaining variables, polarization on the six questions dealing with political ideology form the strongest latent factor, accounting for 44 percent of the total variation in polarization in the remaining 17 questions (A0173, Exxx, Fxxx). This, in addition to the argument based on communality and KMO criteria, is another reason to focus our attention on polarization on these six questions.

6. A closer analysis of the questions regarding "morally debatable behavior" (questions 8–17 in table 2) indicates that they are characterized by high correlation (around 0.8) between mean scores and diversity scores. This is because people tend to answer relatively extreme on these questions, implying that, as the mean score increases or decreases, the diversity in answers automatically increases or decreases. In addition to their low KMO and communality scores, this is another reason to exclude them from our measure of value diversity.

7. Results based on linguistic fractionalization are very similar.

References

Alesina, A., Baqir, R., and Easterly, W. 1999. Public goods and ethnic divisions. *Quarterly Journal of Economics* 114 (4): 1243–1284.

Alesina, A., Devleeschauwer, A., Easterly, W., Kurlat, S., and Wacziarg, R. 2003. Fractionalization. *Journal of Economic Growth* 8: 155–194.

Alesina, A., and La Ferrara, E. 2002. Who trusts others? *Journal of Public Economics* 85: 207–234.

Aghion, P., Algan, Y., Cahuc, P., and Shleifer, A. 2010. Religion and distrust. *Quarterly Journal of Economics* 125 (3): 1015–1049.

Andreoni, J., Payne, A., Smith, J. D., and Karp, D. 2011. Diversity and donations, The effect of ethnic and religious diversity on charitable giving, Working Paper 17618, National Bureau of Economic Research.

Ashraf, Q., and Galor, O. 2013. The Out of Africa hypothesis, human genetic diversity and comparative economic development. *American Economic Review* 103 (1): 1–46.

Baumgartner, H., and Steenkamp, J. B. 2001. Response styles in marketing research: A cross national investigation. *Journal of Marketing Research* 38 (2): 143–156.

Beugelsdijk, S., and Maseland, R. 2010. *Culture in Economics: History, Methodological Reflections and Contemporary Applications.* Cambridge University Press.

Crissman, P. 1942. Temporal changes and sexual difference in moral judgments. *Journal of Social Psychology* 16: 29–38.

Dahlberg, M., Edmark, K., and Lundqvist, H. 2012. Ethnic diversity and preferences for redistribution. *Journal of Political Economy* 120 (1): 41–76.

Duclos, J. Y., Esteban, J., and Ray, D. 2004. Polarization, concepts, measurement, estimation. *Econometrica* 72 (6): 1737–1772.

Easterly, W., and Levine, R. 1997. Africa's growth tragedy: Policies and ethnic divisions. *Quarterly Journal of Economics* 111 (4): 1203–1250.

Esteban, J., and Ray, D. 1994. On the measurement of polarization. *Econometrica* 62 (4): 819–851.

Glaeser, E. L., Laibson, D. I., Scheinkman, J. A., and Souter, C. L. 2000. Measuring trust. *Quarterly Journal of Economics* 115: 811–846.

Glaeser, E. L., Scheinkman, J. A., and Shleifer, A. 1995. Economic growth in a cross-section of cities. *Journal of Monetary Economics* 36 (1): 117–143.

Guiso, L., Sapienza, P., and Zingales, L. 2003. People's opium, religion and economic attitudes. *Journal of Monetary Economics* 50 (1): 225–282.

Harding, S., and Phillips, D. 1986. *Contrasting Values in Western Europe: Unity, Diversity and Change.* Macmillan.

Harzing, A. W. 2006. Response styles in cross-national mail survey research: A 26-country study. *International Journal of Cross Cultural Management* 6 (2): 243–266.

Hofstede, G. 1980. *Culture's Consequences: International Differences in Work Related Values*. SAGE.

Hofstede, G. 2001. *Culture's Consequences: Comparing Values, Behaviors, Institutions, and Organizations across Nations*, second edition. SAGE.

House, R. J., Hanges, P. J., Javidan, M., Dorfman, P. W., and Gupta, V. 2004. *Culture, Leadership and Organizations: The GLOBE Study of 62 Societies.* SAGE.

Inglehart, R. 1997. *Modernization and Postmodernization: Cultural, Economic and Political Change in 43 Societies*. Princeton University Press.

Jost, J. T., Frederico, C. M., and Napier, J. L. 2009. Political ideology: Its structure, functions, and elective affinities. *Annual Review of Psychology* 60: 307–337.

Jost, J. T., Nosek, B. A., and Gosling, S. D. 2008. Ideology: Its resurgence in social, personality, and political psychology. *Perspectives on Psychological Science* 3 (2): 126–136.

Kaiser, H. F. (1974). An index of factorial simplicity. *Psychometrika*, 39(1), 31–36.

Katz, R. C., Santman, J., and Lonero, P. 1994. Findings on the revised morally desirable behaviors scale. *Journal of Psychology* 128 (1): 15–21.

Klasing, M. 2012. Cultural dimensions, collective values, and their importance for institutions. *Journal of Comparative Economics* 41 (2): 447–467.

Keefer, P., & Knack, S. (2002). Polarization, politics and property rights: Links between inequality and growth. *Public Choice*, 111(1–2), 127–154.

La Porta, R., Lopez-de-Silanes, F., Shleifer, A., and Vishny, R. 1999. The quality of government. *Journal of Law Economics and Organization* 15 (1): 222–279.

Lindqvist, E., and Östling, R. 2010. Political polarization and the size of government. *American Political Science Review* 104 (3): 543–565.

Lynn, R., and Martin, T. 1995. National differences for thirty-seven nations in extraversion, neuroticism, psychoticism and economic, demographic and other correlates. *Personality and Individual Differences* 19 (3): 403–406.

MacCallum, R. C., Widaman, K. F., Zhang, S., and Hong, S. 1999. Sample size in factor analysis. *Psychological Methods* 4 (1): 84–99.

Montalvo, J. G., and Reynal-Querol, M. 2005. Ethnic polarization, potential conflict, and civil wars. *American Economic Review* 95 (3): 796–816.

Rokeach, M. 1973. *The Nature of Human Values*. Free Press.

Schwartz, S. H. 1994. Beyond individualism/collectivism: New cultural dimensions of values. In *Individualism and Collectivism: Theory, Method, and Applications*, ed. U. Kim, H. Triandis, C. Kagitçibasi, S. Choi, and G. Yoon. SAGE.

Schwartz, S. H. 1999. A theory of cultural values and some implications for work. *Applied Psychology* 48 (1): 12–47.

Schwartz, S. H. 2004. Mapping and interpreting cultural differences around the world. In *Comparing cultures*, ed. H. Vinken, J. Soeters, and P. Ester. Brill.

Schwartz, S. H. (2006). A theory of cultural value orientations: Explication and applications. *Comparative Sociology*, 5(2–3), 137–182.

Smith, T. W. 2003. Developing comparable questions in cross-national surveys. In *Cross-Cultural Survey Methods*, ed. J. Harkness, F. Van de Vijver, and P. Mohler. Wiley.

Tomkins, S. 1963. *Affect/Imagery/Consciousness*, volume 2: *The Negative Affects*. Springer.

Van Hemert, D. A., van de Vijver, F., Poortinga, Y. H., and Georgas, J. 2002. Structural and functional equivalence of the Eysenck Personality Questionnaire within and between countries. *Personality and Individual Differences* 33: 1229–1249.

8

(Sweden)

Cultural Persistence and the Pill

Kelly Ragan

N33 N34 J13
J12 B55 Z13

Recently, economists have echoed demographers and sociologists, arguing that preference formation is important in shaping fertility decisions. Lesthaeghe and Surkyn (1988), prominent demographers, challenged economists to take up the role of preference formation in fertility outcomes more than 25 years ago. A recent literature on culture in economics has delivered empirical evidence on preference transmission mechanisms as well as quantitative general-equilibrium models of how families, communities, and other institutions interact with regard to the transmission of norms regulating sexual behavior and fertility. I review this literature on culture and fertility and discuss how social norms played an important role in shaping illegitimacy rates more than a hundred years ago as well as the take-up of modern contraceptive methods in Sweden. I present new data on the use of oral contraceptives ("the Pill") and compile measures of illegitimacy from more than a hundred years ago to illustrate the important role of historical behavior in shaping present-day contraceptive take-up.

The setting when the Pill was introduced and the availability of unique data on contraceptive sales make Sweden an ideal setting for the analysis of how cultural forces shaped the adoption of new contraceptive technologies. Putting current contraceptive innovations in historical perspective is aided by Sweden's rich data on historical fertility patterns, which have been studied extensively by biologists, ethnographers, and statisticians. Although methods of inquiry have differed across fields, there has been general consensus that fertility patterns in nineteenth-century Sweden were shaped by powerful social norms regulating sexual activity and promiscuity. I discuss the means through which these norms were enforced.

Although social constraints were strong, they were not uniform. Illegitimacy differed dramatically across Swedish communities at the turn of the twentieth century, and had done so since the first population statistics were collected. I present alternative measures of illegitimacy as a means of quantifying social constraints on premarital sex and illustrate how non-marital fertility patterns from more than a hundred years ago are prescient predictors of demand for new contraceptive methods such as the Pill.

A review of the literature on the role of preferences in fertility outcomes and contraceptive use in economics and other disciplines is followed by a detailed review of the literature specific to nonmarital fertility in Sweden and the supporting evidence regarding the importance of social norms in shaping sex, marriage, and fertility-control behavior in Sweden in the nineteenth century and earlier. An overview of the institutional setting in Sweden surrounding the Pill's introduction highlights how the Swedish setting is ideally suited to the study of social norms and contraceptive take-up. Historical data on illegitimacy and use of the Pill are presented and compared through tables, graphs, and maps. The strong positive correlation between the take-up of the Pill and nonmarital fertility 100 or 150 years earlier follow a distinctive geographical pattern that is not simply a result of north-south development differentials or of urbanization patterns. The geographical presentation of the data makes clear that variations in Pill take-up within regions are highly correlated with out-of-wedlock childbearing many generations earlier. The chapter concludes by connecting the correlations found in the data with the broader literature on the role of culture in economics.

A Review of the Literature on the Economics of Fertility and Contraception

Becker's *Treatise on the Family* laid the foundation for modern economic inquiry into the family and fertility decisions. Although economists from Malthus to Marshall had posited an important role for norms in shaping population dynamics, modern theories of the family and fertility focus on incomes, time investments, and other characteristics of the labor market and the marriage market.[1] This fruitful approach has been widely used in the theoretical and empirical literature on contraceptive demand.

Easterlin and Crimmins (1985) present a supply-and-demand analysis of the forces that lie behind the variations in fertility and contraceptive use that underlie recent demographic transitions. Their framework is similar to the one Becker used when modeling utility maximizing parents, but by allowing social norms as a means to shift preference they take a first step in defining a role for culture in contraception demand. Fertility control is a function of regulation costs (RC), demand for children (Cd), and the potential supply of children (Cn). The demand for children is determined by income, prices, and tastes, as in Becker 1965. On the production side, the potential supply of children is the number of surviving children a household would have if fertility were not deliberately limited. The supply of children may depend as much on biological factors as on cultural factors, as Easterlin and Crimmins note, arguing that customs that affect coital frequency or fecundity in a society may result in a natural fertility rate that is below the physiological maximum. The potential supply of and demand for children (Cn − Cd) jointly determine the motivation for fertility regulation. In the "excess supply" situation (Cn > Cd), parents would be faced with the prospect of having unwanted children and would be motivated to regulate fertility and hence to adopt contraception. Although Easterlin and Crimmins (1985) provide motivation for how social norms could affect fertility supply and demand, they do not consider the long-run evolution of these norms, nor do they define a role for the historical illegitimacy patterns discussed here.

Theoretical models of nonmarital fertility such as those put forth in Willis and Haaga 1996 and in Willis 1999 are very explicit with regard to the labor-market and marriage-market forces that drive illegitimacy and minimize the role of social norms. Social norms and preference heterogeneity play roles in the model of contraceptive innovation and illegitimate childbearing developed by Akerlof, Yellen, and Katz (1996). Unfortunately, the sources of preference heterogeneity are not explored, nor compared in a systematic way to historical behavior. The detailed discussion of Swedish fertility patterns below and the analysis of how these patterns affect the adoption of new contraceptive methods suggests that the differences in preferences regarding contraception, central to the model of Akerlof et al., may have historical roots.

Empirical work on the economic impact of the adoption of modern contraceptives following Goldin and Katz (2002) has not explored the role of culture in shaping the take-up of the Pill. Bailey 2006, Bailey 2010, and other empirical studies that focus on the differential pattern of access to the Pill across US states rely on strong identifying assumptions; differences in legislative and legal outcomes cannot be correlated with local cultures and institutions. Such assumptions preclude any evaluation of culture's role in the take-up of new contraceptive technologies such as the Pill. The data presented here suggest a potentially large role for social determinants in the take-up of the Pill across communities.

The social aspects of fertility have received more attention than contraceptive demand or premarital sexual activity in recent empirical work exploiting data on immigrants and their fertility decisions. Blau (1992) and Guinnane, Moehling, and O'Grada (2006) study immigrants to the US and find that home-country differences in fertility have a significant effect on immigrants' fertility decisions even after accounting for differences in observed characteristics. Fernandez and Fogli (2006, 2009) emphasize culture as a feature of the preference environment that shapes fertility decisions. Fernandez and Fogli focus on observed fertility, but contraception is a closely related latent variable. Their papers, and other papers on culture transmission (e.g., Bisin and Verdier 2000 and Bisin and Verdier 2001), emphasize the joint influence of culture as transmitted by parents (direct) and the communities in which women reside (oblique). The correlations I present embody the composite effect of both forces as proxied for by observed behavior of previous generations of women in a locality. The focus on contraception as a specific channel through which culture influences fertility is unique to this chapter.

The institutional setting of this chapter differs from those of the papers by Fernandez and Fogli and by Blau et al. (2008), which analyze the behavior of second-generation immigrants using measures of behavior in the parents' home country to proxy for norms. This approach addresses the challenge of separating cultural and institutional influences by looking at immigrants residing in an institutional setting not related to the cultural background of their parents. I avoid this challenge since the localities examined here have all the same legal, educational, medical, and retail drug market institutions.

Fernandez (2011) notes the dearth of studies on the interaction of culture and the economic and institutional environment with regard to contraception. This is not surprising; norms about sex, marriage, and reproduction are difficult to elicit. Fernandez-Villaverde, Greenwood, and Guner (2014) present a model in which supply-side shocks in the form of contraceptive innovations alter norms of behavior among the young. The current chapter helps fill the gaps between empirical studies of the introduction of the Pill in the US, which have largely ignored culture; theoretical contributions such as those Akerlof et al. (1996) and Willis (1999), and recent quantitative work emphasizing how technology alters culture. Here I ask whether there is evidence that long-standing patterns of fertility behavior that are argued to be culturally determined influence the adoption of birth-control innovations.

Another strand of the recent literature on the role of culture in regulating fertility outcomes closely mirrors the sociological literature on social disorganization. Kearney and Levine (2011) interpret the importance of year/state fixed effects in nonmarital fertility as an outcome of "cultural' differences across localities with respect to the incidence of teenage childbearing. Kearney and Levine (ibid. and 2012) focus on a "culture of despair" as a driving force behind teenagers' decision underpinning their fertility, and quantify "despair cultures" by using local measures of income inequality. In contrast with the literature following Fernandez and Fogli, the cultural forces emphasized by Kearney and Levine need not operate through differential preferences, but may only be the product of low-social-status women living in highly unequal communities facing little economic penalty for teenage childbearing. Hence, the degree of contemporaneous income inequality is shown to be important in explaining the geographic variation in illegitimacy among women of low socioeconomic status.

Whereas I have focused on the literature in economics, Becker (1981) makes mention of the dramatic changes afoot for families in the nineteenth and twentieth centuries, making reference to literatures in history, demography, anthropology, and biology. The recent literature in economics, which has placed preference formation and the transmission of social norms at the forefront, has parallels in demographic studies of the fertility transition in Europe. The Princeton fertility project and its descendants, such as the work of Bongaarts and Watkins (1996), emphasize the role of changing norms in the context of historical demographic transitions as to date. My focus on the recent literature on culture, contraception, and fertility in economics is not intended to minimize the importance of the related literature to the topic, but instead to provide an introduction.

A Review of the Literature

Fertility and Contraception in Nineteenth-Century Sweden

Studies of Swedish fertility patterns from a variety of fields have emphasized the importance of community customs and social norms regarding contraception.[2] Some studies of eighteenth-century population statistics emphasized that geographic differences in population growth rates were due not only to differences in urbanization and socioeconomic structures but also to regional differences in contraceptive use. For example: "Furthermore, it seems very probable that some form of birth control was practiced in Eastern Sweden at least as early as the eighteenth century. Eastern Sweden supplemented epidemics and war with vice to keep down the population, while Western Sweden relied to a greater extent on moral restraint." (Utterström 1965, p. 530)

Past illegitimacy may reflect persistent differences in community customs and social sanctions, both facets of culture. These facets of culture are similar to the explanation for the divergent illegitimacy patterns proposed by Gustav Sundbärg (1910), the father of Swedish population statistics, who argued that inherited community characteristics, persistent across generations, drove differences in nonmarital fertility; Sundbärg coined the term "public mood" to refer to these characteristics.[3] Persistent nonmarital fertility patterns formed the basis of Sundbärg's division of Sweden into the distinct demographic regions depicted in figure 8.1.[4]

Sundbärg's hypothesis, in keeping with Guiso, Sapienza, and Zingales' (2006) definition of culture as "those customary beliefs and values that ethnic, religious, and social groups transmit fairly unchanged from generation to generation," argues that culture played an important role in the marriage and fertility decisions of Swedes through the early twentieth century. This section reviews the extensive literature from several fields related to contraception and nonmarital fertility from Sweden in the nineteenth century and earlier. The consensus from this review is that differences in social controls on the sexual, contraceptive, and marriage behavior of the young were important factors in shaping the very different patterns of non-marital fertility observed in Sweden during the nineteenth century and earlier. In this chapter, I investigate whether these same social forces from centuries earlier persisted and correlate with the geographic pattern of per capita demand for modern contraceptive technologies such as the Pill.

Social Sanctions and Courting Customs in Sweden

Social constraints on individuals' reproductive decisions were particularly strong in nineteenth-century Sweden. The evolutionary biologist Bobbi Low (1990) described the setting: "19th century Sweden represents an extreme of societal constraints on people's reproduction: highly monogamous, little remarriage, essentially no divorce, and a low rate of illegitimacy." Societal constraints took many forms; ethnological studies emphasize social sanction against premarital sex and courting customs that regulated sexual behavior among the young and meted out punishment on those who violated local customs.

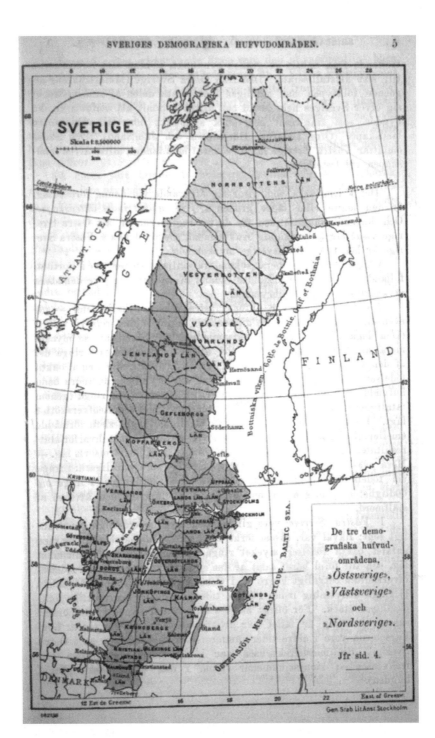

Figure 8.1
Gustav Sundbärg's three demographic regions of Sweden.

A woman who engaged in sex outside of marriage was a *hora* (whore) or a *löndahora* (immoral woman). If her sexual encounter resulted in a birth, the child would be referred to as a *horunge* (whore youngster). Unmarried women whom engaged in *lönskaläge* (affairs with unmarried men) or *enkelt hor* (with married men) were subject to punishment under the law.[5]

In addition to legal sanctions, women also faced social and financial penalties levied by the church. Such penalties required unmarried mothers to confess their transgressions in conjunction with ceremonies designed to publicly humiliate them before their children could be baptized. Confession as penance for unlawful intercourse was abolished in 1855 but continued to be practiced into the twentieth century in some parts of Sweden. These ceremonies culminated in absolution, but women who confessed illicit sexual behavior would never regain their status and sat apart from the community during church services. The church also imposed fines and work levies on women who conceived children in relationships that did not lead to marriage.

Community sanctions (social and financial) against women who engaged in premarital sex were extensive. The most visible included the wearing of a red cap, called a *horluva* (whore cap). Folk customs attributed any number of the consequences of poor nutrition among children or livestock to whores. Rickets was commonly believed to be caused by whores, and suspected whores were banned from working near children or livestock.[6] Instead, these women were relegated to heavy field work at reduced wages.

Other women were the main monitors of sexual behavior. In parts of Skåne, in southern Sweden, married women inspected the breasts of single women in conjunction with the tending of geese to find out if they had given birth or were pregnant. Such monitoring had been used to catch child murderers since the Middle Ages.

Courting customs also operated as a check on illicit sex and a means for enforcing marriage among the young. Sweden has several distinct courting customs, as discussed by Wikman (1937), all of which carried with them severe penalties for women who had children outside of legitimate marriages. Regions or social groups that were tolerant of premarital sex within courting rituals were strictly opposed to loose sexual relations. Families played an important role in monitoring courting behavior in the south, while in the north courting was monitored by gangs of young men who punished and excluded individuals who violated *nattfrieri* (night courtship) customs. According to Frykman (1975), customs differed by region; social sanctions were stronger in southern Sweden, while monitoring and enforcement of courting customs was stronger north of the limes norrlandicus.[7]

Fertility Control: Coitus Interruptus and Abortion

Differences in nonmarital fertility have been a consistent feature of Swedish population statistics since the eighteenth century. The agrarian society that typified Sweden in the nineteenth century relied heavily on social control as a substitute for contraception. Reduced coition through prolonged abstinence and late marriage was a primary means of fertility control, but methods for preventing conception or inducing abortion played a role.

Early explanations of nonmarital fertility patterns made little direct reference to contraception. For example, Eli Heckscher (1949) argued that regional differences in urbanization rates led to the differential pattern of out-of-wedlock fertility, and Nils Wohlin (1915), a statistician of the same era, argued that marital fertility patterns were the result of differences in land tenure systems.[8] Gigi Santow (1995) provides a thorough discussion of the quantitative and descriptive evidence on the use of fertility control, coitus interruptus in particular, during the eighteenth and nineteenth centuries. Quantitative evidence from Gotland suggests that interrupted intercourse had been practiced among married couples since the 1700s and throughout the rest of Sweden by the end of the nineteenth century.[9] Utterström (1965) emphasized regional differences in contraceptive use as contributing to differential rates of population growth across Sweden. Anecdotal and quantitative evidence led Frykman (1975) to conclude that knowledge about coitus interruptus was widespread by the late nineteenth century.[10] This is consistent with the findings of the Swedish Population Commission, which found that the most common form of birth control at the turn of the nineteenth century was coitus interruptus together with abstinence and abortion.[11]

Although family planning and the spread of neo-Malthusian ideas among intellectual circles was underway in Europe during the 1870s, the spread of contraceptive technologies was limited.[12] Detailed historical analysis of contraceptive practices is scant. The lack of attention paid to contraception in nineteenth-century historical studies may be due to widely held views of family planning as immoral. Wohlin, for example, regarded family planning as a sign of moral weakness, and that view was codified by the Swedish anti-contraceptive laws of 1910. From 1911 until 1938, it was illegal to provide knowledge of contraceptive techniques or to publicly sell contraceptives "intended for immoral use or to prevent the results of sexual intercourse."[13]

Knut Wicksell aided in spreading information regarding contraception in the period before and after the anti-contraceptive laws went into force. Wicksell advocated for the formation of societies to promote family planning while a student in Uppsala in 1880, giving lectures and distributing pamphlets throughout the country. Wicksell was nearly expelled from Uppsala University, but he continued touring the country to lecture on family planning.[14] Wicksell was denounced as an "apostle of promiscuity" and jailed for spreading birth-control propaganda. The anti-contraceptive laws were ultimately abandoned in 1938.

The regulation of abortion has a long history in Sweden.[15] In the thirteenth century, the Västergötland Law forbade any form of induced abortion under threat of severe penalty. The criminal code of 173 punished abortion along the same lines as infanticide and made it punishable by death. In 1864, and again in 1890, the law was liberalized, and the maximum sentence for abortion was reduced to six years of penal servitude. The law was further liberalized in 1921, but abortion remained illegal in Sweden until 1975.

Although knowledge of abortifacients was rudimentary, many women attempted to use home remedies to induce abortion.[16] In the second half of the nineteenth century, provincial doctors were required to perform autopsies on suspected suicides, and evidence from these autopsies shows that attempted abortion was widespread, according to Hédren (1901). During the 1890s, more than 90 percent of the suicides by attempted abortion captured in the autopsy records were of unmarried women, the majority of them under the age of 25. Autopsy records for the years 1851–1855 revealed fewer than three suicides by attempted abortion per year, but by 1894 this had risen to 119, increasing rapidly from 1870 onward and far outstripping population growth.

The cross-sectional pattern of suicides by pregnant women is striking. The frequencies per the population varied dramatically. Hédren (1901) focused on the city of Uppsala, which accounted for 2.5 percent of the population and in which 41 suicides by attempted abortion occurred in the period 1891–1900. In Kopparberg, a twice as large population, they recorded six suicides by attempted abortion occurred over the same period. The regional variations in the incidence of these suicides could not be explained by urbanization patterns, according to Hédren, as the growth of cities was not met with an increase in abortion-related suicides, but instead much of the increase in the 1880s and the 1890s occurred in largely rural districts.[17]

The majority of women captured in the suicide statistics were in the final stages of pregnancy, and most such suicides were by poison (phosphorus in 90 percent of cases).[18] Many of the women included in the death statistics had had earlier abortions. Although estimates from the 1930s suggested that 10,000 abortions were performed in Sweden annually, Frykman (1975) presents extensive survey evidence to conclude that abortion as a means of birth control was not condoned by the Swedish peasant culture of the nineteenth century.

Child Mortality

The data show that during the early nineteenth century half the children born outside of marriage died during infancy, as compared with one sixth of children born to married women. That the high death rate among children born to unmarried mothers may have been a result of social sanctions is given credence by the motivation for a royal proclamation issued in 1778. The proclamation, which granted unwed mothers the right to remain anonymous when the child was enrolled in church records, was issued for the purpose of reducing the high mortality rate among extramarital children.[19]

Frykman (1975) argues that extramarital infant mortality showed a "very definite" regional pattern. It was far more common for infants born out of wedlock to die in Småland than in Jamtland or other districts in Norrland. Frykman argues that this was not due to any genetic or environmental factors, but to variations on normative pressures against premarital sex: "The fewer children born out of wedlock, the stronger the sanction against those who deviated from the narrow path seems to be the conclusion one can draw from this example [infant mortality]." (ibid., p. 137)

The Geography of Swedish Illegitimacy

Illegitimacy differed dramatically across Swedish communities at the turn of the twentieth century. These differences formed the basis of a division of Sweden into demographic regions as described by Sundbärg (1910) and as depicted in figure 8.1.[20] Before 1850 illegitimacy was highest in the area west of Stockholm and in the southernmost parts of Sweden. A single characteristic that defines illegitimacy patterns is difficult to discern; high rates of illegitimacy are seen north and south of the limes norrlandicus, along coasts and plains. Mining and industrial regions have relatively high occurrence of unwed birth, but many areas with high levels of illegitimacy were primarily agrarian. Heckscher (1949) argued that urbanization led to the differential pattern of out-of-wedlock fertility, but Frykman (1975) shows how areas with high illegitimacy had population densities no different from central Småland, an area of low illegitimacy.

Sundbärg's (1910) compilation of data going back to the seventeenth century illustrates that relative rates of illegitimacy were highly persistent over hundreds of years. Sklar (1977) presents a detailed history of the forces which contributed to rising illegitimacy during the late nineteenth century. A series of land reforms disrupted rural communities, making it difficult to monitor and enforce norms related to sex and marriage among the young. Growing resource-extraction industries in the middle of Sweden led to migration of single men to that region. Women were also more mobile, moving to regions that offered employment in textile industries. Sklar concludes that migration weakened communities' capacity to enforce norms related to marriage and premarital sex, consistent with the hypothesis presented here that social norms are important in shaping premarital sexual behavior and demand for contraception.

The Introduction of the Pill in Sweden: Homogeneous Institutions

The Pill was approved for prescription use by the Swedish National Board of Health and Welfare in May of 1964. By the early 1970s, oral contraception had become one of the most common methods of family planning. In 1968, of those couples using some type of preventive method at their most recent intercourse, condoms and coitus interruptus were the most common methods, followed by the Pill.[21] There are no recurring surveys on contraceptive practices in Sweden, so it is not possible to trace how use of oral contraceptives evolved alongside other forms of contraception, but a detailed study of the Pill conducted by the Swedish Board of Medicine in 1984 (Swedish Board of Health and Welfare 1984) followed sales of oral contraceptives. According to that study, sales of the Pill in 1969 amounted to one year of use for 25 percent of women in the reproductive age span. The age distribution of Pill users was heavily skewed toward young women, with 25 percent of oral contraceptive prescriptions written for women aged 15–19 and 29 percent to women aged 20–24 in 1979.[22] By 1981, 61 percent of women 21–45 were using contraception and the Pill was the second most common method (used by 32 percent of these women), just behind barrier methods (used by 33 percent).

As the statistics from the two decades following the Pill's introduction illustrate, use of oral contraceptives was widespread, especially among young women. The popularity of the Pill among young women in Sweden, in contrast to similar statistics for the US, may have been due in part to the legal environment in Sweden. Swedish law allowed for women as young as 15 to have access to contraceptive services without parental knowledge or approval.[23]

The extensive regulatory environment in place in Sweden during the period gave rise the unprecedented homogeneity of institutions across the country. The assumption of uniform institutions is difficult to support in some settings, but in the context of Sweden in the early 1970s this assumption is accurate in both a de jure and a de facto sense. In addition to the uniformity of laws regulating contraceptives, the medical and retail pharmacy sectors were operated directly by public entities and subject to uniform administration. Pharmacies offered the same assortment of contraceptives, at the same prices, throughout the country. Private insurance was virtually non-existent during this period, so the prices set by the pharmacy monopoly reflect the cost faced by consumers.[24]

The year 1970, the first year for which data is available following the approval of the Pill for contraceptive use, predates changes in abortion access brought about by the Swedish Abortion Act of 1974.[25] Although abortion was illegal, performing abortions in cases of clear medical, social, or humanitarian necessity, as determined by a medical board that reviewed individual petitions for abortion, had become unofficially accepted. The Abortion Act granted women access to abortion without the approval of a medical board or two physicians, as was required during the period considered here.

A common sex-education curriculum had been in place since 1956. In addition to the curriculum in the schools, all maternal health clinics provided information about contraceptives and supplied diaphragms to women regardless of their marital status, and had done so since the 1950s. The Riksförbundet för Sexuell Upplysning kept a list of doctors known to provide contraceptives, but by the late 1960s that body deemed such a list unnecessary, as doctors were universally willing to provide contraceptive services to women. It should also be noted that advertising by pharmaceutical companies to consumers was prohibited during this period.

Sweden's institutional setting is well suited for an analysis of culture's effect on demand for the Pill. The legal, medical, retail pharmacy and educational institutions that played a role in the supply of the Pill and of contraceptive information were all subject to uniform rules when the Pill was introduced. In this unique environment, in which all communities face the same supply curve for the Pill, differences in quantities sold arguably reflect differences in demand. As the next section will show, these differences in demand are closely related to levels of illegitimacy from a century earlier.

The Geography of Nineteenth-Century Illegitimacy and the Adoption of the Pill

Sundbärg (1910) argued that community characteristics, persistent across generations, drove the differences in nonmarital fertility he documented back through the seventeenth century. In keeping with Sundbärg's focus on nonmarital fertility as an important characteristic of differences in culture across communities, I compile measures of illegitimacy and compare them relative to measures of Pill use in 1970. Regardless of the measure used, illegitimacy is highly correlated with demand for the Pill.

Summary statistics on Pill expenditures per woman and on out-of-wedlock births per 100 live births from 1910 and 1860 are presented in table 8.1. The source of the data on Pill expenditures was a quarterly publication on the Swedish Drug Market from Läkemedelsstatistik, AB. Unique sales data from 70 markets constitute the entire universe of oral contraceptive sales in Sweden. These data have not been analyzed before, and compiling and analyzing them is a primary contribution of this project.[26]

Population data are from Statistiska Central Byrån (SCB), as are the historical birth and illegitimacy data reported in the SCB publication *Befolkning Statistisk Årsbok* for each year. The data are from population censuses performed every decade, supplemented by data from local church books. Church books contain extensive birth, death, and marriage records in addition to the minutes of the husförhör (home interrogations) conducted by local priests. The 1900 census resulted in a discrepancy of only 310 missing individuals in the church records of a total population of just over 5 million. The dual collection of population statistics and the high level of agreement between these measures argue for the reliability of the historical birth statistics used here.

Table 8.1 reports average summary statistics computed across the 70 markets over which Pill sales data is collected, as well as population weighted summary statistics. Pill expenditures per woman are 8.6 SEK (Swedish krona) per woman (9.4 SEK per woman when weighted by the population of women aged 15–40 in 1970). Conlunett, introduced by

Table 8.1
Summary statistics on pill use and historical unwed births.

		Unweighted		Weighted			
Variable	N	Mean	S.D.	Mean	S.D.	Min	Max
Pill expenditure per woman 15–40 in 1970	70	8.64	1.51	9.42	1.56	5.09	12.55
Unwed births per 100 births in 1910	70	12.28	4.00	15.81	6.68	6.11	27.58
Unwed births per 100 births in 1860	70	7.98	3.10	11.59	7.54	3.98	26.33

	Cross-Correlations					
	Unweighted			Weighted		
Pill expenditure per woman 15–40 in 1970	1.00			1.00		
Unwed births per 100 births in 1910	0.52	1.00		0.52	1.00	
Unwed births per 100 births in 1860	0.46	0.75	1.00	0.41	0.93	1.00

Astra during the second quarter of 1967, was the most popular variety of oral contraceptive (OC), accounting for more than 27 percent of OC sales in 1970. A 21-day regimen of Conlunett was priced at 3.17 SEK. The average expenditure per fecund female translates into almost 3 months of the most popular variety of the Pill. This is consistent with the computations by the Swedish Board of Health and Welfare that total oral contraceptive sales equated to a quarter of the fecund population using the Pill in 1969.

There is significant variation in take-up of the Pill across communities. As the lower panel of table 8.1 shows, this is highly correlated with historical nonmarital fertility. That panel also shows how nonmarital fertility is highly correlated over time, having a correlation coefficient of 0.75 across communities, or 0.93 when weighted by the distribution of the female population in 1970.

A scatter plot of Pill use per woman aged 15–40 versus the rate of unwed births in 1910 and 1860 is presented in figure 8.2. The data are weighted by the population of women in a market in 1970, as denoted by the varying size of the circles in the plot. The strong positive correlation between illegitimacy 100 or 150 years earlier is apparent regardless of the measure used. Excluding Stockholm leads to a steeper slope between Pill take-up and past illegitimacy. The linear regression line is also plotted in figure 8.2, and it should be noted that the coefficients on historical out-of-wedlock birth are positive and significantly different from zero at the 0.001 level in both specifications.

The strong positive correlation between illegitimacy a century earlier and take-up of the Pill in 1970 is striking, but one may wonder if this correlation is driven north/south development differences, population densities, or other geographical factors. The right panel of figure 8.3 presents the geographical pattern of Pill use per woman aged 15–40 in 1970; the left panel presents a map of nonmarital fertility as a share of live births in 1910 at the market level. The similarities between the maps of Pill use and illegitimacy from more than a half century earlier are remarkable. Areas of high and low demand are found in the north and the south, and in both densely and sparsely populated areas. Urban areas, such as Stockholm and Malmö, are among the areas of highest demand for the Pill, but Gothenburg, the second-largest city, is not among the top ten

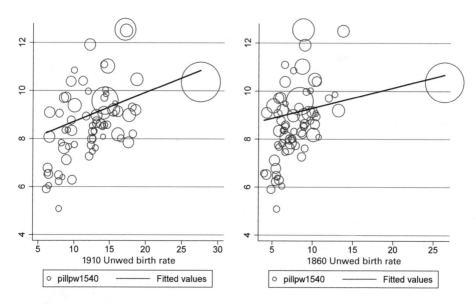

Figure 8.2
Pill use per woman in 1070 vs. historical out-of-wedlock birth rates per 100 births (women 15–40, population weighted).

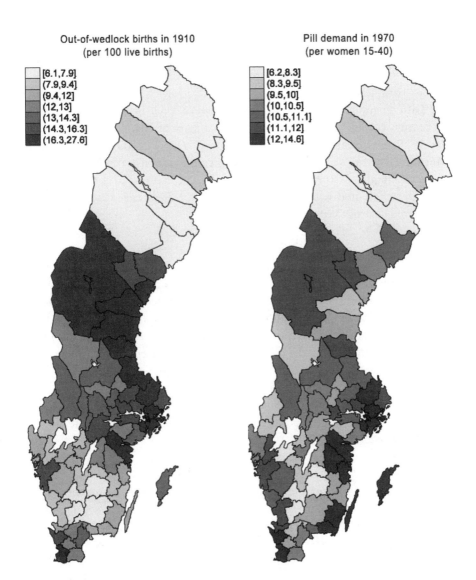

Figure 8.3
Maps of out-of-wedlock births and pill use.

markets. The maps make clear that the correlation is not simply a north/south or urban/rural story, as there are regions of high and low demand throughout the country that correlate with the geographic variation in nonmarital fertility in 1910.

Differences in demand are closely related to levels of illegitimacy from a century earlier. Communities with higher rates of unwed births in 1860 or 1910 have greater demand for the Pill when it is introduced. It remains for future work to establish whether this result is robust to other contemporaneous and historical factors, but the correlations and geographic patterns presented here suggest that historical illegitimacy is an important predictor of take-up of the Pill.

Conclusion

Economists from Malthus (1807) to Marshall (1922) have long recognized the importance of social forces in fertility control. Despite this, theoretical and empirical studies of the introduction of the Pill in the economics literature have ignored the importance of social constraints and customs in shaping the adoption of new contraceptive technologies. Recent empirical work by Fernandez and Fogli (2006, 2009) and quantitative models such as those of Fernandez-Villaverde, Greenwood, and Guner (2014) and Greenwood and Guner (2010) have refocused attention on the role of culture and social constraints on fertility and contraceptive behavior.

In this chapter I have focused on the case of Sweden and the introduction of the Pill. I have presented historical data on nonmarital fertility patterns from the nineteenth century and the early twentieth century. I have discussed these patterns in the context of the historical setting and survey the related ethnographic and demographic literature. The literature, in particular Frykman (1975, 1977) emphasizes how differential nonmarital fertility behavior was largely a product of differences in social constraints such as customs regulating marriage, norms regarding premarital sex, and moral attitudes about the use of contraception and abortion. I have discussed how early demographic studies emphasized the persistence of nonmarital fertility across communities, and I have looked at data on nonmarital childbearing spanning a half decade to show how these fertility patterns are highly correlated over time.

Pill take-up is highly correlated with historical rates of illegitimacy. Communities with higher rates of nonmarital fertility a century earlier have greater demand for the Pill when it is introduced. This is true regardless of the specific time period we consider (1860 or 1910), or whether the data is weighted. The geographic pattern of Pill adoption closely mirrors the geography of illegitimacy from generations earlier. Historical illegitimacy may proxy for differences in social norms regarding premarital sex and may provide a useful way to quantify how important culture is in determining the adoption of contraceptive innovations as well as other related behaviors. The strong correlation between nineteenth-century illegitimacy and the take-up of modern contraception a century later points to the importance of culture in shaping the adoption of contraceptive innovations.

Notes

1. See, for example, Mincer 1962.

2. A detailed review of the fertility patterns of Sweden in the eighteenth and nineteenth centuries is provided by Gustav Sundbärg as part of his contribution to the extensive Swedish emigration investigation of 1907–1914. See also chapter 8 in Low 2000 for several examples; also see Low, Clarke, and Lockridge 1992 and Low 1990. Sundin and Söderlund (1979) have edited a volume with many detailed demographic studies of nineteenth-century Sweden. An interesting summary of general trends in fertility by Santow (1995) makes some reference to the particular case of Sweden.

3. See Sundbärg 1907 and Sundbärg 1910.

4. Figure 8.1 is reproduced from page 5 of Sundbärg 1910. Low levels of nonmarital fertility in the West were coupled with very late ages of first marriage and with high marital fertility rates. The east was characterized by high nonmarital fertility rates and very low marital fertility rates, and by early ages of first marriage. The north had relatively low levels of nonmarital childbearing, and the highest rates of marital birth.

5. See chapters 2 and 13 of the *Giftermålsbalken* and chapter 17 of the *Strafflagen*.

6. Rickets was referred to as *horeskäver*.

7. The limes norrlandicus roughly marks the frontier of medieval society and a biological divide between different climate zones with different types of plant growth.

8. Wohlin's (1915) thesis has not found support (see Gaunt 1973), and the data on which he based his analysis have been shown to be flawed.

9. See Carlsson 1966 and Gaunt 1973.

10. Frykman (1975) provides an account of an exchange between a mother and her son (aged approximately 20) that occurred in 1916. The mother implores her son to be careful while visiting a dance that evening: "Olle, my dear, I tell you: don't let it drip where it sits unprotected." Her son, recently returned from

military service, responds "Oh no, Mum! I'll push all of it up their arses!" Frykman argues that coitus interruptus was known to both the mother's generation and the son's.

11. See Santow 1995 and Sklar 1977.

12. Technical contraceptive measures that preceded the Pill were a very recent phenomenon in Sweden, according to Frykman (1975).

13. See Myrdal 1968 and Linner 1967.

14. See also Myrdal 1968.

15. The lack of geographically disaggregated abortion data precludes a study of the demand for abortion.

16. Informal measures included phosphorus, arsenic, quicksilver, ergot, saffron, and strong laxatives such as aloe.

17. See Hedrén 1901, p. 20.

18. Matches containing phosphorus were banned in 1901 because of their use in abortions, which in many cases were fatal to women. In 1902 only eleven women died from phosphorus poisoning.

19. Statistics compiled in the 1900s suggest that 5 percent of all births were anonymously registered.

20. The figure is from Sundbärg 1910. Sundbärg also included characteristics based on the incidence of suicides, age of marriage, and rates of marital fertility in his analysis.

21. See Lewin 2000.

22. Source: Swedish Board of Health and Welfare 1984, table 2.

23. Laws regulating the prescription and sale of contraceptives are set by national regulatory bodies and don't differ by jurisdiction.

24. This period predates the introduction of uniform subsidies on oral contraceptives.

25. Lack of disaggregated abortion data precludes an analysis of culture on abortion demand.

26. Previous studies have relied on retrospective surveys to determine which types of contraception women had used at different points in time. These surveys are useful in eliciting information on the birth-control methods women have used, but they present an incomplete picture of demand for the Pill.

References

Akerlof, G., J. Yellen, and M. Katz. 1996. An analysis of out-of-wedlock childbearing in the United States. *Quarterly Journal of Economics* 111 (2): 277–317.

Bailey, Martha J. 2006. More power to the pill: The impact of contraceptive freedom on women's life cycle labor supply. *Quarterly Journal of Economics* 121 (1): 289–320.

Bailey, Martha J. 2010. "Momma's got the pill": How Anthony Comstock and *Griswold v. Connecticut* shaped US childbearing. *American Economic Review* 100 (1): 98–129.

Becker, G. 1965. A theory of the allocation of time. *Economic Journal (Oxford)* 75:493–517.

Becker, G. 1981. *A Treatise on the Family*. Harvard University Press.

Bisin, Alberto, and Thierry Verdier. 2000. "Beyond the melting pot": Cultural transmission, marriage, and the evolution of ethnic and religious traits. *Quarterly Journal of Economics* 115 (3): 955–988.

Bisin, Alberto, and Thierry Verdier. 2001. The economics of cultural transmission and the dynamics of preferences. *Journal of Economic Theory* 97 (2): 298–319.

Blau, Francine. 1992. The fertility of immigrant women: Evidence from high-fertility source countries. In *Immigration and the Work Force: Economic Consequences for the United States and Source Areas*, ed. G. Borjas and R. Freeman. University of Chicago Press.

Blau, Francine, Lawrence M. Kahn, Albert Yung-Hsu Liu, and Kerry L. Papps. 2008. The Transmission of Women's Fertility, Human Capital and Work Orientation Across Immigrant Generations. Working Paper 14388, National Bureau of Economic Research.

Bongaarts, J., and S. Watkins. 1996. Social interactions and contemporary fertility transitions. *Population and Development Review* 22 (4): 639–682.

Carlsson, G. 1966. The decline of fertility: Innovation or adjustment process. *Population Studies* 20 (2): 149–174.

Easterlin, R., and E. Crimmins. 1985. *The Fertility Revolution A Supply-Demand Analysis*. University of Chicago Press.

Fernandez, R. 2011. Does culture matter? In *Handbook of Social Economics*, ed. J. Benhabib, A. Bisin, and M. Jackson. Elsevier.

Fernandez, R., and A. Fogli. 2006. Fertility: The role of culture and family experience. *Journal of the European Economic Association* 4 (2–3): 552–561.

Fernandez, R., and A. Fogli. 2009. Culture: An empirical investigation of beliefs, work, and fertility. *American Economic Journal. Macroeconomics* 1 (1): 146–177.

Fernandez-Villaverde, J., J. Greenwood, and N. Guner. 2014. From shame to game in one hundred years: An economic model of the rise in premarital sex and its de-stigmatization. *Journal of the European Economic Association* 12 (1): 25–61.

Frykman, J. 1975. Sexual intercourse and social norms: A study of illegitimate births in Sweden 1831–1933. *Ethnologia Scandinavica* 3: 111–150.

Frykman, J. 1977. *Horan i Bonde Samhället*. LiborLäromedel.

Gaunt, D. 1973. Family planning and the preindustrial society: Some Swedish evidence. In *Aristocrats, Farmers, Proletarians: Essays in Swedish Demographic History*. Almqvist and Wiksell.

Goldin, C., and L. Katz. 2002. The power of the Pill: Oral contraceptives and women's career and marriage decisions. *Journal of Political Economy* 110 (4): 730–770.

Greenwood, J., and N. Guner. 2010. Social change: The Sexual Revolution. *International Economic Review* 51 (4): 893–923.

Guinnane, T., C. Moehling, and C. O'Grada. 2006. The fertility of the Irish in the United States. *Explorations in Economic History* 43 (3): 465–485.

Guiso, L., P. Sapienza, and L. Zingales. 2006. Does culture affect economic outcomes? *Journal of Economic Perspectives* 20 (2): 23–48.

Heckscher, Eli. 1949. *Sveriges Ekonomiska Historia Från Gustav Vasa: Andra Delen Det Moderna Sveriges Grundlägning Fösta Halvbandet.* Albert Bonniers.

Hedrén, Gunnar. 1901. Om fosterfördrivning från rättsmedicinsk synpunkt. Dissertation, Karolinska Institute.

Helmfrid, S. 1961. The Storskifte, Enskifte adn Laga skifte in Sweden—General features. *Geografiska Annaler* 43 (1): 114–144.

Kearney, M., and P. Levine. 2011. Income Inequality and Early Non-Marital Childbearing: An Economic Exploration of the "Culture of Despair." Working Paper 17157, National Bureau of Economic Research.

Kearney, M., and P. Levine. 2012. Why is the teen birth rate in the United States so high and why does it matter? *Journal of Economic Perspectives* 26 (2): 141–163.

Läkemedelstatistik, AB. 1974. Swedish Drug Market: Statistical Survey of Registered Pharmaceutical Specialties in Sweden.

Lesthaeghe, R., and K. Neels. 2001. From the First to the Second Demographic Transition: An interpretation of the spatial continuity of demographic innovation in France, Belgium and Switzerland. *European Journal of Population* 18: 325–360.

Lesthaeghe, R., and J. Surkyn. 1988. Cultural dynamics and economic theories of fertility change. *Population and Development Review* 14 (1): 1–45.

Lewin, Bo. 2000. *Sex in Sweden: On the Swedish Sexual Life 1996.* Stockholm: National Institute of Public Health.

Liljeström. Rita. 1974. A Study of Abortion in Sweden: A Contribution to the United Nations World Population Conference. Royal Ministry of Foreign Affairs, Stockholm.

Linner, Birgitta. 1967. *Sex and Society in Sweden.* Pantheon.

Low, Bobbi. 2000. *Why Sex Matters: A Darwinian Look at Human Behavior.* Princeton University Press.

Low, B. S. 1990. Occupational status, landownership, and reproductive behavior in 19th-century Sweden: Tuna Parish. *American Anthropologist* 92 (2): 457–468.

Low, B. S., A. L. Clarke, and K. A. Lockridge. 1992. Toward an ecological demography. *Population and Development Review* 18 (1): 1–31.

Malthus, T. R. 1807. *An Essay on the Principle of Population*, fourth edition, volume I. J. Johnson.

Marshall, A. 1922. *Principles of Economics: An Introductory Volume*. Macmillan.

McLaren, Angus. 1992. *A History of Contraception: From Antiquity to the Present Day*. Wiley Blackwell.

Mincer, J. 1962. On-the-job training: Costs, returns, and some implications. *Journal of Political Economy* 70 (5), part 2 (suppl.): 50–79.

Myrdal, Alva. 1968. *Nation and Family*. MIT Press.

Santow, Gigi. 1995. Coitus interruptus in the twentieth century. *Population and Development Review* 19 (4): 767–792.

Sklar, June. 1977. Marriage and nonmarital fertility: A comparison of Ireland and Sweden. *Population and Development Review* 3 (4): 359–375.

Statistics Central Byrån. 1864. *Befolkning Statistisk Årsbok 1860*. Stockholm: SOS.

Statistics Central Byrån. 1914. *Befolkning Statistisk Årsbok 1910*. Stockholm: SOS.

Statistiska Central Byrån. 1970. *Statistisk Årsbok 1970*. Stockholm: SOS.

Sundbärg, Gustav. 1907. *Bevölkerungsstatistik Schwedens 1750–1900*. *Reprinted in Urval 3*. Statistika Central Byrån.

Sundbärg. Gustav. 1910. *Emigrationsutredningen Bilaga V: Ekonomisk-statistisk beskrifning öfver Sveriges olika landsdelar*. Norstedt.

Sundin, Jan, and Erik Söderlund. 1979. *Time, Space and Man: Essays on Microdemography*. Almqvist & Wiksell.

Swedish Board of Health and Welfare. 1984. Workshop: Hormonal Contraceptives.

Utterström, G. 1965. Two essays on population in eighteenth-century Scandinavia. In *Population in History*, ed. D. Glass and D. Eversley. Aldine.

Wikman, K. 1937. Die Einleitung der Ehe: Eine Vergleichend Ethno-Soziologische Untersuchung über die Vorstufe der Ehe. In *Den Schwedischen Volkstums*. Institut für Nordische Ethnologie an der Åbo Akademie.

Willis, Robert J. 1999. A theory of out-of-wedlock childbearing. *Journal of Political Economy* 107 (S6): S33–S64.

Willis, Robert J., and John G. Haaga. 1996. Economic approaches to understanding nonmarital fertility. *Population and Development Review* 22: 67–86.

Wohlin, N. 1915. *Den Äktenskapliga Fruktsamhetens Tillbakagång på Gotland*. Stockholm.

9

(Europe)

Cultural Determinants of Gender Roles: "Pragmatism" as an Underpinning Attitude toward Gender Equality among Children of Immigrants

J16 B55

J15 Z13

Martin Ljunge

Gender equality, the equal opportunity of men and women to influence the course of their lives, has increasingly become a goal of social policy. The focus on gender equality may be most apparent in the Nordic countries, which have high rates of labor-force participation by women and policies that support work and family. The trend toward more gender equality applies broadly, particularly among developed countries.

Underpinning the opportunities of women and men are attitudes toward what roles women and men have both in the labor market and in family life. These gender norms shape what individuals value and what options are available in society. Both the preferences and the opportunity sets affect individual choices and aggregate social outcomes.

At the individual level there is evidence that gender norms affect fertility and labor-market outcomes (Fernández and Fogli 2006, 2009; Levine 1993; Fortin 2005; Farré and Vella 2013). At the aggregate level there is evidence that gender equality promotes economic development. Women's participation in the labor force has a strong positive correlation with economic development. The fertility rate has negative correlation, although there is evidence of a U-shaped relationship at very high development levels; see Myrskylä et al. 2009.

The analysis in this chapter is based on a comprehensive measure of cultural norms, and on studies of how they shape gender norms across generations. Transmission of norms is studied on both the mother's and the father's side. The literature so far has focused on formation of gender norms based on either indirect proxies or survey questions. Fernandez and Fogli (2006, 2009) use women's participation in the labor force and fertility rates to measure gender attitudes . Farré and Vella (2013) correlate the answers to survey questions on gender norms between mothers and children.

Hofstede et al. (2010) report six cultural dimensions that vary across cultures: power distance, individualism (versus collectivism), masculinity (versus femininity), uncertainty avoidance, pragmatism (versus normative), and indulgence (versus restraint). Of these dimensions, the previous literature has focused on the masculinity dimension, as it most directly incorporates gender norms. More masculine cultures embrace more "male" values; they focus on achievement, think that boys fight and don't cry, and embrace a traditional family structure. This could, of course, be an important dimension shaping gender norms, but it may not be the only or the most important one. Other dimensions may be important. Individualism, which focuses on individual opportunities and achievement, may be a force toward greater gender equality. The transition toward more gender equality may also be facilitated by pragmatism, meaning that social norms and behavior are allowed to change rather than that old ways should be maintained. One such old norm could be traditional gender roles.

The perspective applied in the analysis is that the six cultural dimensions characterize the ancestral country. Other aspects of the ancestral country could be seen as products the underlying cultural dimensions. The analysis will hence avoid using proxies of cultural norms (such as women's participation in the labor force) or specific attitudes (such as the role of women in the labor market).

Another innovation is to look at influences on both the mother's and the father's side. The existing literature has focused on influences on the mother's side; see, for example, Fernandez and Fogli 2006, 2009; Farré and Vella 2013; Moen et al. 1997. Studying how gender norms are shaped also on the father's side adds to this literature.

Moreover, daughters and sons are studied separately to examine the cultural dimensions both on the father's and the mother's side. This provides evidence of gender differences among parents and among children. The evidence points to many similarities but also to some differences between parents and children.

To provide a clear direction of causality from the cultural dimensions to gender norms, I study children of immigrants. The gender norms of the children are compared within country of birth and related to the six cultural dimensions in the father's or the mother's country of birth. Since the gender norms of an individual in one country cannot determine the cultural dimensions in another country, the influence, if there is any, must run from the cultural dimensions to the gender norms. Moreover, since the comparisons are done within the country of birth, all common factors affecting gender norms in that country are accounted for. This avoids confounding the influence of the cultural dimensions on gender norms with common unobserved factors in the birth country.

The chapter proceeds as follows: Section 9.1 presents the data. Section 9.2 discusses the empirical model. The results are discussed in section 9.3. Section 9.4 concludes the chapter.

9.1   Data

The main data set is the European Social Survey (ESS). The second, fourth, and fifth rounds are used as the questions that are the main dependent variables are asked in these waves.[1] The survey asks about the country of birth of the respondent as well as the country of birth of both parents.[2] This information allows me to identify children of immigrants and which countries their parents originate from. Studying 30 countries of residence for children of immigrants reduces the concern that the results are driven by conditions in one particular country. The cultural dimensions can be linked to individuals with ancestry from 78 countries. The wide range of countries reduces the concern that the results are particular to a small number of ancestral backgrounds. The summary statistics are presented in table 9A.2 in the appendix to the chapter. The children of immigrants are similar to the general population on observables.

The sample is children of immigrants. Children with an immigrant mother and those with an immigrant father are studied separately. In the immigrant-mother sample the individual is born in the same country as he or she resides, while the mother is born in a different country. The father may be an immigrant or a native of the individual's country. The immigrant-father sample is defined correspondingly.

Gender-Role Attitudes

There are two questions in the ESS that assess gender attitudes. The respondent is read two statements to which he or she can agree or disagree. The first statement is "A woman should be prepared to cut down on her paid work for the sake of her family." The statement is "When jobs are scarce, men should have more right to a job than women." For both statements the respondent can pick a category from the same scale. The options are "Agree strongly," "Agree," "Neither agree nor disagree," "Disagree," and "Disagree strongly." The answers are coded from 1 through 5 such that a higher number represents stronger disagreement.

The variables hence have increasing values for more gender-equal attitudes. The distributions for the full population and by the individual's gender are reported in figures 9.1 and 9.2. The distributions are very similar in the immigrant-mother and immigrant-father samples, so the distributions in the figures include both samples.

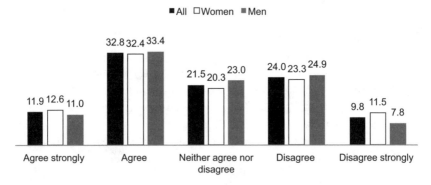

Figure 9.1
Attitudes toward the role of women in the home. The complete statement is "A woman should be prepared to cut down on her paid work for the sake of her family." Bars depict percentages. Individual data from the European Social Survey, rounds 2, 4, and 5. The figure includes both those with an immigrant father and those with an immigrant mother.

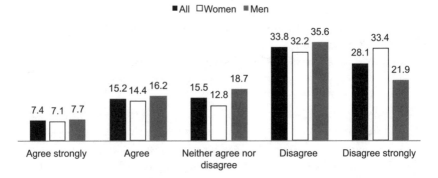

Figure 9.2
Attitudes toward the role of women in the labor market. The complete statement is "When jobs are scarce, men should have more right to a job than women." Bars depict percentages. Individual data from the European Social Survey, rounds 2, 4, and 5. The figure includes both those with an immigrant father and those with an immigrant mother.

For the first question, the wording of which is "Women should take care of the family," the median response is neither to agree nor to disagree. The most common response is to agree. Women have somewhat less traditional attitudes, but the difference is muted. For the second question, "Men should have priority to jobs," the median response, in total as well as for women and for men, is to disagree. There are clear differences at the upper end of the scale between women and men in this respect, women having stronger gender-equality attitudes. One third of the women strongly disagree with the statement; only one fifth of the men have the same attitude.

The gender-role attitudes of children of immigrants are very similar to those of the general population on average, as can be seen in table 9A.2. This indicates a large degree of assimilation. Yet this similarity in means masks systematic differences across ancestries among children of immigrants.

Hofstede's Cultural Dimensions

The cultural dimensions studied in this chapter are based on the work of Geert Hofstede and collaborators. The work was initiated by studying how culture affected workplace organization in IBM offices across the world. The initial studies were conducted between 1967 and 1973. Subsequent work has extended the analysis to more countries and wider populations.

The source for the cultural dimensions used in this chapter is Hofstede et al. 2010, in which scores on six cultural dimensions are reported for 78 countries. The original scores are between 0 and 100, but I have scaled them between 0 and 1 in the analysis in order to get fewer decimal points in the reported point estimates. Table 9A.2 displays similar scores on the cultural dimensions across the immigrant-father and immigrant-mother samples. The country scores on the cultural dimensions are presented in table 9A.3.

Descriptions of the six cultural dimensions based on Hofstede et al. (2010) are given below. Table 9A.4 presents correlations of the dimensions across the 78 countries in the sample. Note that the strongest correlation is −0.7 (between power distance and individualism); other correlations are fairly modest. It indicates that the dimensions are not collinear and one should be able to include all in a regression analysis.

Power distance   This dimension expresses the degree to which the less powerful members of a society accept and expect that power is distributed unequally. The fundamental issue here is how a society handles inequalities among people. People in societies exhibiting a large degree of power distance accept a hierarchical order in which everyone has a place and one that needs no further justification. In societies with low power distance, people strive to equalize the distribution of power and demand justification for inequalities of power.

Societies with a low score on Power distance tend to be more independent, hierarchies only result from convenience, they display equal rights and easy access to superiors, and coaching leaders are common. Power is decentralized, and managers count on the experience of their team members. Employees expect to be consulted. Control is disliked, and attitude toward managers are informal and on a first-name basis. Communication is direct and participative.

Societies with a high score believe that hierarchy should be respected and that inequalities among people are acceptable. The different distribution of power justifies the fact that power holders have more benefits than the less powerful in society. In such societies it is important to show respect to the elderly, and children care for their elderly parents. In companies there is one boss who takes complete responsibility. Status symbols of power are very important in order to indicate social position and "communicate" the respect that could be shown. The largest power-distance scores in the sample are for Slovakia and Malaysia; the lowest are for Austria and Denmark.

Individualism versus collectivism   The high side of this dimension, called individualism, can be defined as a preference for a loosely knit social framework in which individuals are expected to take care of only themselves and their immediate families. In individualistic societies, offense causes guilt and a loss of self-esteem, the employer/employee relationship is a contract based on mutual advantage, hiring and promotion decisions are supposed to be based on merit only, and management is the management of individuals.

Collectivism, the opposite of individualism, represents a preference for a tightly knit framework in which individuals can expect their relatives or members of a particular in-group to look after them in exchange for unquestioning loyalty. A society's position on this dimension is reflected in whether people's self-image is defined in terms of "I" or "we." In collectivist societies, people are, from birth, integrated into strong, cohesive groups (especially extended families including uncles, aunts, grandparents, and cousins) that continue to protect their members in exchange for loyalty. This is an important aspect in the working environment too; for instance, an older and powerful member of a family is expected to help a younger nephew get hired for a job in his own company. In business it is important to build up trustworthy and long-lasting relationships; a meeting usually starts with general conversations so that people to get to know one another before doing business. The preferred communication style is context-rich, so people will often speak profusely and write in an elaborate fashion. The most collectivist countries are Venezuela and Colombia. The most individualist societies are the United States and Australia.

Masculinity versus femininity   The masculinity side of this dimension represents a preference in society for achievement, heroism, assertiveness, and material rewards for success. Society at large is more competitive. Its opposite, femininity, stands for a preference for cooperation, modesty, caring for the weak, and quality of life. Society at large is more oriented toward consensus. In the business context, masculinity versus femininity is sometimes also referred to as "tough versus tender."

In feminine countries it is important to maintain a balance between life and work and to make sure that all are included. An effective manager is supportive, and decision making is achieved through involvement. Managers strive for consensus, and people value equality, solidarity, and quality in their working lives. Conflicts are resolved by compromise. Incentives such as free time and flexibility in work hours and places are favored. In masculine countries, people "live in order to work"; managers are expected to be decisive and assertive; the emphasis is on equity, competition, and performance; and conflicts are resolved by fighting them out. The most masculine societies are Slovakia and Japan; the most feminine are Sweden and Norway.

Uncertainty avoidance   The dimension of uncertainty avoidance expresses the degree to which the members of a society feel uncomfortable with uncertainty and ambiguity. The fundamental issue here is how a society deals with the fact that the future can never be known; the question is "Should we try to control the future, or just let it happen?" Countries exhibiting strong uncertainty avoidance maintain rigid codes of belief and behavior and are intolerant of unorthodox behavior and ideas. In these cultures there is an emotional need for rules (even if the rules never seem to work), time is money, people have an inner urge to be busy and work hard, precision and punctuality are norms, innovation may be resisted, and security is an important element in individual motivation.

Societies weak in uncertainty avoidance maintain a more relaxed attitude in which practice counts more than principles and deviance from the norm is more easily tolerated. In societies exhibiting low uncertainty avoidance, people believe there should be no more rules than are necessary and that rules that are ambiguous or that don't work they should be abandoned or changed. Schedules are flexible, hard work is undertaken when it is necessary but not for its own sake, precision and punctuality do not come naturally, and innovation is not seen as threatening. The most relaxed countries with respect to uncertainty are Singapore and Denmark. The countries most averse to uncertainty are Greece, Portugal, and Uruguay.

Pragmatism (or short-term normative) versus normative   Every society has to maintain some links with its own past while dealing with the challenges of the present and the future. Societies prioritize these two existential goals differently. Societies that score low on this dimension, for example, prefer to maintain time-honored traditions and norms and view societal change with suspicion. Those with a culture that scores high, on the other hand, take a more pragmatic approach; they encourage thrift and efforts in modern education as a way to prepare for the future.

In the business context and in the country comparison tool of Hofstede et al. (2010) this dimension is related to as "(short term) normative versus (long term) pragmatic." People in normative societies have a strong concern with establishing the absolute Truth; they are normative in their thinking. They exhibit great respect for traditions, a relatively small propensity to save for the future, and a focus on achieving quick results. In societies with a pragmatic orientation, people believe that truth depends very much on situation, context, and time. They show an ability to adapt traditions easily to changed conditions, a strong propensity to save and invest, thriftiness, and perseverance in achieving results. The most normative countries in the sample are Ghana and Egypt. The most pragmatic are Korea and Taiwan.

Indulgence versus restraint   A society characterized by indulgence allows relatively free gratification of basic and natural human drives related to enjoying life and having fun. People possess a positive attitude and have a tendency toward optimism. In addition, they place a higher degree of importance on leisure time, act as they please, and spend money as they wish.

A society characterized by restraint suppresses gratification of needs and regulates it by means of strict social norms. Societies with a low score on indulgence have a tendency to cynicism and pessimism. Also, in contrast to indulgent societies, restrained societies do not put much emphasis on leisure time and control the gratification of their desires. People with this orientation have the perception that their actions are restrained by social norms and feel that indulging themselves is somewhat wrong. The two societies most prone to indulgence are Venezuela and Mexico; the most restrained are Egypt and Latvia.

Development of Ancestral Country
The log of the ancestral country's gross domestic product per capita is used to measure the effect of ancestry from a higher-income country.[3] This measure is taken from the World Development Indicators (WDI) provided by the World Bank. Although the main focus is on the transmission of the six cultural dimensions, there are also results conditioning on the level of development to rule out the possibility that the cultural influences are collinear with development.

Individual Control Variables
The ESS includes a rich set of individual controls. Age, gender, marital status, education, income, and religious affiliation are observed. Marital status is captured by two dummies for married and never married, with widowed and divorced being the excluded category. Education is captured by one dummy for tertiary (university) degree and above and one dummy for upper secondary as the highest attained degree. Lower education is the excluded category. Income is measured by income decile, based on the country specific income distribution. I create one dummy for the bottom three deciles (Low Income) and one dummy for the middle four deciles (Middle Income). Religion dummies for being a Catholic or a Protestant are included; other religious denominations are in the excluded category.

9.2 Empirical Specification

To separate the influence of cultural transmission in the family from influences in the society in which the individual lives, I use the "epidemiological approach" (as the method is labeled in Fernandez 2010. The main type of analysis is ordinary least-squares regressions of the form

$$\text{GenderRole}_{icat} = \alpha_0 + \alpha_1 \text{PDI}_a + \alpha_2 \text{IDV}_a + \alpha_3 \text{MAS}_a + \alpha_4 \text{PRA}_a + \alpha_5 \text{UAI}_a$$
$$+ \alpha_6 \text{IND}_a + \alpha_7 X_{icat} + \gamma_{ct} + \varepsilon_{icat}. \qquad (1)$$

GenderRole$_{ict}$ measures the gender-role attitude by individual i, born and residing in country c with a parent born in country a, and a ≠ c, in period t. This regression is run on a sample of second-generation immigrants. The six cultural dimensions in the ancestral country are captured by the variables PDI$_a$, IDV$_a$, MAS$_a$, PRA$_a$, UAI$_a$, and IND$_a$. They measure the scores on power distance, individualism, masculinity, pragmatism, uncertainty avoidance, and indulgence, respectively. These variables are common to all individuals with a parent born in country a. X$_{icat}$ captures individual demographic and economic controls that may affect gender attitudes. The country of residence-by-year fixed effect is denoted by γ_{ct}, and ε_{icat} is the error term. All standard errors are clustered by the parent's birth country to allow for arbitrary correlations of the error terms among individuals with the same ancestral country.

Reverse causality is not a concern in equation 1, since the attitudes of a person born and residing in country c cannot affect the cultural dimensions in the parent's birth country a. The inclusion of the country-by-year fixed effect γ_{ct} means that the institutional structure and all other unobserved differences that apply to all residents in country c in period t are accounted for. It also means that the method used to identify the estimates on the cultural dimensions is to compare the attitudes of second-generation immigrants within each country of residence and year relative to the values in their countries of ancestry. Since the country fixed effects are included for each year, they account for non-linear trends in gender norms that may differ across countries. The method and the related literature are discussed in more detail in Fernandez 2010.[4]

The main specification in the analysis relates the cultural dimension in the ancestral country to the relative gender attitudes of children of immigrants within country of residence. The cultural dimensions' capture broad features of the ancestral country that could be transmitted across generations and shape gender attitudes. The transmission channel from parent to child is labeled "direct vertical transmission" in the model of Bisin and Verdier (2001, 2010). Gender attitudes may also be shaped by the society in which the child grows up in, labeled "oblique horizontal transmission" in their model. These social influences may change as a result of changes in the political system or anti-discrimination laws, and may introduce a time-varying component of gender attitudes. As children of immigrants are studied within a country and a year, all individuals face similar social influences in their residence countries. Including the country and year fixed effects hence focuses attention on the deviations of gender attitudes around the time trends.

9.3 Results

This section presents the estimation results on how cultural dimensions' shape attitudes toward gender roles in the home and the market sector. The focus is on Hofstede's six cultural dimensions. The idea is that these dimensions characterize the ancestral country, and the analysis tells us which dimensions shape the gender attitudes. The analysis is done separately on the father's and the mother's side. The literature has thus far focused on transmission of norms on the mother's side and my analysis can shed light on differences in how gender attitudes are shaped on the maternal and paternal sides. Moreover, the analysis is done separately for daughters and sons on both the paternal and maternal sides, in order to assess gender differences both among the children and among the parents.

Father's Side

The first question examined is if women should care for the family rather than work.[5] A higher value captures stronger disagreement with the statement and more gender-equal attitudes. The first column in table 9.1 includes controls for the six cultural dimensions, age and its square, gender, and country of birth by year fixed effects. Two cultural dimensions have significant estimates: Masculinity (with a negative sign) and Pragmatism (with a positive sign).

The negative estimate on Masculinity is as one would expect from the previous literature. Cultures emphasizing more Masculinity shape more traditional gender attitudes. Masculinity would encapsulate previously used measures based on women's participation in the labor force rate and specific gender attitudes. More surprising may be the second significant estimate, Pragmatism. The positive estimate indicates that more pragmatic cultures shape more gender-equal attitudes. As the trend in the European countries studied is toward more gender equality, it makes sense that pragmatic cultures embrace this shift faster than more normatively orthodox cultures. Interestingly, there is no significant difference between men and women on this question once the cultural dimensions are accounted for.[6]

The main perspective in the analysis is that the six cultural dimensions characterize the ancestral country. Yet it may be interesting to assess the influence of the cultural dimensions separate from the level of development. Column 2 of table 9.1 adds the logarithm of the GDP per capita in

Table 9.1
Gender norms and Hofstede's cultural dimensions; father's side. Sample: children of immigrants with an immigrant father.

Dependent variable:	Women should care for family			Men should have priority to jobs		
	(1)	(2)	(3)	(4)	(5)	(6)
Power Distance, father's birth country	0.105	0.007	−0.015	−0.157	−0.122	−0.151
	(0.115)	(0.130)	(0.148)	(0.119)	(0.129)	(0.107)
Individualism, father's birth country	0.066	0.169	0.107	−0.128	−0.199	−0.303
	(0.200)	(0.200)	(0.196)	(0.174)	(0.204)	(0.181)*
Masculinity, father's birth country	−0.253	−0.261	−0.240	−0.288	−0.268	−0.231
	(0.109)**	(0.118)**	(0.112)**	(0.118)**	(0.133)**	(0.116)*
Uncertainty avoidance, father's birth country	−0.123	−0.080	−0.123	−0.025	−0.104	−0.174
	(0.193)	(0.209)	(0.193)	(0.168)	(0.176)	(0.152)
Pragmatism, father's birth country	0.377	0.414	0.313	0.500	0.439	0.289
	(0.128)***	(0.125)***	(0.127)**	(0.137)***	(0.152)***	(0.132)**
Indulgence, father's birth country	0.138	0.177	0.087	0.089	0.035	−0.094
	(0.178)	(0.191)	(0.185)	(0.210)	(0.237)	(0.198)
Log of GDP per capita, father's birth country		−0.059	−0.039		0.049	0.083
		(0.051)	(0.052)		(0.064)	(0.058)

Table 9.1 (continued)

Dependent variable:	Women should care for family			Men should have priority to jobs		
	(1)	(2)	(3)	(4)	(5)	(6)
Age	0.022	0.021	0.026	0.026	0.025	0.016
	(0.005)***	(0.005)***	(0.005)***	(0.004)***	(0.004)***	(0.005)***
Age²/100	−0.029	−0.029	−0.030	−0.038	−0.037	−0.025
	(0.006)***	(0.006)***	(0.005)***	(0.005)***	(0.005)***	(0.005)***
Female	0.037	0.037	0.043	0.238	0.239	0.236
	(0.028)	(0.028)	(0.032)	(0.030)***	(0.032)***	(0.029)***
Married			−0.104			−0.117
			(0.047)**			(0.045)**
Never married			0.120			0.036
			(0.070)*			(0.060)
Upper secondary			0.150			0.274
			(0.043)***			(0.048)***
College or university			0.368			0.598
			(0.059)***			(0.059)***

Table 9.1 (continued)

Dependent variable:	Women should care for family			Men should have priority to jobs		
	(1)	(2)	(3)	(4)	(5)	(6)
Low income			-0.136			-0.223
			(0.061)**			(0.076)***
Middle income			-0.126			-0.193
			(0.043)***			(0.037)***
Catholic			-0.151			-0.138
			(0.035)***			(0.049)***
Protestant			-0.113			-0.136
			(0.062)*			(0.058)**
Country-by-year fixed effects	Yes	Yes	Yes	Yes	Yes	Yes
R^2	0.113	0.119	0.141	0.182	0.187	0.225
Observations	5819	5442	5224	5863	5478	5267

The dependent variable in columns 1–3 is attitudes toward that women should care for the family. In columns 4–6 the dependent variable is attitudes toward that men should have priority to jobs. In all cases the answers range from "Agree strongly," coded as 1, to "Disagree strongly," coded as 5. The first six explanatory variables are scores on the cultural dimensions in Hofstede et al. 2010. Country of residence by year fixed effects included in all specifications. Individual data are from the second, fourth, and fifth waves of the European Social Survey. Standard errors are in parenthesis. Standard errors allow for clustering on the mother's birth country. Significance: *$p < 0.1$; **$p < 0.05$; ***$p < 0.01$.

the ancestral country to the specification, which broadly accounts for development.

The estimates on the cultural dimensions in the first and second columns in table 9.1 are very similar. Masculinity and Pragmatism remain strongly significant, with the same signs as in the base-line model. The development measure, GDP per capita, is insignificant, indicating a strong influence of the cultural dimensions over and above the level of development.

The third specification in table 9.1 adds a set of individual controls frequently used in the literature. One issue with adding these controls is that they shut down any influence of the cultural dimensions on gender attitudes that works through the included controls. For example, one could imagine that the cultural dimensions affect education, and that education in turn shapes gender attitudes. Controlling for education effectively shuts down this influence of culture on gender attitudes.

In the extensive model represented in column 3 of table 9.1, the two cultural dimensions Masculinity and Pragmatism remain strongly significant as before. The point estimate on Pragmatism is somewhat lower. Individual characteristic associated with more gender-equal attitudes are high education and high income. Married individuals and those with an expressed religion (Catholic or Protestant) express more traditional views.

The second half of table 9.1 has to do with whether men should have priority to work when jobs are scarce. The estimates follow the same pattern as the previous question. Masculinity is negative and significant; Pragmatism is positive and significant. The level of development is insignificant. The life-cycle pattern is inversely U-shaped; in particular, old individuals express more traditional gender attitudes. In contrast to the previous question, women now express substantially stronger gender-equality attitudes. Attitudes toward women in the labor market appear more divisive across gender lines than the role of women in the home. In column 6 of table 9.1, with extensive individual controls, the estimate on Masculinity loses some significance but remains significant at conventional levels. There is also a weakly significant estimate on Individualism.

The estimates on the individual characteristics in columns 3 and 6 of table 9.1 reveal larger point estimates (in magnitude) on education and income in column 6. Individual characteristics hence appear more important in explaining gender roles in the market sector than in the home. The weaker estimate on Masculinity in column 6 of table 9.1 indicates that some of the previously estimated influence may have affected education and other individual characteristics. Both in the market sector and at home, low education and low income is associated with more traditional gender roles.

Mother's Side

This subsection performs analysis of the same questions as in the previous subsection but with the distinct difference that the gender attitudes are related to the six cultural dimensions on the *mother's* side. The specifications include the same set of controls as in the previous analysis.

First are the specifications analyzing attitudes toward women prioritizing home work ("Women should care for the family"). The first column of table 9.2 presents the results with only the most exogenous individual controls. The estimate on Masculinity is negative and significant, and the estimate on Pragmatism is positive and significant at the 10 percent level, both similar to the estimates on the father's side. However, there is a positive and significant estimate on the Power Distance, and a weakly significant estimate on Indulgence. The robustness of the last estimate is not clear, as Indulgence loses significance in the second column of table 9.2, where the level of development is accounted for. Also, Pragmatism loses its significance at conventional levels in this specification. Power Distance and Masculinity remains significant. In the third column of table 9.2, where extensive individual controls are included, Power Distance remains strongly significant and Masculinity is significant at the 10 percent level.

The positive sign on the Power Distance estimate means that those with ancestry from more hierarchical countries express more gender-equal attitudes. This may seem surprising at first if one expects that less hierarchical cultures would be more likely to embrace gender equality. Yet the estimates indicate a "counterculture" in which the children of mothers from more hierarchical cultures have a stronger embrace of gender equality in the home than those with ancestry from countries with less power distance.

Next, consider the estimates on what shapes attitudes to women in the labor market ("Men should have priority to jobs"). The estimate on Masculinity remains negative and significant, as in previous regressions. The estimate on Pragmatism is positive and significant in columns 4 and 5 of table 9.2. Pragmatism loses significance in column 6 of table 9.2 because the point estimate drops somewhat, so it does not appear as a

Table 9.2
Gender norms and Hofstede's cultural dimensions, mother's side. Sample: children of immigrants with an immigrant mother.

Dependent variable:	Women should care for family			Men should have priority to jobs		
	(1)	(2)	(3)	(4)	(5)	(6)
Power distance, mother's birth country	0.393	0.432	0.481	0.058	0.173	0.163
	(0.110)***	(0.123)***	(0.121)***	(0.102)	(0.119)	(0.113)
Individualism, mother's birth country	0.235	0.198	0.117	0.218	0.092	−0.041
	(0.198)	(0.215)	(0.209)	(0.178)	(0.184)	(0.149)
Masculinity, mother's birth country	−0.418	−0.380	−0.311	−0.384	−0.345	−0.246
	(0.138)***	(0.149)**	(0.162)*	(0.103)***	(0.105)***	(0.109)**
Uncertainty avoidance, mother's birth country	−0.106	−0.196	−0.249	−0.143	−0.289	−0.324
	(0.201)	(0.207)	(0.191)	(0.164)	(0.189)	(0.156)**
Pragmatism, mother's birth country	0.240	0.166	0.104	0.335	0.255	0.147
	(0.144)*	(0.131)	(0.128)	(0.119)***	(0.122)**	(0.097)
Indulgence, mother's birth country	0.300	0.225	0.171	0.093	−0.007	−0.085
	(0.176)*	(0.169)	(0.167)	(0.222)	(0.242)	(0.193)
Log of GDP per capita, mother's birth country		0.049	0.073		0.089	0.117
		(0.045)	(0.044)*		(0.047)*	(0.040)***

Table 9.2 (continued)

Dependent variable:	Women should care for family			Men should have priority to jobs		
	(1)	(2)	(3)	(4)	(5)	(6)
Age	0.018	0.016	0.019	0.025	0.023	0.012
	(0.004)***	(0.004)***	(0.005)***	(0.004)***	(0.004)***	(0.005)**
Age²/100	−0.025	−0.024	−0.024	−0.036	−0.034	−0.020
	(0.005)***	(0.005)***	(0.005)***	(0.005)***	(0.005)***	(0.006)***
Female	0.071	0.070	0.072	0.249	0.250	0.245
	(0.030)**	(0.031)**	(0.035)**	(0.044)***	(0.046)***	(0.043)***
Married			−0.181			−0.118
			(0.050)***			(0.046)**
Never married			0.030			0.003
			(0.070)			(0.070)
Upper secondary			0.111			0.323
			(0.032)***			(0.050)***
College or university			0.323			0.609
			(0.067)***			(0.063)***

Table 9.2 (continued)

Dependent variable:	Women should care for family			Men should have priority to jobs		
	(1)	(2)	(3)	(4)	(5)	(6)
Low income			-0.160			-0.166
			(0.044)***			(0.061)***
Middle income			-0.045			-0.092
			(0.032)			(0.038)**
Catholic			-0.122			-0.136
			(0.050)**			(0.047)***
Protestant			-0.143			-0.145
			(0.049)***			(0.063)**
Country–by–year fixed effects	Yes	Yes	Yes	Yes	Yes	Yes
R^2	0.130	0.135	0.154	0.179	0.184	0.220
Observations	5,701	5,403	5,202	5,722	5,420	5,228

The dependent variable in columns 1–3 is attitudes toward that women should care for the family. In columns 4–6 the dependent variable is attitudes toward that men should have priority to jobs. In all cases the answers range from "Agree strongly," coded as 1, to "Disagree strongly," coded as 5. The first six explanatory variables are scores on the cultural dimensions in Hofstede et al. 2010. Individual data are from the second, fourth, and fifth waves of the European Social Survey. Standard errors are in parenthesis. Standard errors allow for clustering on the mother's birth country. Significance: *p < 0.1; **p < 0.05; ***p < 0.01.

significant change across specifications. New in column 6 of table 9.2 is a negative and significant estimate on Uncertainty Avoidance.

The estimates on the individual characteristics in specifications 3 and 6 are broadly similar across the immigrant-father and immigrant-mother samples in tables 9.4 and 9.5. Women are significantly more likely to express gender-equal attitudes, and the magnitude is now significant in the case of women prioritizing the family, while the magnitude is larger in the case of men having priority to jobs. Higher education and income are associated with more gender-equal attitudes, as before. Those married and expressly Protestant or Catholic are more traditional in their gender attitudes.

Daughters and Sons

This subsection examines heterogeneity across the child's gender. Different cultural dimensions may influence daughters and sons. Moreover, these influences may differ between a father and mother. The following analysis sheds some light on these issues. Transmission of the father's side is studied before we turn to the mother's side. All the results are estimated in the base-line model, controlling for age, its square, and the country-by-year effects.

Father's side Attitudes toward if women should care for the family are examined in the first two specifications of table 9.3. Column 1 studies daughters and related their attitude to the six cultural dimensions on the father's birth country.

The estimate on Masculinity is negative and significant, and the estimate on Pragmatism is positive and significant. This is similar to the joint sample in table 9.1. For sons, the estimate on Masculinity is negative but no longer significant. The magnitudes of the estimates are comparable between sons and daughters (indicating similar influences), yet the estimate among sons is not significant (indicating a weaker influence in this group). The estimate on Pragmatism among the sons in column 2 of table 9.3 is positive and significant at the 10 percent level. Again, the magnitudes are comparable across daughters and sons; however, the significance is lower among sons, indicating a weaker influence.

Next is the study of attitudes toward whether men should have priority to jobs. For daughters the estimate on Masculinity is negative and significant at the 10 percent level. The estimate on Pragmatism is large, positive, and strongly significant. The estimates indicate that Pragmatism

Table 9.3
Estimates by daughters and sons. father's side. Sample: children of immigrants with an immigrant father.

Dependent variable:	Women should care for family		Men should have priority to jobs			
Child's gender:	Female	Male	Female	Male		
	(1)	(2)	(3)	(4)	(6)	(7)
Power distance,	0.042	0.130	−0.036	−0.291	−0.264	−0.206
father's birth country	(0.120)	(0.192)	(0.150)	(0.155)*	(0.108)**	(0.083)**
Individualism,	0.017	0.140	−0.030	−0.219	0.043	0.039
father's birth country	(0.239)	(0.224)	(0.209)	(0.196)	(0.068)	(0.052)
Masculinity,	−0.282	−0.258	−0.289	−0.296	0.017	0.015
father's birth country	(0.113)**	(0.161)	(0.156)*	(0.151)*	(0.029)	(0.022)
Uncertainty avoidance,	−0.222	−0.004	−0.102	0.033	0.010	0.008
father's birth country	(0.208)	(0.225)	(0.169)	(0.222)	(0.081)	(0.066)
Pragmatism,	0.412	0.343	0.640	0.346	−0.009	−0.007
father's birth country	(0.118)***	(0.197)*	(0.145)***	(0.174)*		

Table 9.3 (continued)

Dependent variable:	Women should care for family		Men should have priority to jobs			
Child's gender:	Female	Male	Female	Male		
	(1)	(2)	(3)	(4)	(6)	(7)
Indulgence, father's birth country	0.154 (0.208)	0.090 (0.227)	-0.044 (0.264)	0.191 (0.241)	0.008 (0.005)	0.005 (0.004)
Age and age² controls	Yes	Yes	Yes	Yes	Yes	Yes
Country-by-year fixed effects	Yes	Yes	Yes	Yes	Yes	Yes
R²	0.108	0.121	0.184	0.170	0.143	
Observations	3162	2657	3179	2684	6,847	6,847

The dependent variable in columns 1 and 2 is attitudes toward that women should care for the family. In columns 3 and 4 the dependent variable is attitudes toward that men should have priority to jobs. In all cases the answers range from "Agree strongly," coded as 1, to "Disagree strongly," coded as 5. Columns 1 and 3 include women (daughters) and columns 2 and 4 men (sons). The six explanatory variables are scores on the cultural dimensions in Hofstede et al. 2010. Individual controls include age and age squared. Country of residence by year fixed effects included in all specifications. Individual data are from the second, fourth, and fifth waves of the European Social Survey. Standard errors are in parenthesis. Standard errors allow for clustering on the mother's birth country. Significance: $*p < 0.1$; $**p < 0.05$; $***p < 0.01$.

appears to be most important dimension shaping the paternal transmission of gender attitudes in the workplace.

For the sons in column 4 of table 9.3 there are three estimates that are significant at the 10 percent level. The estimates on Power Distance and Masculinity are negative, and the estimate on Pragmatism is positive.

The estimates on the father-to-daughter transmission of gender norms given in columns 1 and 3 in table 9.3 indicate that Pragmatism may be the strongest influence. Influences from the father to the son are, on the whole weaker, as can be seen in columns 2 and 4 of table 9.3. Still, pragmatism appears to be the most important influence for sons too.

Mother's side   This subsection examines how daughters' and sons' attitudes are shaped through influences on the mother's side. The first question is whether women should care for the family. The estimate on Power Distance is positive and significant both for daughters and sons, as seen in the first two specifications of table 9.4. The point estimate is a little larger and more significant for daughter than for sons.

The point estimate on Masculinity is negative for both groups, not significant for daughters, and strongly significant for sons. The magnitude is substantially higher for sons. The estimate on Pragmatism is positive and significant for daughters; the positive estimate is smaller in magnitude and insignificant for sons. For daughters there is a fairly large positive estimate on Indulgence that is significant at the 10 percent level.

Columns 3 and 4 of table 9.4 represent attitudes toward women in the labor market. The estimate on Power Distance is positive and significant for daughters; the point estimate is negative and of similar magnitude for sons. This indicates a difference in the influence across the gender of the child.

The estimate on Masculinity is negative and significant for both daughters and sons. However, the size of the estimate for sons is twice that for daughters, indicating a differential impact. Masculinity imparted through the mother seems to have a stronger influence on the attitudes of sons than on those of daughters both in the labor market and in the family.

The point estimates on Pragmatism in columns 3 and 4 of table 9.4 are positive for both sons and daughters. However, the estimate is not significant for daughters, while it is significant for sons. Comparing the estimates on Pragmatism across table 9.4, one notices that it is a significant influence for daughters in the case of attitudes in the home while it is

Table 9.4
Estimates by daughters and sons, mother's side. Sample: children of immigrants with an immigrant mother.

Dependent variable:	Women should care for family		Men should have priority to jobs	
Child's gender:	Female	Male	Female	Male
	(1)	(2)	(3)	(4)
Power distance, mother's birth country	0.440 (0.162)***	0.348 (0.134)**	0.331 (0.167)*	−0.247 (0.170)
Individualism, mother's birth country	0.061 (0.251)	0.398 (0.202)*	0.249 (0.205)	0.159 (0.241)
Masculinity, mother's birth country	−0.265 (0.165)	−0.565 (0.180)***	−0.277 (0.105)***	−0.532 (0.211)**
Uncertainty avoidance, mother's birth country	−0.131 (0.244)	−0.108 (0.216)	−0.301 (0.202)	0.051 (0.213)
Pragmatism, mother's birth country	0.350 (0.174)**	0.153 (0.130)	0.270 (0.169)	0.445 (0.119)***

Table 9.4 (continued)

Dependent variable:	Women should care for family		Men should have priority to jobs	
Child's gender:	Female	Male	Female	Male
	(1)	(2)	(3)	(4)
Indulgence, mother's birth country	0.440 (0.231)*	0.183 (0.174)	0.173 (0.251)	0.043 (0.291)
Age and age^2 controls	Yes	Yes	Yes	Yes
Country–by–year fixed effects	Yes	Yes	Yes	Yes
R^2	0.132	0.130	0.174	0.180
Observations	3,089	2,612	3,091	2,631

The dependent variable in columns 1 and 2 is attitudes toward that women should care for the family. In columns 3 and 4 the dependent variable is attitudes toward that men should have priority to jobs. In all cases the answers range from "Agree strongly," coded as 1, to "Disagree strongly," coded as 5. Columns 1 and 3 include women (daughters) and columns 2 and 4 men (sons). The six explanatory variables are scores on the cultural dimensions in Hofstede et al. 2010. Individual controls include age and age squared. Country of residence by year fixed effects included in all specifications. Individual data are from the second, fourth, and fifth waves of the European Social Survey. Standard errors are in parenthesis. Standard errors allow for clustering on the mother's birth country. Significance: *$p < 0.1$; **$p < 0.05$; ***$p < 0.01$.

significant for sons regarding attitudes in the market. The estimates reveal differential strength in the influences across gender and type of gender norm.

9.4   Discussion

This chapter finds evidence of how gender norms are shaped by a broad set of cultural influences. The analysis goes beyond the study of how the mother's attitudes are transmitted to the daughter by studying transmission both through fathers and through mothers, and by studying both daughters and sons. Moreover, the analysis considers a broad range of cultural influences rather than measures aimed at capturing gender attitudes only. For example, Farré and Vella (2013) and Thornton et al. (1983) focus on the influence on attitudes toward women and men, while Fernandez and Fogli (2006, 2009) focus on indirect measures such as women's participation in the labor force and fertility rates.

I study a wide-ranging set of cultural factors based on work on cultural traits across the world done by Hofstede et al. (2010). They identify six important and largely independent cultural dimensions: Power Distance, Individualism, Masculinity, Uncertainty Avoidance, Pragmatism, and Indulgence. Of these factors, Masculinity fits with the focus of the previous literature. Yet it is not know whether this is the most important factor shaping gender norms once other dimensions are accounted for.

The analysis finds that ancestry from a country that scores high on Masculinity has negative and significant influence on gender-equality norms, as one might expect. More unexpectedly, Pragmatism reveals itself as an important influence behind promoting gender-equality norms. In some cases the effect size of Pragmatism is twice that of Masculinity (in magnitude). The results point to the importance of broadening the perspective beyond direct transmission of gender norms.

There is also interesting heterogeneity in the influence of Pragmatism on gender attitudes. This influence seems to be stronger on the father's side than on the mother's. Moreover, on the father's side the results indicate that the positive influence of Pragmatism on gender equality is stronger on daughters than on sons.

The results show that both mothers and fathers are important in shaping gender norms. They indicate that the previous literature's focus on transmission on the mother's side omits important channels through which gender norms are shaped and in turn potentially affect choices and outcomes. This study points to the importance of including the fathers in such studies.

The results may have implications for integration policy in countries that want to promote more gender equality. For example, in Sweden gender equality is an important political and social objective. It is though that men and women should have the same possibilities to influence their lives. Underlying the equal possibilities are norms about what men and women should do, which in turn affect both individual choices and the available options in society. Sweden also has significant immigration from countries with more traditional gender roles. There is a conflict between the indigenous Swedish values and migrant groups. Integration, from the Swedish perspective, seem to require the migrant groups to adopt more gender-equal attitudes. The results presented here point to the need for integration policy to recognize the role of promoting pragmatism among these groups as a means to influence gender attitudes.

Pragmatism could make integration of immigrants faster, beyond the influence on gender norms. It is plausible that Pragmatism (in which one adapts the norms to the current context) may make life easier for migrants along many dimensions than holding on to their ancestral culture's "truth" when living in a country that may embrace other convictions. The potentially wider influence of Pragmatism on attitudes and behavior is a topic for my future research.

Notable is also that the gender norms are quite similar for men and women. In one case (that regarding the statement that women should take care of the family on the father's side), there is no significant difference between women and men. On the mother's side the estimate on being female is significant but modest in magnitude. Regarding the statement that men should have priority to jobs, there is a significant difference across gender. However, on a scale from one to five it does not represent a dramatic difference. If one would play with the idea that all men changed gender it would result in more gender-equal attitudes by one eighth of a point. It seems that gender equality does not follow if all men become like women, at least not with respect to the two attitudes examined.

This study points to the importance of broadening the perspective when studying the formation of gender norms and their potential influence on individual choices and policy. First, it appears important to consider how gender norms are transmitted both through the mother and the father. Second, the results point to the significance of accounting for a broader set of cultural influences than just gender norms of the mother or her birth country. Although Masculinity is an important influence on gender norms, the estimates indicate that Pragmatism is more important in several circumstances.

Acknowledgments

I acknowledge financial support from the Swedish Council for Working Life and Social Research (Forte) under grant 2012:1261, from the Swedish Research Council under grant 2012–643, and from the Torsten Söderberg Foundation under grant E1–14.

Appendix

Table 9A.1
Countries participating in the ESS by survey round.

	Survey round				
	1	2	3	4	5
Austria	X	X	X		
Belgium	X	X	X	X	X
Bulgaria			X	X	X
Croatia					X
Cyprus			X	X	X
Czech Republic	X	X		X	X
Denmark	X	X	X	X	X
Estonia		X	X	X	X
Finland	X	X	X	X	X
France	X	X	X	X	X
Germany	X	X	X	X	X
Greece	X	X		X	X

Table 9A.1 (continued)

	Survey round				
	1	2	3	4	5
Hungary	X	X	X	X	X
Ireland	X	X	X	X	X
Israel	X			X	X
Italy	X	X			
Luxembourg	X	X			
Netherlands	X	X	X	X	X
Norway	X	X	X	X	X
Poland	X	X	X	X	X
Portugal	X	X	X	X	X
Russian Federation			X	X	X
Slovakia		X	X	X	X
Slovenia	X	X	X	X	X
Spain	X	X	X	X	X
Sweden	X	X	X	X	X
Switzerland	X	X	X	X	X
Turkey		X		X	
Ukraine		X	X	X	X
United Kingdom	X	X	X	X	X

Edition 2.0 of ESS round 5 is used, and the cumulative file for earlier rounds. Rounds 2,4, and 5 are used in the analysis. Survey years: round 1 in 2002, round 2 in 2004, round 3 in 2006, round 4 in 2008, round 5 in 2010.

Table 9A.2
Summary statistics.

Variable	Immigrant-father sample		Immigrant-mother sample		Native population sample	
	Mean	S.D.	Mean	S.D.	Mean	S.D.
Women should care for family	2.85	1.19	2.85	1.20	2.82	1.17
Men should have priority to jobs	3.56	1.25	3.57	1.26	3.46	1.26
Power distance, parent's birth country	0.637	0.223	0.628	0.229		
Individualism, parent's birth country	0.526	0.189	0.530	0.186		
Masculinity, parent's birth country	0.527	0.183	0.521	0.190		
Uncertainty avoidance, parent's birth country	0.750	0.189	0.743	0.188		
Pragmatism, parent's birth country	0.532	0.222	0.542	0.226		
Indulgence, parent's birth country	0.366	0.169	0.373	0.168		
GDP per capita (log), parent's birth country	9.524	0.795	9.561	0.793		
Age	44.5	17.9	44.5	17.9	47.7	18.6
Female	0.543	0.498	0.542	0.498	0.538	0.499
Married	0.504	0.500	0.492	0.500	0.535	0.499
Never married	0.314	0.464	0.322	0.467	0.274	0.446
Upper secondary degree	0.499	0.500	0.503	0.500	0.440	0.496
College/university degree	0.258	0.438	0.263	0.440	0.225	0.417
Middle income	0.223	0.416	0.220	0.414	0.259	0.438
High income	0.321	0.467	0.322	0.467	0.294	0.456
Catholic	0.176	0.381	0.198	0.398	0.307	0.461
Protestant	0.066	0.249	0.070	0.256	0.136	0.342

Data on individuals are from the European Social Survey, rounds 2, 4, and 5. The immigrant-father sample refers to individuals born in the country of residence whose father is born in a different country. The immigrant-mother sample refers to individuals born in the country of residence whose mother is born in a different country. Data on the cultural dimensions are from Hofstede et al. 2010. The parent's birth country is the father's in the immigrant-father sample and the mother's in the immigrant-mother sample.

Table 9A.3
Scores on Hofstede's cultural dimensions by country.

Country	Cultural dimension						Country	Cultural dimension					
	PDI	IDV	MAS	UAI	PRA	IND		PDI	IDV	MAS	UAI	PRA	IND
AL	90	20	80	70	61	15	JP	54	46	95	92	88	42
AO	83	18	20	60	15	83	KR	60	18	39	85	100	29
AR	49	46	56	86	20	62	LB	75	40	65	50	14	25
AT	11	55	79	70	60	63	LT	42	60	19	65	82	16
AU	36	90	61	51	21	71	LU	40	60	50	70	64	56
BD	80	20	55	60	47	20	LV	44	70	9	63	69	13
BE	65	75	54	94	82	57	LY	80	38	52	68	23	34
BF	70	15	50	55	27	18	MA	70	46	53	68	14	25
BG	70	30	40	85	69	16	MT	56	59	47	96	47	66
BR	69	38	49	76	44	59	MX	81	30	69	82	24	97
CA	39	80	52	48	36	68	MY	100	26	50	36	41	57
CH	34	68	70	58	74	66	MZ	85	15	38	44	11	80
CL	63	23	28	86	31	68	NG	80	30	60	55	13	84
CN	80	20	66	30	87	24	NL	38	80	14	53	67	38

Table 9A.3 (continued)

Country	Cultural dimension						Country	Cultural dimension					
	PDI	IDV	MAS	UAI	PRA	IND		PDI	IDV	MAS	UAI	PRA	IND
CO	67	13	64	80	13	83	NO	31	69	8	50	35	55
CV	75	20	15	40	12	83	NZ	22	79	58	49	33	75
CZ	57	58	57	74	70	29	PE	64	16	42	87	25	46
DE	35	67	66	65	83	40	PH	94	32	64	44	27	42
DK	18	74	16	23	35	70	PL	68	60	64	93	38	29
DO	65	30	65	45	13	54	PT	63	27	31	99	28	33
EE	40	60	30	60	82	16	RO	90	30	42	90	52	20
EG	70	25	45	80	7	4	RU	93	39	36	95	81	20
ES	57	51	42	86	48	44	SA	95	25	60	80	36	52
FI	33	63	26	59	38	57	SE	31	71	5	29	53	78
FR	68	71	43	86	63	48	SG	74	20	48	8	72	46
GB	35	89	66	35	51	69	SI	71	27	19	88	49	48
GH	80	15	40	65	4	72	SK	100	52	100	51	77	28
GR	60	35	57	100	45	50	SV	66	19	40	94	20	89

Table 9A.3 (continued)

Country	Cultural dimension						Country	Cultural dimension					
	PDI	IDV	MAS	UAI	PRA	IND		PDI	IDV	MAS	UAI	PRA	IND
HK	68	25	57	29	61	17	TH	64	20	34	64	32	45
HR	73	33	40	80	58	33	TR	66	37	45	85	46	49
HU	46	80	88	82	58	31	TT	47	16	58	55	13	80
ID	78	14	46	48	62	38	TW	58	17	45	69	93	49
IE	28	70	68	35	24	65	TZ	70	25	40	50	34	38
IN	77	48	56	40	51	26	US	40	91	62	46	26	68
IQ	95	30	70	85	25	17	UY	61	36	38	99	26	53
IR	58	41	43	59	14	40	VE	81	12	73	76	16	100
IS	30	60	10	50	28	67	VN	70	20	40	30	57	35
IT	50	76	70	75	61	30	ZA	49	65	63	49	34	63
JO	70	30	45	65	16	43	ZM	60	35	40	50	30	42

Data by country are from Hofstede et al. 2010. Country codes follow ISO-3166. Cultural dimensions are abbreviated as follows: PDI is the power distance index, IDV is individualism, MAS is masculinity, UAI is the uncertainty avoidance index, PRA is pragmatism, IND is indulgence.

Table 9A.4
Cross-country correlations of Hofstede's cultural dimension ($n = 78$).

	Power distance	Individualism	Masculinity	Uncertainty avoidance	Pragmatism	Indulgence
Power distance	1					
Individualism	−0.70	1				
Masculinity	0.19	0.03	1			
Uncertainty avoidance	0.17	−0.12	0.08	1		
Pragmatism	−0.13	0.23	0.07	0.06	1	
Indulgence	−0.24	0.05	−0.04	−0.11	−0.44	1

Data by country are from Hofstede et al. 2010.

Notes

1. See table 9A.1 for the participating countries in each round. Round 2 was collected in 2004, round 3 in 2006, round 4 in 2008, and round 5 in 2010.

2. Extensive documentation of the data is available at http://ess.nsd.uib.no/.

3. Current measures of gross domestic product are used since data for more countries are available in recent years. As the rank of income across countries is fairly stable the current measure captures differences in development. Moreover, the results are robust to using national income measures from 1960, 1970, and 1980, or averages across those periods.

4. The method has been applied to the cultural transmission of trust on the mother's and father's side. See Ljunge 2014a,b.

5. The full question is as follows "A woman should be prepared to cut down on her paid work for the sake of her family."

6. Women express somewhat stronger gender-equal attitudes if the cultural dimensions are not included in the model.

References

Bisin, Alberto, and Thierry Verdier. 2001. The economics of cultural transmission and the dynamics of preferences. *Journal of Economic Theory* 97: 298–319.

Bisin, Alberto, and Thierry Verdier. 2010. The economics of cultural transmission and socialization. In *Handbook of Social Economics*, ed. J. Benhabib, A. Bisin, and M. Jackson. Elsevier.

Farré, Lídia, and Francis Vella. 2013. The intergenerational transmission of gender role attitudes and its implications for female labour force participation. *Economica* 80: 219–247.

Fernandez, Raquel. 2010. Does culture matter? In *Handbook of Social Economics*, ed. J. Benhabib, A. Bisin, and M. Jackson. Elsevier.

Fernández, Raquel, and Alessandra Fogli. 2006. Fertility: The role of culture and family experience. *Journal of the European Economic Association* 4 (2–3): 552–561.

Fernández, Raquel, and Alessandra Fogli. 2009. Culture: An empirical investigation of beliefs, work, and fertility. *American Economic Journal. Macroeconomics* 1 (1): 146–177.

Fortin, Nicole M. 2005. Gender role attitudes and the labour-market outcomes of women across OECD countries. *Oxford Review of Economic Policy* 21 (3): 416–438.

Hofstede, Geert, Gert Jan Hofstede, and Michael Minkov. 2010. *Cultures and Organizations: Software of the Mind*, third edition. McGraw-Hill.

Levine, David I. 1993. The effect of non-traditional attitudes on married women's labor supply. *Journal of Economic Psychology* 14 (4): 665–679.

Ljunge, Martin. 2014a. Trust issues: Evidence on the intergenerational trust transmission from children of immigrants. *Journal of Economic Behavior and Organization* 106: 175–196.

Ljunge, Martin. 2014b. Social capital and political institutions: Evidence that democracy fosters trust. *Economics Letters* 122 (1): 44–49.

Moen, Phyllis, Mary Ann Erickson, and Donna Dempster-McClain. 1997. Their mother's daughters? The intergenerational transmission of gender attitudes in a world of changing roles. *Journal of Marriage and the Family* 59 (2): 281–293.

Myrskylä, Mikko, Hans-Peter Kohler, and Francesco C. Billari. 2009. Advances in development reverse fertility declines. *Nature* 460: 741–743.

Thornton, A., D. F. Alwin, and D. Camburn. 1983. Causes and consequences of sex-role attitudes and attitude change. *American Sociological Review* 48 (2): 211–227.

10

The Role of Repugnance in the Development of Markets: The Case of the Market for Transplantable Kidneys

Julio Jorge Elias

D47 B55
I11 Z13

[E]thics is not a branch of statistics; one thing continues to be atrocious even if thousands of people have hailed or executed it.
Jorge Luis Borges, "Un Curioso Método," in *Revista Ficcion* no. 6, 1957

Economic efficiency is a criterion commonly used in economic analysis to establish an order of priority or preference among policy alternatives in a given context. However, in many situations efficiency is not the criterion that wins out, as a more visceral societal reaction may prevail in the development of policy. Roth (2007) suggests that the reason why purchasing or selling kidneys for transplantation is illegal in many places is that a large number of people find such practices repugnant, rather than a law or a policy determined solely by cost-benefit analysis. One may also consider the example of a black market for the purchase and sale of infants.

This chapter analyzes repugnance, also called disgust or the "yuck factor," and discusses how it restricts certain transactions in the marketplace and the consequences of such restrictions. What is repugnant may depend on various circumstances, and the degree to which something is repugnant is closely related to the social and ethical costs associated with prohibition or regulation.

To develop the analysis, I considered instances and jurisdictions in which purchasing and selling human organs for transplantation is prohibited. The demand for transplantable organs and the lengthy waiting lists for them have become pressing public-policy issues in countries with organ-transplantation programs. Generally, when economists mark persistent gaps between supply and demand the next step is to identify obstacles to the equilibrium of the marketplace. In the case of the market for transplantable organs, a substantial obstacle is the prohibition of monetary incentives to acquire organs either from living individuals or from cadavers.

Using tools of the new economy of mortality and other areas of economic analysis, Becker and Elias (2007) show that the introduction of monetary incentives would increase the supply of kidneys sufficiently to eliminate the long queues in the market without greatly increasing the total cost of a kidney transplant. In most countries, markets for organs are illegal. One exception is Iran, which permits the sale of kidneys by living donors. There are many complex ethical and moral issues involved in the use and promotion of financial incentives to solicit increased organ donors. The repugnance factor explains, in part, why people feel that there is something wrong with having markets or financial incentives for kidneys. This is despite the presentation of an economic analysis which demonstrates that these incentives work well, increase the supply, and keep costs in check, and this factor represents a substantial and perhaps insuperable obstacle. In discussing the role of repugnance in the marketplaces of kidneys intended for transplantation, Roth (2007) said "the laws against buying or selling kidneys reflect a reasonably widespread repugnance, and this repugnance may make it difficult for arguments that focus only on the gains from trade to make headway in changing these laws" As Sandel (2012) argues, the efficiency of markets is not a virtue in itself; there are often other considerations. The question at hand is whether introducing a new market mechanism will corrupt the "good things of life."

I begin by discussing some salient features of the market for transplantable kidneys in the United States. The emphasis is on the gap between demand and supply, which is responsible for the growing list of persons in need of transplant surgery. I formalize the idea of a "repugnance" factor that operates as an obstacle in the market. I analyze how policy is determined and how it may change. Finally, I present some examples in which the social costs were affected by a policy or by a regulation.

10.1   The Ban on the Market for Transplantable Kidneys

In the United States, in 2012, there were 95,000 patients on the waiting list for new kidneys, the most commonly transplanted organ; however, only about 16,500 kidney transplants were performed that year. Taking into account the number of people who die while waiting for a transplant, this indicates an average wait of 4.5 years for a kidney transplant. The situation is far worse than it was only ten years earlier, when nearly 54,000 people were on the waiting list, with an average wait of 2.9 years. (See figure 10.1.) The waiting list has grown by more than 4,000

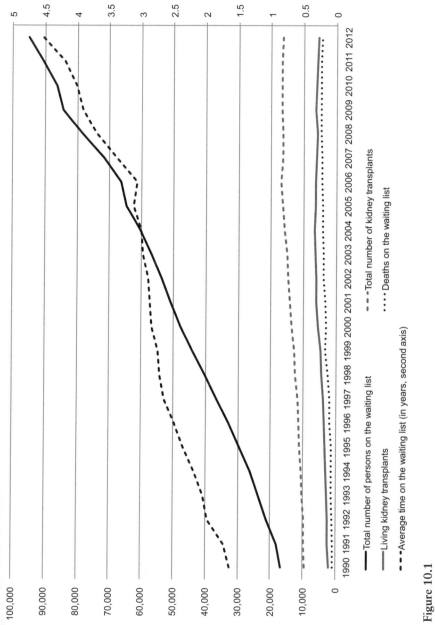

Figure 10.1
Total kidney transplants, patients waiting for transplants, deaths on the waiting list, and average waiting time to receive a transplant in the United States, 1990–2012. Based on Organ Procurement and Transplantation Network (OPTN) data as of December 1, 2013. The data on average time on the waiting list are my own calculations using OPTN data.

individuals each year, while the number of transplants has increased by only about 250 per year. The waiting list has continued to grow because in each year the new demand for kidneys exceeds the number of transplants conducted that year. The malfunctioning of the current system of kidney procurement has not only continued but has also become much worse (Becker and Elias 2007, 2014; Cronin and Elias 2009).

If social altruism were sufficiently powerful, or if other alternatives (such as the use of pig kidneys in transplantation or a cure for kidney diseases) were to be developed, the supply of organs would be large enough to satisfy the demand. Therefore, there would be no need to change the present system, beyond these proposed measures. The only effective way to eliminate the large queues in the market for kidney transplants is by increasing the supply of kidneys. Becker and Elias (2007) show that the introduction of monetary incentives could increase the supply of organs sufficiently to eliminate the large queues without increasing the total cost of kidney transplants by a large percent. Even though the benefits of eliminating the organ shortage are significant, many people have opposed proposals to create financial incentives for people to donate organs, and financial payments are prohibited by law in almost every country.

Most organ-procurement efforts in the United States, such as kidney-exchange programs, have concentrated on increasing the pool of altruistic donors. Although these efforts have resulted in modest gains, they have failed to significantly increase the number of transplantable kidneys enough to alleviate the large and growing shortage. The most important gains in transplantations over the last ten years have been in finding living, unrelated donors, but at the same time direct donation by relatives has declined, offsetting those gains. In my analysis, I consider how the repugnance factor operates as a restriction on certain markets and to what extent it is malleable. Following Roth, I use repugnancy to contextualize a proposed transaction in which the would-be participants are willing to make a sale but third parties disapprove and work to prevent such transactions.

10.2   A Simple Formalization of Repugnance and Its Interaction with the Market

In order to formalize repugnance as a factor affecting regulations, I consider this variable in the sale of kidneys for transplantation as dependent on a series of factors. For instance, repugnance could be affected by the expected price of a kidney up for sale: if the price is too low, it may resemble a form of exploitation, a form of coercion to the poor for a desperately needed source of income. Additionally, medical doctors may be repulsed in dealing with paid providers instead of altruistic donors. On the other hand, there may be other factors that work to reduce repugnancy. Other examples that reduce repugnancy could include that there are so many people on the waiting list, that some will die while waiting, or that the system is not working efficiently.

Let us assume that repugnance of a person i can be represented by a function:

$$\text{Repugnance}_i = R_i(\text{Factors}). \tag{1}$$

This relationship may vary across different persons.

In what follows, using the proposed framework, I will analyze how repugnance influences the acceptance of financial incentives for organ transactions.[1] First, let us consider the welfare or well-being of individuals under two different regimes: a regime in which payments or any other form of financial incentives for kidneys providers are not allowed and a regime in which payments are allowed. Again, I use a function to represent individual well-being, and I assume that the individual welfare is a function of three factors only: consumption, health, and repugnance. The welfare of an individual i in regime j is given by

$$\text{Individual Welfare}_{i,j} = U(C_{i,j}, H_{i,j}, R_{i,j}) \qquad j = \text{No Market, Market.} \tag{2}$$

Notice that these three factors may vary across persons (i) and across regimes (j). Different individuals will have different level of well-being within and across systems because C, H, and R may vary. For non-direct participant in the market, consumption and health are going to be approximately the same under the two regimes. For example, this is likely to be the case for individuals who are not in need of a kidney transplant, or for those that do not plan to provide a kidney for transplantation. According to our representation, the individual welfare of person i under the two different regimes are given by the following expressions:

$$\text{Individual Welfare}_{\text{No Market},i} = U(C_{\text{No Market},i}, H_{\text{No Market},i}, R_{\text{No Market},i}), \tag{3}$$

$$\text{Individual Welfare}_{\text{Market},i} = U(C_{\text{Market},i}, H_{\text{Market},i}, R_{\text{Market},i}). \tag{4}$$

Not having a market for kidneys represents a cost in terms of welfare for some individuals (i.e., individuals for whom

$$U(C_{\text{No Market},i}, H_{\text{No Market},i}, R_{\text{No Market},i}) < U(C_{\text{Market},i}, H_{\text{Market},i}, R_{\text{Market},i})),$$

whereas for others it represents a benefit—i.e., individuals for whom

$$U(C_{\text{No Market},i}, H_{\text{No Market},i}, R_{\text{No Market},i}) > U(C_{\text{Market},i}, H_{\text{Market},i}, R_{\text{Market},i}).$$

For instance, friends and family members of those needing organs might have strong preferences surrounding the existence of the market, and it is important to notice that this group grows proportionally with the waiting list. To quantify the disagreement with a market allocation, we ask the same question on equalizing differences as Adam Smith did: How much consumption, or money, do we have to give to an individual in order for her to be indifferent between the two regimes or systems? Let's call this amount δ. We calculate δ using the individual welfare function

$$U(C_{\text{No Market},i}, H_{\text{No Market},i}, R_{\text{No Market},i}) = U(C_{\text{Market},i} + \delta, H_{\text{Market},i}, R_{\text{Market},i}). \qquad (5)$$

According to equation 5, the value δ may vary across individuals not only because the level of repugnance is different for the individual in the two regimes, but also because their health and consumption could vary across them. As a consequence, there is going to be a distribution of δ in the population. The distribution depends on consumption, on health, and on the underlying factors that determines repugnance:

$$\delta\, (C_{\text{No Market},i}, H_{\text{No Market},i}, R_{\text{No Market},i}, C_{\text{Market},i}, H_{\text{Market},i}, R_{\text{Market},i}) = \delta_i. \qquad (6)$$

For example, for a person in need for an organ, δ is likely to be negative, not because the person's repugnance toward the market is low, but simply because his or her health status will improve, or is expected to improve under the current market system. Thus, the opinion of the populace may be inferred as follows:

If $\delta_i < 0$, the person likes the idea of a market for kidneys.

If $\delta_i > 0$. the person does not like the idea of a market for kidneys.

If $\delta_i = 0$,. the person is indifferent.

It is worth noting that the consumption level and the health status of the great majority of people will be almost independent of whether there is a market for kidneys or not. As a consequence, for this group δ fully reflect the quantitative dollar value or implicit price of repugnance.

Now that a value has been assigned to introducing financial compensation in the market according to each individual, we can turn to the question of how the kind of system or regime chosen is determined. Let us consider two choice criteria: a compensation principle (i.e., cost-benefit analysis) and majority vote (i.e., a referendum).

10.3   A Market-Based System? A Compensation Principle versus Majority Vote

In order to determine whether a market-based system is desirable, the first thing an economist is likely to do is perform a cost-benefit analysis. The economist will try to determine the "gains" from implementing or removing a regulation (and will try to see whether the winners can compensate the losers). In our framework, we can compute the net gains of removing the ban on the selling of organs by adding up the deltas of the different individuals across the population. If the sum is negative (understanding that a negative δ signifies willingness to pay to obtain a change in the system), then the "winners" of moving to a market-based system can compensate the "losers"; the reverse is true if the sum of deltas is positive. The compensation principle criteria are as follows:

If $\Sigma \delta_i < 0$, the winners can compensate the losers, and the market should be legalized.

If $\Sigma \delta_i > 0$, the winners cannot compensate the losers, and the market should be banned.

However, in practice this may not be enough to determine the policy outcome, as Elias and Roth (2007) noted: "It is illegal to sell horsemeat for human consumption in California, not because a persuasive case was made that the costs exceed the benefits, but because 4,670,524 people voted to make it illegal in a 1998 referendum." According to our framework, in a referendum scenario a person with negative δ will vote against the ban and a person with positive δ will vote in favor. We can easily compute the result of the referendum as follows: Let $V_i = 1$ if the person votes against the ban (i.e., $\delta_i < 0$) and $V_i = -1$ if the person votes for the ban (i.e., $\delta_i > 0$). Then

If $\Sigma V_i > 0$, legalize the market

and

If $\Sigma V_i < 0$, ban the market.

As above, for both criteria the outcome depends on the distribution of δ in the population. However, with the first criterion (the compensation principle) the intensity (the magnitude of δ), matters, whereas with the second criterion (majority vote) all that matters is whether individuals agree with the ban (i.e., whether δ is positive or negative).

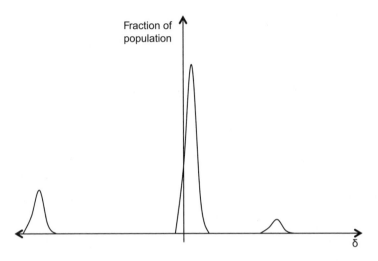

Figure 10.2
Example of a distribution of δs in the population.

Figure 10.2 shows, as an example, a distribution of deltas in the population. On right tail of the distribution we find a relatively small group of individuals who are fiercely opposed to the idea of a market for transplantable kidneys. On the left tail of the distribution we have a small group of people, who we surmise are in need of an organ or have a relative who needs one, who are in favor of a market system. In the middle we have most of the population, who may feel that there is something wrong or repugnant about a market system but who do not expect to participate in such a proposed market and whose feelings, for that reason, are not very strong. In the example from figure 10.2, a referendum will lead to a ban on organ sales and markets, whereas a cost-benefit analysis might indicate that there is a social gain from having such a market. As a consequence, there is a conflict between market efficiency and the practice and principles of a majority vote.

10.4   Shifting Repugnance: Effect of an Increase in the Waiting List

According to Roth's (2007) analysis of repugnance as a constraint on markets, "predicting when repugnance will play a decisive role is difficult, because apparently similar activities and transactions are often judged differently." However, in our framework what is repugnant is determined by underlying factors, and they may change in a predictable way. In particular, the social cost of banning certain transactions at a particular time is an important implicit factor. In particular, in the case of transplantable kidneys, the potential benefits of a market system may have seemed low in comparison with the costs of implementing a new system under severe legal constraints when the shortage was not so severe. Currently the kidney waiting list has more than 100,000 names, and in the past ten years it has grown at a rate of 7 percent per year. Additionally, technological progress that has made transplants safer and more effective during the past 15 years has significantly increased the potential benefits.

Both the growth in the waiting list and the improvements in the safety and effectiveness of kidney transplantation reduce repugnance toward a market system and, at the same time, increase the social costs of the ban. The toll for those on waiting for kidneys and on their families is enormous, including both greatly reduced life expectancy and the many hardships associated with dialysis. A large waiting list increases the burden imposed on them and, as a consequence, negatively affects the well-being of non-direct participants in the market, assuming that they show some altruism toward those in need of an organ. According to equations 1 and 6, an increase in the waiting list would lead to a shift to the left of the distribution of δ in the population, and the votes of some individuals may change. The sign of δ, and as a consequence the vote, is less likely to change for groups with radical positions (i.e., with high δ as an absolute value) than for non-direct participants in the market (i.e., those for whom δ fully measures repugnance).

Assuming a distribution like the one displayed in figure 10.3, a small change in δ may lead to a change in the result of the referendum. The repugnance factor and the existence of the market are jointly determined by the size of the waiting list. In practice things work differently; in most countries a political process determines the final outcome. In our example, we have two groups with radical positions, and they are likely to confront one another in a political arena. Becker (1985) analyzes a similar problem in his paper on the theory of pressure groups; one of his main results is that a major determinant of the final outcome of the political process is the social costs of the policy.

10.5 What Is Repugnant Depends on Circumstances

There are other cases in history in which bans or transactions restrictions were removed because of the large social costs of maintaining them.

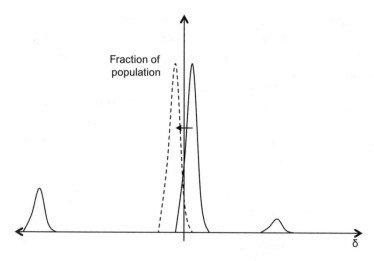

Figure 10.3
The effect of an increase in the waiting list on the distribution of δs.

Someone might say that prohibition was enacted in the United States in 1920 because Americans found the drinking of alcohol repugnant. Fifteen years later, people changed their minds because the costs of prohibition appeared to be high. Life insurance was once considered repugnant. As late as 1853, a *New York Times* editorial contended that "he who insures his life or health must be victim of his own folly or other's knavery." Before the institution of life insurance, widows and their orphans were assisted by their neighbors and relatives and by mutual aid groups. In the nineteenth century, the financial protection of American families became a purchasable commodity. The funeral was another "family and neighborhood" affair that became a business. Now life insurance is considered a form of institutionalized altruism.

If the prices of beef and other meats were to rise astronomically, the repugnance toward horse meat would be reduced and might even disappear. In fact, during World War II, owing to the low supply and the high price of beef, New Jersey legalized the sale of horse meat, but at the war's end that state again prohibited it.[2] The press release for the awarding of the Nobel Prize in Medicine to the father of *in vitro* fertilization in 2010 notes the great opposition Robert G. Edwards faced: "These early studies were promising but the Medical Research Council decided not to fund a continuation of the project. However, a private donation allowed the work to continue. The research also became the topic of a lively ethical debate that was initiated by Edwards himself. Several religious leaders, ethicists, and scientists demanded that the project be stopped, while others gave it their support." However, the press release continues as follows: "Approximately four million individuals have so far been born following IVF. Many of them are now adult and some have already become parents. A new field of medicine has emerged, with Robert Edwards leading the process all the way from the fundamental discoveries to the current, successful IVF therapy. His contributions represent a milestone in the development of modern medicine."

10.6   Conclusion

The present system imposes an intolerable burden on thousands of very ill individuals who suffer and sometimes die while waiting years until suitable organs become available. People suffer and die while waiting for organ transplants. Increasing supply through a form of financial incentive would largely eliminate their wait. There may be a repugnance factor that finds the sale of organ repulsive, but that has to be balanced against the benefits from permitting this market. I have shown in this chapter that what is repugnant depends on the circumstances and is closely associated with the social economic costs generated by the ban or by regulation. The analysis also indicates that, as was shown by Roth (2007), economists cannot ignore the importance of the repugnance factor, because it may have important consequences for the types of markets and transactions that manifest and can be observed.

Acknowledgments

A previous version of this chapter was presented at the 2014 CESifo Conference on Social Economics in Munich, at a symposium on "the ethics of the organ bazaar" co-sponsored by the Harvard University Program on Ethics and Health and the Department of Population and International Health and held at Harvard University in 2008, and at the III Congreso Internacional de Economía y Gestión, held at the Universidad de Buenos Aires in 2009. I am grateful for comments I received at these conferences and at seminars in economics at the Central Bank of Chile, FIEL, Universidade Federal do Rio Grande do Sul, Universidad de San Andrés, Universidad Nacional de San Martin, Universidad Nacional de Tucuman and the National University of Singapore. An earlier version of this chapter was published in Spanish in *Avances en Microeconomía*, ed. O. Chissari (AAEP, 2011).

Notes

1. Another view is to think on repugnance as the residual or the unexplained component of the distaste factor.
2. Source: "Horse meat," Wikipedia (http://en.wikipedia.org/wiki/Horse_meat).

References

Becker, Gary S. 1985. Public policies, pressure groups, and dead weight costs. *Journal of Public Economics* 28 (3): 329–347.

Becker, Gary S., and Julio J. Elias. 2007. Introducing incentives in the market for live and cadaveric organ donations. *Journal of Economic Perspectives* 21 (3): 3–24.

Becker, Gary S., and Julio J. Elias. 2014: Cash for Kidneys: The Case for a Market for Organs. *Wall Street Journal*, January 18.

Cohen, Patricia. 2008. Economists dissects the "Yuck" factor. *New York Times*, January 31.

Cronin, David, and Julio J. Elias. 2009. Operational organization of a system for compensated living organ providers. In *When Altruism Isn't Enough: The Case for Compensating Kidney Donors*, ed. S. Satel. AEI Press.

Elias, Julio J., and Alvin E. Roth. 2007. A market for kidneys? *Wall Street Journal* Online.

Roth, Alvin E. 2007. Repugnance as a constraint on markets. *Journal of Economic Perspectives* 21 (3): 37–58.

Roth, Alvin E. 2007. What Have We Learned From Market Design? Working Paper 13530, National Bureau of Economic Research.

Sandel, Michael. 2012. *What Money Can't Buy: The Moral Limits of Markets*. Farrar, Straus and Giroux.

11

Cultural Attitudes and the "Traditional Medicines Paradox": Evidence from Ghana and the Philippines

Joan Costa-Font and Azusa Sato

ɔlʃ I ll
ʑl 3 Bʃʃ

Traditional medicines continue to be widely used worldwide despite the increasing availability of modern medicines. We coin this phenomenon the "traditional medicines paradox" and argue that entrenched cultural beliefs contribute to the endurance of traditional medicines despite the existence and expansion of modern health technologies. Following the ethnographic literature, we test how beliefs and attitudes toward traditional medicines and healers (TM/H) affect their utilization (Evans-Pritchard 1937; Kleinman 1980; Helman 2000; World Health Organization 2002).

Our study seeks to close the gap in literature by exploring six beliefs that underlie TM/H utilization. This chapter draws upon unique data collected in Ghana and comparable evidence from the Philippines.

In section 11.1 we discuss the role of cultural attitudes. In section 11.2 we outline empirical strategies. In sections 11.3 and 11.4 we present results and discussions. In section 11.5 we provide a brief summary of the findings.

11.1   Culture and the "Traditional Medicines Paradox"

Anthropologists have long argued that health-seeking behavior and the use of use of traditional medicines can be attributed to culture. Rivers (1924) argues that people take appropriate actions after first understanding and perceiving why their disease or illness exists.[1] Explanatory models have distinguished between "emic" ideologies learned from local populations and "etic" ideologies of professionals outside local communities (Kleinman 1980). Consistently, culture is at the heart of beliefs about TM/H and of explanations of people's interpretations of—and therefore their reactions to—illness (Helman 2000; Winkelman 2009). In turn, beliefs may be transmitted from ethnic, religious, and social groups and remain fairly unchanged from generation to generation (Guiso, Sapienza, and Zingales 2006, p. 23).[2] It has previously been documented that religion and ethnicity are associated with differing attitudes and beliefs. For example, Roy et al. (2004, p. 26) find that ethnicity is significantly associated with the belief that "some (traditional) home remedies are still better than prescribed drugs for curing illnesses." Similarly, Winkler et al. (2010) find that stronger beliefs (such as symptoms and causes) about traditional healing methods for epilepsy in Tanzania are held by men and are influenced by tribe, religion, and non-urban location. In modern medicine, cultural background is also significantly associated with health beliefs (Horne et al. 2004) and, in turn, treatment-seeking patterns (Karasz and McKinley 2007).

The literature also shows that continued use of traditional medicines is a product of societal norms. Folk theories of causation in Africa find that societal ills can manifest within an individual, at which point social responses are crucial (Hevi 1989). Legitimacy of medicinal products is attributed to local communities, institutions, and symbolic values (van der Geest and Whyte 1988; van der Geest, Whyte, and Hardon 1996), and under such scenarios healers would be important sources of care.

The idea that beliefs linger and evolve only slowly is also well documented, pointing to evidence that people will continue to utilize traditional medicines even when alternatives become available. Owusu-Daaku and Smith (2005) show that Ghanaian women who have moved to the United Kingdom uphold Ghanaian perspectives about health and illness while adapting to the British system. Barimah and van Teijlingen (2008) studied the attitudes toward TM of Ghanaians living in Canada and found that 73 percent of respondents had not changed their views as a result of emigration. There were no significant differences in results between individuals who had been abroad for a long time and those who had been abroad for a short time, and qualitative evidence showed strong acts of agency whereby Ghanaians imported TM back to Canada from their homeland.

The use of traditional medicines is known to be a result of both belief and structural barriers to accessing formal health care (Ransford, Carrillo, and Rivera 2010; Young and Garro 1994).[3] However, attitudes and beliefs are not always the classified as the main drivers of the utilization of health care. Jenkins et al. (1996), for example, show no significant associations between traditional beliefs held by Vietnamese immigrants and access to modern preventive care. Young and Garro (1994) examine medical choices made in two Mexican villages and find that, despite similar attitudes and beliefs toward traditional and folk medical knowledge, the village with better accessibility (easier transport links and cheaper cost of care) utilized physicians significantly more than the village with poor accessibility. Young and Garro calculate that only a fifth of traditional care users stated cultural preference as an important reason for utilization, whereas half of them stated transport issues as their primary reason.

11.2 Methods

Data Collection

A total of 772 households—consisting of information on 4,713 individuals—were surveyed using methods approved by the World Health Organization (Arhinful 2011). Specifically, this involved sampling in two regions of Ghana (Greater Accra and Upper West) that were purposely chosen for their contrasting characteristics. Using public health facilities as reference points, household clusters were randomly selected within three radii (0.5–5 kilometers, 5–10 kilometers, and more than 10 kilometers). Within households, a representative answered the majority of questions except when individuals were able to answer questions of their own experiences. The household representative fulfilled at least three of the following criteria: main health-care decision maker most knowledgeable about health of household members, most knowledgeable about health expenditures of the household, most knowledgeable about health utilization by household members, designated care giver for sick household members. Before fieldwork was done, ethical approval was obtained from the London School of Economics and the host institution in Ghana, the Kwame Nkrumah University of Science and Technology.

Database I: Ghana A summary of data from Ghana is given in table 11.1. The dependent variable is a dummy variable indicating utilization (0 = no utilization, 1 = utilization) of TM/H conditioned on health need. The independent variables include level of agreement (using a Likert scale from 1 to 5, where 1 indicates strong agreement and 5 indicates strong disagreement) on six opinions reflecting attitudes on TM/H and these are used as the primary dependent variables: "THs are knowledgeable about illnesses that doctors do not know about" (knowledge), "some diseases can only be cured by THs" (cure), "I trust THs" (trust), "in this region, THs are well accepted" (accept), "TM are safer to use than modern medicines" (safe), and "TM can be used without a TH" (without). Other independent variables include ethnicity (categorized as dummy variables into the following: Akan; Ga/Dangbe; Ewe and others; Dagaare; Waale); religion (categorized as dummy variables of Christian, Muslim, other, and none); information on financial background (income—proxied by equivalent monthly expenditure using OECD formula and logged, and insurance); type of health-care need (whether chronic, defined as requirement of medicines in the past month for previously diagnosed illnesses and severity of illness); socio-demographic background (age, sex, education and occupation); and supply characteristics (closeness to healers, urbanity, region).

Database II: The Philippines   We also draw upon data from the Philippines, to examine how attitudes carry over to other lower middle-income countries. Using data from the ISSP (see http://www.issp.org/index.php for further details), regressions are ran using answers to two questions:

1. "Alternative medicines offer better solutions than conventional medicine" ("Better")

2. "During the past 12 months, how often did you visit or were you visited by an alternative/traditional/folk health-care practitioner?" ("Alternative/traditional/folk health-care practitioner" was defined as someone who was not trained in mainstream medicine or did not practice it.)

As in the Ghana model, answers to these questions were re-categorized into three measures of attitudes (strongly agree and agree; neutral; strongly disagree and disagree) and utilization into "never" and "once or more." All controls remain the same (as far as possible), and all regressions take sampling weights into account.

Empirical Strategy
We do not have access to experimental data that allow for a causal identification of the determinants of TM use. Instead, we examine survey evidence that contains records which then can be confirmed in other studies. Given the binary nature of the data on use of traditional medicines, we estimate a series of probit models using standard maximum-likelihood estimators of the probability of use of traditional medicines (y_i = 1 or 0). The multivariate probit model is as follows:

$$P(y_i | \text{need}) = \Phi \left(X'_i \beta + Y'_i \gamma + D'_i \delta + S'_i \tau + U_i \omega + \varepsilon_i \right),$$

Table 11.1
The effect of attitudes on utilization in Ghana.

Variable code	Variable definition	Without controls	With controls
Knowledge	Neutral	0.099*** [0.026]	0.180*** [0.035]
	Disagree/Strongly disagree	0.145*** [0.055]	0.202*** [0.050]
Cure	Neutral	−0.144*** [0.009]	−0.141** [0.058]
	Disagree/Strongly disagree	−0.071*** [0.026]	−0.003 [0.076]
Trust	Neutral	−0.047 [0.044]	−0.067 [0.059]
	Disagree/Strongly disagree	−0.166** [0.072]	−0.161** [0.081]
Region	Neutral	−0.064*** [0.018]	−0.084*** [0.013]
	Disagree/Strongly disagree	−0.037 [0.047]	−0.01 [0.086]
Safety	Neutral	0.019 [0.031]	0.021 [0.049]
	Disagree/Strongly disagree	−0.046 [0.103]	−0.075 [0.074]
Tmwithout	Neutral	−0.018 [0.110]	−0.011 [0.146]
	Disagree/Strongly disagree	0.01 [0.016]	0.038 [0.065]
Ethnicity	Ga/Dangbe		−0.056 [0.066]
	Ewe		−0.093* [0.051]
	Waale		−0.200*** [0.056]

Table 11.1 (continued)

Variable code	Variable definition	Without controls	With controls
	Dagaare		−0.014 [0.053]
Religion	Muslim		0.013 [0.064]
	Other		−0.067 [0.082]
	None		0.032 [0.063]
Financial	logequivtotalexp		−0.042 [0.026]
	insurance		−0.038 [0.084]
Type	Chronic		0.109*** [0.038]
Severity	Serious		−0.091* [0.054]
	Not serious		−0.102 [0.083]
Socio-demographic	Age in years, sex, education	No	Yes
Occupation	Office worker, self-employed, unemployed, full-time employed	No	Yes
Urbanization	Urban	No	Yes
Observations		712	584
Adjusted R^2		0.042	0.157

Robust standard errors in brackets. * significant at 10%; ** significant at 5%; *** significant at 1%

where X' denotes vector of the main variables of interest (attitudes and beliefs), Y' represents financial background, D' represents disease characteristics, S' represents socio-demographic characteristics, U' represents supply characteristics, ε_i represents errors, and $\Phi(\cdot)$ is the standard normal cumulative distribution function. When running the models, categories were regrouped into three (strongly agree and agree; neutral; disagree and strongly disagree), as there were a limited number of observations of TM/H users. Variance inflation factors (VIFs) are checked for multicollinearity in robustness checks, and all regressions are clustered by radius to reflect the sampling methodology. We considered some subsample analysis as well as alternative specifications that account for potential sample selection and endogeneity (which we do not report, as they do not alter the results).

There are also some methodological limitations. In the utilization regressions, attitudes and beliefs of the individual are proxied by the household representative. It may be the case that different individuals within households harbor different views, but unfortunately it was not practicable to draw upon multiple respondents. However, given that respondents fulfilled the criteria that they were the main decision maker, or had greatest knowledge about health-care needs of the household, some of the errors in reporting may have been removed. Traditional medicines and traditional healers were also grouped together for ease of analysis and data limitations, but some of the results highlighted how opinions on these two categories may vary. In the future, separate analysis is would allow us to gain a more accurate picture. Finally, some ethnicities and religious groups are more prevalent in certain regions. This was controlled for by including region dummies, but further investigation of this aspect is necessary.

Preliminary Evidence

A descriptive exploration of the available data on the effect of attitudes on traditional medicines utilization in Ghana (table 11.1) shows that on all dimensions except knowledge and safety more users than non-users cited strong agreement or agreement with statements. More non-users than users were inclined to be concerned about safety (39.7 percent and 29.5 percent, respectively, citing disagreement or strong disagreement). However, users did not necessarily believe that TH had greater knowledge than doctors, with 27 percent and 10.4 percent of all users disagreeing and strongly disagreeing with the statement, respectively.

11.3   Results

Results from Ghana

To shed some light to the TM paradox, we estimate the impact of beliefs on the probability of using TM. Probit models are presented with and without controls in table 11.1. All coefficients are marginal effects, so outputs are given as percentage changes in the probability. Standard errors are corrected for clustering by radius. For all attitudes and beliefs, the omitted category is "strongly agree/agree." Both models indicate that four attitudes—knowledge, cure, trust, and region—are significantly associated with utilization. Contrary to what might have been expected, individuals who felt neutral or disagreed that healers had knowledge about diseases that doctors did not were more likely than those who agreed with the statement to utilize TM/H. Belief that some diseases can be cured only by healers, in contrast, is strongly associated with utilization. Specifically, in comparison with individuals who state that they strongly agree/agree, individuals in the "neutral" and "disagree/strongly disagree" categories are 14.4 and 7.1 percentage points less likely to utilize TM/H, respectively. Generally, trust is also associated with utilization: the more one disagrees that healers cannot be trusted, the likelihood of utilization falls. In the case of perceived acceptability of TM/H within region, individuals who disagreed that TM/H was well accepted were on the whole less likely to utilize than those who agreed. Individuals who disagreed on TM safety were marginally less likely to utilize them, whereas on the whole there were no significant effects of attitudes about using TM without healers on utilization.

The second specification with controls largely confirms findings from the previous one. When controls are added, magnitudes of some attitudes and beliefs (e.g., healer knowledge, ability to cure) change slightly but on the whole signs remain constant and the same dimensions retain significance. Individuals from Waale and "Ewe/other" groups were significantly less likely to utilize TM/H than Akans, while there were no significant effects of religion on utilization. Higher income and holding insurance reduce utilization rates, but the findings are not significant. The probability of utilization increases with age and being female or having a chronic illness. The effect of education is mixed, as results show those with basic education have a slightly higher propensity to utilize TM/H than those without, but individuals with the higher qualifications appear to use less. However, both these results are insignificant. An individual whose household head has his/her own business or is not in employment is less likely than households headed by farmers/fishermen/manual laborers to utilize TM/H, whereas the unemployed and those working in office jobs are more likely than farmers to utilize. Supply characteristics show that having a healer within 15 minutes' walking distance and living in an urban area also increases likelihood of use.

Robustness checks   Four main robustness checks were carried out. Firstly, multicollinearity of probit models were checked, which revealed that in the regression including controls, log income was correlated with some other variables. Consequently, interaction terms for income and ethnicity were included, but were largely found to be insignificant and made little difference to the main results. To investigate this issue further, individuals were divided into income quintiles and those in the highest income category were excluded from analysis. Many marginal effects retaining both their significance and magnitudes. Thirdly, endogeneity of utilization models is considered by using ethnicity as an instrumental variable (thus, having only an indirect effect on utilization). On the whole, while significance of attitudes toward utilization holds robust; however, the lack of appropriate instrumental variables may render this analysis unsuitable.

Results from the Philippines

To further expand on the robustness of our results, we take a different country altogether, the Philippines, to examine how attitudes carry over to other lower middle income countries. The results presented in table 11.2 show that attitudes still account for much of utilization; in the first column, a strong relationship between thinking that alternative medicines are better than modern medicines and utilization, is seen. Specifically, a one-point increase in probability of responding "neutral" is associated with a 3.9-percentage-point decrease in the probability of utilization of TM relative to those who responded "strongly agree/agree" (the omitted category). A one-point increase in probability of responding "disagree/strongly disagree" is associated with a 18.9-percentage-point decrease in utilization of alternative medicines. In column 2, we take the average attitude according to ethnicity (split into the four major ethnic groups of the Philippines). Here, a one-point increase in average attitude (indicating negativity) is associated with a 12.4-percentage-point decrease likelihood of utilization.

Table 11.2
The effect of attitudes on utilization in the Philippines.

		1	2
		All attitudes	Average attitudes
Better	Neutral	−0.039 [0.059]	−0.124* [0.068]
	Disagree/Strongly disagree	−0.189*** [0.052]	0.001 [0.01]
Religion	Roman Catholic	−0.078* [0.040]	−0.089* [0.047]
Insurance	Yes	0.049 [0.045]	0.041 [0.051]
Chronic	Yes	0.139*** [0.029]	0.143*** [0.025]
Health state (descending order)	2	0.190*** [0.026]	0.180*** [0.054]
	3	0.109*** [0.026]	0.107*** [0.023]
	4	0.102*** [0.030]	0.090*** [0.024]
	5	0.071 [0.101]	0.042 [0.113]
Socio-economic	Age, sex, education, work, wealth	Yes	Yes
Urban		Yes	Yes
Observations		1,148	1,156
Pseudo R^2		0.078	0.062

Robust standard errors in brackets. * significant at 10%; ** significant at 5%; *** significant at 1%

11.4 Discussion

We examined one potential explanation of the "Traditional Medicines Paradox," namely that cultural attitudes underpin utilization of TM. We found that knowledge, trust, ability to cure, and perceived acceptability were strongly associated with utilization consistently with a cultural theory of culture. Such findings were echoed in a larger survey undertaken in the Philippines and were checked for robustness using subsamples. Overall, findings suggest that cultural traits such as ethnicity (but religion not so much) may be "carriers" of attitudes toward TM, which in turn color individuals' actions when they fall ill. However, further (causal) exploration and quantification of attitudes are required to better understand motivations and origins of attitudes and reasons for TM/H utilization.

Contrary to what might have been expected, individuals in Ghana who felt neutral or disagreed that healers had knowledge about diseases that doctors did not have were more likely than those who agreed with the statement to utilize TM/H. This suggests that people do not necessarily dismiss modern health systems, but that even users of traditional medicines acknowledge that healers are limited in their knowledge of certain diseases. This suggests a transformation of "traditional" medicines to "complementary," whereby users pick and choose, sometimes using both, according to perceived need.

Indeed, each of these dimensions has intuitive explanations toward rationalizing an individual's decision. First, trust is arguably a driving force of strong relationships between patients and healthcare providers in imperfect markets and under asymmetry of information. Second, users of TM/H were confident of its ability to cure, a finding supported by a study from Jamaica that shows 87 percent of herb users perceive herbal medicines to be more efficacious than modern medicines and therefore continue to utilize them (Clement et al. 2007). In TM, however, the conceptualization of efficacy is not necessarily aligned with that presented in biomedicine (Audu et al. 2002). Thus, although individuals are potentially "cured" by either form of medicine, traditional systems offer individuals a culturally more acceptable outlet; for example, individuals appreciate that they can talk to somebody they trust and who shares the same view of illness and health. Third, users did not necessarily agree that healers were more knowledgeable about certain illnesses than doctors. This suggests that on the whole, people consider modern systems to have better trained personnel, perhaps reflecting the perceived merit of compulsory qualifications required to practice. Healers, on the other hand, are largely informal and can set up business without certification or training.

Leonard (2003) argues that healers and users depend on culture for outcome contingent payment systems to be successful, as levels of trust and ability to enforce unwritten contracts is high in small communities. In Leonard's model, culture is modeled as a supply variable (with healers' characteristics) whereas here, the emphasis is more on users' demand. Controlling for disease characteristics also demonstrates that chronic illness sufferers and those who rate their illness as less severe, perhaps as a result of normalization, have a larger likelihood of using TM/H. This is highly suggestive that individuals with longer lasting illnesses are likely to try as many alternative modes of therapy as possible in the search for a remedy. Such findings complement studies on multiple-treatment-seeking behavior and polypharmacy (Astin 1998; Clement et al. 2007; Singh et al. 2004b; Turshen 2001) and points to the need for further analysis of utilization patterns. The marginal effects of education reflect the somewhat inconclusive findings of studies looking at associations between education and use of traditional medicines (Ceylan et al. 2009; Kim et al. 2009; Peltzer et al. 2008; Singh et al. 2004b; Stekelenburg et al. 2005; Tabi et al. 2006). Some of these studies also suggest that the more educated hold more self-confidence and are inclined to know better how to self-medicate (Okumura et al. 2002), and this may include traditional medicines. Supply characteristics show that having a healer within 15 minutes' walking distance and living in an urban area also increases likelihood of use. The latter result perhaps reflects urbanites being able to afford multiple forms of care.

Together, these findings suggest that TM/H might be considered an example of a "relational good" (Uhlaner 1989, p. 254), defined as "goods [that] arise as a function of a relationship with others." That is to say, attitudes are most likely formed because others in surrounding areas influence individual perception and consequently, utility levels. In visiting a healer, individuals may be able to maintain an identity, gain social approval or fulfill a norm. Thus, "joint consumption" is intrinsically valuable. On a broader level, our results suggest that it is unlikely that TM/H will be supplanted simply by increasing access to modern drugs without taking into account cultural attitudes, as individuals do not necessarily see them to be substitutes and the systems exhibit divergent logic. Modern medicines have failed to completely displace traditional medicines and a process of "acculturation," in which different cultures merge, has occurred. Consequently, modern and traditional systems coexist, but do so while retaining distinct characteristics and older, traditional systems will remain important for its users who believe that healers are trusted, TM/H remain well accepted in their region and healers possess an ability to cure that doctors do not. Thus, strategies that advocate "integration" to place traditional medicines within a biomedical framework (World Health Organization 2002) will not succeed if the demand side of the equation is sidestepped.

Notes

1. All health-seeking behavior is the result of a process involving identification of causation, followed by etiology, diagnosis then prognosis. Whereas biomedical diagnoses would consider disease to be caused by, or the result of, biological, physical or chemical abnormalities within the body (informed in large part but not exclusively by germ theory), anthropological understandings would deem illness to involve more than simply a biomedical explanation, placing the individual within a societal context.

2. The latter includes demographic traits such as religion, ethnicity and language are all thought to be carriers of information and shape the way an individual views the world (Dein 2004; Anyinam 1987; Evans-Pritchard 1937; Mechanic 1986; Press 1978; Rivers 1924; Stoner 1986; Tsey 1997; Turner 1968; Twumasi 1979; Young 1982).

3. Health beliefs and attitudes are known to be associated with health-care utilization (Aday and Andersen 1974; Peltzer, Preez, Ramlagan, and Fomundam 2008; Ravenell, Johnson, and Whitaker 2006), in line with models such as the theory of planned behavior (Ajzen 1991) and the health beliefs model (Rosenstock, Strecher, and Becker 1988), which model health beliefs as central to shaping actions.

References

Aday, L. A., and R. Andersen. 1974. A framework for the study of access to medical care. *Health Services Research* 9 (3): 208–220.

Ajzen, I. 1991. The theory of planned behavior. *Organizational Behavior and Human Decision Processes* 50 (2): 179–211.

Anyinam, C. 1987. Availability, Accessibility, Acceptability, and Adaptability - 4 Attributes of African Ethno-Medicine. *Social Science and Medicine* 25 (7): 803–811.

Arhinful, D. 2011. WHO Level II Household Survey to Measure Access to and Use of Medicines in Ghana. Ministry of Health, Ghana.

Astin, J. A. 1998. Why patients use alternative medicine—Reply. *Journal of the American Medical Association* 280 (19): 1661–1661.

Audu, R. A., E. O. Idigbe, D. I. Onwujekwe, J. A. Adedoyin, N. Onyejepu, A. G. Mafe, et al. 2002. Possible impact of co-infections on the CD4(+) cell counts of HIV patients in Nigeria. Presented at XIV International AIDS Conference.

Barimah, K. B., and E. R. van Teijlingen. 2008. The use of traditional medicine by Ghanaians in Canada. *BMC Complementary and Alternative Medicine* 8 (30).

Ceylan, S., O. Azal, A. Taslipinar, T. Turker, C. H. Acikel, and M. Gulec. 2009. Complementary and alternative medicine use among Turkish diabetes patients. *Complementary Therapies in Medicine* 17 (2): 78–83.

Clement, Y. N., J. Morton-Gittens, L. Basdeo, A. Blades, M. J. Francis, N. Gomes, et al. 2007. Perceived efficacy of herbal remedies by users accessing primary healthcare in Trinidad. *BMC Complementary and Alternative Medicine* 7: 4.

Dein, S. 2004. Explanatory models of and attitudes towards cancer in different cultures. *Lancet Oncology* 5 (2): 119–124.

Evans-Pritchard, E. E. 1937. *Witchcraft, Oracles and Magic among the Azande*. Clarendon.

Guiso, L., P. Sapienza, and L. Zingales. 2006. Does culture affect economic outcomes? *Journal of Economic Perspectives* 20 (2): 23–48.

Helman, C. 2000. *Culture, Health, and Illness*, fourth edition. Butterworth-Heinemann.

Hevi, J. 1989. In Ghana, conflict and complementarity. *Hastings Center Report* 19 (4): 5–7.

Horne, R., L. Graupner, S. Frost, J. Weinman, S. M. Wright, and M. Hankins. 2004. Medicine in a multi-cultural society: The effect of cultural background on beliefs about medications. *Social Science and Medicine* 59 (6): 1307–1313.

Jenkins, C. N. H., T. Le, S. J. McPhee, S. Stewart, and N. T. Ha. 1996. Health care access and preventive care among Vietnamese immigrants: Do traditional beliefs and practices pose barriers? *Social Science and Medicine* 43 (7): 1049–1056.

Karasz, A., and P. S. McKinley. 2007. Cultural differences in conceptual models of everyday fatigue—A vignette study. *Journal of Health Psychology* 12 (4): 613–626.

Kim, M. J., S. D. Lee, R. B. Kim, Y. H. Kong, W. S. Sohn, S. S. Ki, et al. 2009. Use of complementary and alternative medicine by Korean patients with Parkinson's disease. *Clinical Neurology and Neurosurgery* 111 (2): 156–160.

Kleinman, A. 1980. *Patients and Healers in the Context of Culture: An Exploration of the Border Land between Anthropology, Medicine, and Psychiatry*. University of California Press.

Leonard, K. 2003. African traditional healers and outcome-contingent contracts in health care. *Journal of Development Economics* 71 (1): 1–22.

Mechanic, D. 1986. The concept of illness behavior—Culture, situation and personal predisposition. *Psychological Medicine* 16 (1): 1–7.

Okumura, J., S. Wakai, and T. Umenai. 2002. Drug utilisation and self-medication in rural communities in Vietnam. *Social Science and Medicine* 54 (12): 1875–1886.

Owusu-Daaku, T. K., and F. Smith. 2005. Health-seeking behaviour: Perspectives of Ghanaian women in London and Kumasi. *International Journal of Pharmacy Practice* 13 (1): 72–76.

Peltzer, K. 2009. Utilization and practice of traditional/complementary/alternative medicine (Tm/Cam) in South Africa. *African Journal of Traditional, Complementary, and Alternative Medicines* 6 (2): 175–185.

Peltzer, K., N. F. D. Preez, S. Ramlagan, and H. Fomundam. 2008. Use of traditional complementary and alternative medicine for HIV patients in KwaZulu-Natal, South Africa. *BMC Public Health* 8: 255.

Press, I. 1978. Urban folk medicine—Functional overview. *American Anthropologist* 80 (1): 71–84.

Ransford, H. E., F. R. Carrillo, and Y. Rivera. 2010. Health care-seeking among Latino immigrants: Blocked access, use of traditional medicine, and the role of religion. *Journal of Health Care for the Poor and Underserved* 21 (3): 862–878.

Ravenell, J. E., W. E. Johnson, and E. E. Whitaker. 2006. African-American men's perceptions of health: A focus group study. *Journal of the National Medical Association* 98 (4): 544–550.

Rivers, W. H. R. 1924. *Medicine, Magic and Religion*. Kegan Paul, Trench, Trubner.

Rosenstock, I. M., V. J. Strecher, and M. H. Becker. 1988. Social learning theory and the Health Belief Model. *Health Education Quarterly* 15 (2): 175–183.

Roy, L. C., D. Torrez, and J. C. Dale. 2004. Ethnicity, traditional health beliefs, and health-seeking behavior: Guardians' attitudes regarding their children's medical treatment. *Journal of Pediatric Health Care* 18 (1): 22–29.

Singh, V., D. M. Raidoo, and C. S. Harries. 2004a. The prevalence, patterns of usage and people's attitude towards complementary and alternative medicine (CAM) among the Indian community in Chatsworth, South Africa. *BMC Complementary and Alternative Medicine* 4 (3).

Singh, V., D. M. Raidoo, and C. S. Harries. 2004b. The prevalence, patterns of usage and people's attitude towards complementary and alternative medicine (CAM) among the Indian community in Chatsworth, South Africa. *BMC Complementary and Alternative Medicine* 4 (3).

Stekelenburg, J., B. E. Jager, P. R. Kolk, E. H. M. N. Westen, A. van der Kwaak, and I. N. Wolffers. 2005. Health care seeking behaviour and utilisation of traditional healers in Kalabo, Zambia. *Health Policy (Amsterdam)* 71 (1): 67–81.

Stoner, B. P. 1986. Understanding medical systems: Traditional, modern, and syncretic health care alternatives in medically pluralistic societies. *Medical Anthropology Quarterly* 17 (2): 44–48.

Tabi, M. M., M. Powell, and D. Hodnicki. 2006. Use of traditional healers and modern medicine in Ghana. *International Nursing Review* 53 (1): 52–58.

Tsey, K. 1997. Traditional medicine in contemporary Ghana: A public policy analysis. *Social Science and Medicine* 45 (7): 1065–1074.

Turner, V. W. 1968. *The Drums of Affliction: A Study of Religious Processes among the Ndembu of Zambia.* Clarendon and International African Institute.

Turshen, M. 2001. Doctors and the state: The struggle for professional control in Zimbabwe. *Journal of Public Health Policy* 22 (3): 371–373.

Twumasi, P. A. 1979. A social history of the Ghanaian pluralistic medical system. *Social Science and Medicine. Medical Anthropology* 13B (4): 349–356.

Uhlaner, C. J. 1989. Relational goods and participation—Incorporating sociability into a theory of rational action. *Public Choice* 62 (3): 253–285.

van der Geest, S., and S. R. Whyte. 1988. *The Context of Medicines in Developing Countries: Studies in Pharmaceutical Anthropology.* Dordecht. Kluwer.

van der Geest, S., S. R. Whyte, and A. Hardon. 1996. The anthropology of pharmaceuticals: A biographical approach. *Annual Review of Anthropology* 25: 153–178.

Winkelman, M. 2009. *Culture and Health: Applying Medical Anthropology*, first edition. Jossey-Bass.

Winkler, A. S., M. Mayer, S. Schnaitmann, M. Ombay, B. Mathias, E. Schmutzhard, et al. 2010. Belief systems of epilepsy and attitudes toward people living with epilepsy in a rural community of northern Tanzania. *Epilepsy and Behavior* 19 (4): 596–601.

World Health Organisation. 2002. *WHO Traditional Medicine Strategy*..

Young, A. 1982. The Anthropologies of Illness and Sickness. *Annual Review of Anthropology* 11: 257–285.

Young, J. C., and L. C. Garro. 1994. *Medical Choice in a Mexican Village.* Waveland.

12

Changing Culture to Change Society?

Mireia Borrell-Porta, Joan Costa-Font, and Azusa Sato

(Europe)   JIS

BSS 213

Culture is staging a comeback in economics research, taking center stage in empirical analysis of common behavior in labor markets, in household decisions, in health-care behavior, and, more generally, in partial-equilibrium analysis. The study of "culture" in economics is of fundamental importance if we take seriously the task of describing and predicting social behavior and the bigger endeavor of attempting to bring social change by changing cultural priors. In increasingly multicultural societies, policy makers no longer can assume a "common rationality" to guide behavior. The increasing relevance of culture for economics research, therefore, poses a series of challenges and questions having to do with the meanings of culture, its relationship with identity and other similar concepts, its role as a policy variable, and the validity of its measurement.

Culture, broadly speaking, stands for group-specific "reasons for preferences" ("why people prefer some things to others"), which traditionally have been outside the realm of methodological individualism. Economists instead have prioritized the "operationalization" of culture for modeling and testing with survey data, evaluating the extent to which culture can be measured and its relevance for economic policy research.

In this chapter we attempt to review the evidence of culture in economics and social research to respond to the following questions: Can culture be a policy variable, and hence be used to change society? What can we infer from the existing datasets and methods in economics? We draw on evidence from migrants interviewed in the

European Values Study for 2008–2010 to argue that culture can be a policy variable. To do so we operationalize culture in a way similar to what the economists have done, showing evidence of cultural persistence in a large set of attitudes. We then discuss the caveats of existing approaches to "operationalize" the effect of culture, and then move to discussing the meaning of culture in other social sciences which refers to what economists refer to general-equilibrium effects of culture (including both direct and external effects of culture). We then suggest that it may be possible to bridge the differences of meaning of culture among the disciplines by regarding culture as a driver of individual "social identity" and propose a stronger focus on cultural identity interpreted as summary measure of individually internalized cultural norms. Following such interpretation, we argue that on the basis of the existing evidence, there is some scope for showing that by changing cultural social norms it is possible to shape the locus of value (meaningfulness) in a society. The latter is what we typically refer to as "social change." However, unlike with social norms, core beliefs in a society are likely to be culturally persistent.

12.1   Culture in Economics and in Other Social Sciences

Culture in Economics
Culture has traditionally been ignored by mainstream economics research. Becker and Stigler (1977) claimed that habit and traditions can be thought of as resulting from "investment of time and other resources in the accumulation of knowledge about the environment." Continuously updating information about the existing environment is costly, so habit and tradition are often more efficient ways to deal with moderate changes. In a similar vein, macroeconomists[1] have considered traditions and habits to be an "error term" under otherwise "rational" expectations. In contrast, institutionalist traditions have acknowledged the role of informal institutions and culture more specifically in understanding economic and social phenomena. (See, e.g., North 1990.) Indeed, institutionalists have generally assumed that individuals devise general strategies (heuristics) to solve problems with little effort using ready-made solutions (such as those determined by cultural priors), so that they can "blindly follow without rethinking the problem each time anew" (Mantzavinos 2001, p. 100).

   More recently, claims that culture is a major determinant of economic outcomes have emerged (there are multiple examples; see Fernandez

2007) for a review), and have complemented research on the effect of the market mechanisms on culture (Bowles 2011a). Indeed, not only do cultures affect markets; markets also affect cultural transmission of preferences. Hence one can speak of a "cultural market failure" whereby unregulated free markets erode or crowd out culture, because markets underprovide civic virtue (as in Titmuss' story of blood donations), which gives rise to a cultural market failure). Although proponents of the free market argue that the best outcomes are achieved without virtues, Bowles' models show that this can lead to a downward spiral and ultimately to market-induced erosion of socially beneficial ethical values (virtues).

The conceptualization of culture used in economics generally refers to "the customary beliefs, social forms, and material traits of a racial, religious, or social group; (and) the set of shared attitudes, values, goals, and practices that characterizes an institution or organization" (Fernandez 2010). Beyond this definition, some discrepancies can be identified, some having to do with the speed of change. Some research emphasizes minimal changes in culture (see, e.g., Guiso, Sapienza, and Zingales 2003), assuming that being of a certain ethnic background or religious group is path dependent (David 2007) and difficult to change or defect from. Others argue explicitly that culture can change slowly or rapidly depending on the environment and on external shocks. (See, e.g., Fernandez 2007 or Fernandez 2010.) Andrew Postlewaite makes a stronger effort to reconnect with the work of Becker and Stigler (1977) and emphasizes that there is no need to assume away stable and similar preferences and, at the same time, account for social norms. In order to do so, Postlewaite (1998) makes a useful distinction between *deep preferences* (those involving immediate alternatives irrespectively of the environment), assuming that the choice doesn't trigger a response from others, and *reduced-form preferences* (those involving actions today given the equilibrium in specific environment). These different views lead not only to different ways of measuring culture but also to different results on its effects on economic outcomes. More generally, these problems can be attributed to the limited discussion within the discipline of economics of the conceptualization of culture, an issue we will discuss in section 12.2.

Culture in Other Social Sciences

In contrast to economists, social scientists do not adopt a single definition of culture. Instead they rely on multiple definitions. Culture is "embedded" within social relations (Granovetter 1985), and thus markets result not only from formal institutions and regulation but also from values and market-related attitudes. "Culture" refers to human action passed on from generation to generation, independent of the biological genes (Useem and Useem 1963). Hence, "culture" defined in this way refers to a vague environmental influence embedding learned (and therefore taught) actions transmitted through common knowledge (Linton 1945), or through social recognition and conformity (Rao and Walton 2004). Hence, culture can be argued to give rise to collective identities (Levin 2008).

Nonetheless, unlike the economists' definition, *cultural identity is not fixed*. Instead, cultural identity speaks to a central issue in the economics debate: that of rational choice. The idea is that actions take place under a cultural identity that embeds current actions to past actions (Kluckhohn and Kelly 1945). The latter can explain a long list of behaviors, including why some individuals do not eat pork and why homosexuality is stigmatized. Similarly, Banks et al. (1989) argue that culture "in its essence lies in the values, symbols, interpretations, and perspectives that distinguish one people from another" and that "people within a culture usually interpret the meaning of symbols, artefacts, and behaviors in the same or in similar ways." This stance interprets culture as the channel through which identities are formed and ideas are disseminated, which allows people to interpret the meanings of their behaviors and actions (Lederach 1995).

A more restrictive definition is that of Kroeber and Kluckhohn (1952), who define culture as explicit and implicit behavior acquired and transmitted by symbols, constituting the distinctive achievements of human groups. Consistently, Hofstede (1984) defines culture as the mechanisms to define identity as "the collective programming of the mind which distinguishes the members of one category of people from another."

In some social sciences, such as anthropology, acculturation is defined as a "phenomenon resulting from different cultures coming into continuous first hand contact, with subsequent changes in the original cultural patterns of either or both groups" (Redfield et al. 1936). An important clarification is provided by Wildavsky (1987), who distinguishes between first-level choices, which refer to the choice of "culture," and different courses of action, which are second-level choices. Economists have traditionally focused on second-level choices, and only recently have cultural economists acknowledged that "culture" is a first-level choice.

Cultural Measurement

The first steps towards the economic measurement of culture were very much focused on trust and religion proxying cultural variables in explaining economic growth. Greif (1989, p. 914) compared Maghribi and Genovese traders of the eleventh and twelfth centuries and concluded that "differences in the societal organization of the two trading societies can be consistently accounted for as reflecting diverse cultural beliefs." La Porta et al. (1996) documented a strong correlation between trust and the existence of large organizations. Similarly, Knack and Keefer (1997) found trust to be positively and significantly correlated with growth. Barro and McCleary (2003) analyzed the influence of religion on the growth rates of per capita GDP in 59 countries all over the world. Algan and Cahuc (2006) found that religion exerts and influence in individuals demand for job protection and male breadwinner values. Trust is found to correlate with preferences for higher levels of regulation, according to Aghion et al. (2009).

Nonetheless, more recent economic studies of culture have expanded the scope of culture as a study variable. For instance, Ichino and Maggi (2000) study the influence of the individual's regional background on shirking behavior in Italy. Pryor (2007) groups OECD nations into five distinct clusters of culture—a finding echoed by Inglehart et al. (1998), who argued that cultural characteristics of more developed countries are different from those of less developed countries when one looks at product markets, labor markets, the business sector, the government sector, and the financial sector. Uy (2009) and Williamson and Mathers (2011) show how belief systems influence the economy and an constrain growth rate.

Another important group of studies focus on family choices. Algan and Cahuc (2006) have analyzed the role of family values in influencing gender roles and employment rates of different demographic groups. Similarly, Giavazzi et al. (2013) look at the attitudes toward women and young people and their effects on employment rates and hours worked. Fernandez and Fogli (2009) show how culture can explain women's participation in the labor market and their fertility decisions. More recently, Alesina and Giuliano (2011, 2013) have looked at the role of family ties in the choice of labor-market regulation and in several economic outcomes. They have found that individuals with strong family ties are less mobile, more likely to be unemployed, and likely to choose more rigid labor markets.

Methodologically, studies examining cultural effects can be generally classified as using either an epidemiological (migrants data) or a historical approach (historical institutions) to identify the influence of culture. One example of research using historical proxies is provided by Tabellini (2008), whose empirical account shows that trust is stronger in countries with a long history of liberal political institutions. On the other hand, epidemiological approaches to culture focus instead on how culture is a portable trait over generations.

Migration is a quasi-laboratory experiment in which to examine non-random cultural transmission, specifically among second-generation migrants, if certain conditions (e.g., citizenship acquisition) make it possible to isolate the effects of institutions in the host country. Luttmer and Singhal (2011) show that the redistribution preferences of immigrants who come from pro-redistribution countries are stronger than those who do not come from pro-redistribution countries. Ljunge (2014) follows a similar strategy to examine the portability of generalized trust. Similarly, Fernandez and Fogli (2009) study the work behavior and the fertility behavior of second-generation American women (i.e., women born in the United States to parents who were born elsewhere). The effect of culture is proxied by the past female labor-force participation and total fertility rate from a woman's country of ancestry (from 1950). Giuliano (2007) finds that children of West European immigrants in the US replicate family living arrangements of their country of origin. (For a more exhaustive review of the literature, see Fernandez and Fogli 2009.)

However, while some subjects have taken to measuring culture, others abhor the idea that culture might even be quantified in the first place. Most social sciences assume that culture exert a contextual effect that can be controlled for but not measured. De Jong (2011) argues that we need a multifaceted approach that includes historical analysis, comparative analysis, and regression analysis.

Empirical Evidence from the European Values Study
In this section, to illustrate the role of culture and its complexity, we carry out an empirical exercise. Specifically, we evaluate, for a sample of migrants living in different European countries, the association between their self-reported attitudes and the same average attitudes of their country of origin. We use the European Values Survey for 2008–2010, as the information on the country of origin and parental country of origin are available for those years. The variables (listed below in table 12A.1) have

been dichotomized,[2] and two groups of regressions have been carried out. The first sample group consists of first-generation migrants, the second of second-generation migrants (raised in the same institutions as natives). For both samples we have regressed individuals' attitudes against the average attitude from their country of origin or the parental country of origin, controlling for country fixed effects and individual characteristics such as age, education, income, marital status, gender, employment status, and town. We have dropped countries with fewer than 60 observations, leaving us with about 3,300 observations for the first-generation migrants sample and about 1,700 observations for the sample of second-generation migrants.

The results partially confirm those from the previously cited studies in which the epidemiological approach was used. We find that attitudes from parental or own country of origin significantly explain migrants' attitudes. However, the strength of this relationship varies largely across attitudes. For instance, attitudes which reflect "core values" such as attitudes toward God and toward labor ethics are strongly related with attitudes from parental or own country of origin. Similarly, in examining how attitudes vary over time, we find that some attitudes seem to be more persistently related to attitudes from parental or own country of origin than others.

The importance of parental and own country of origin attitudes   Figure 12.1 depicts the average impact of average attitudes from country of origin on the attitudes of first-generation migrants. Attitudes toward God and religion are very culturally persistent, with a positive and significant coefficient above 0.50. Such findings relating to the importance of religion and God are in line with existing literature (Guiso et al. 2006). Another group of variables that yield interesting results are those related to the role of men and women at work and within the family.[3] *A priori*, this group of variables do not exhibit clear patterns, and we could simply refer to the explanation provided by Giavazzi et al. (2014): that attitudes more subject to environmental (horizontal transmission) effects are less likely to be culturally persistent. Another explanation, following Schwartz et al. 2010, is that attitudes that reflect practical norms about "good or acceptable behavior" are more likely to be shaped by a change in the social environment.[4]

The rest of the variables—whether women need children in order to be fulfilled, whether when jobs are scarce men should have priority, whether children need two parents in order to be fulfilled—seem to be

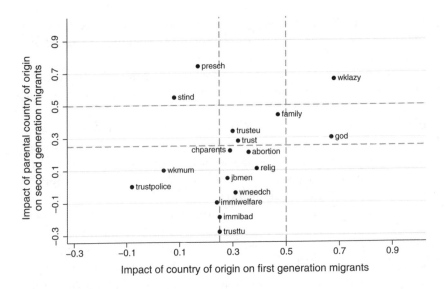

Figure 12.1
Impact of average attitudes from country of origin on first-generation migrants' attitudes. Attitudes in bold and larger font represent statistically significant results. Persistence of country of origin influences on migrants' attitudes.

reflecting the principles guiding one's life, or rules that point to "acceptable" behavior, more than a belief about whether something is true or not, which makes them less subject to existing institutions and more subject to the underlying family values of the country of origin. The same interpretation is also useful to understand the significance of the coefficients of the rest of the variables. Within the variables related to trust, trust in police and trust in trade unions are found to be the ones for which existing average attitudes at the country of origin have a lower relevance, suggesting that people adjust their attitudes to what they see in the country of residence. Conversely, trust in general and trust in the European Union seem to be more engrained and more difficult to change as institutional settings change (Ljunge 2014). The findings for trust therefore reflect the findings presented in the existing literature (Guiso, Sapienza, and Zingales 2009). Attitudes toward people who do not work and toward migrants are also strongly influenced by the attitudes in the country of origin.

Figure 12.2 plots the correlation between the effect of attitudes from country of origin on first-generation migrants' attitudes and the effect of attitudes from parental country of origin on second-generation migrants'

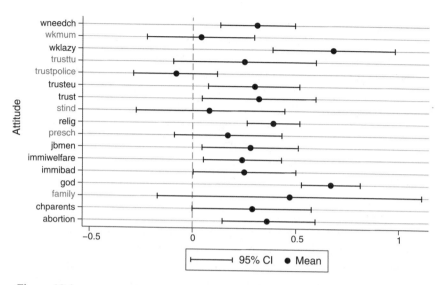

Figure 12.2
Correlation between impact of attitudes from country of origin in first-generation and second-generation migrants.

attitudes. This comparison can give us an idea of the persistence of ideas from the country of origin. The figure seems to point at a decreasing influence of attitudes in country of origin or parental country of origin. Up to eight attitudinal statements, including attitudes toward migrants, trust in some institutions, attitudes toward religion, and attitudes toward the roles of women in society and at home show lower correlation with attitudes in the country of origin for second-generation migrants than for first-generation migrants. This would be in line with the hypothesis in the literature that assimilation happens at a slower pace but still happens.

However, for other attitudinal statements—such as trust in the EU or general trust, the importance of God and family, and attitudes toward jobless people—attitudes from country of origin seem to be rather persistent. The opposite happens for attitudes toward working mothers with pre-school children, for which the data suggest that the attitudes of second-generation migrants are more influenced by attitudes in the country of origin than by the attitudes of first-generation migrants. This finding is in line with another hypothesis in the literature: that second-generation migrants sometimes identify more with their parents' country of origin than their parents do (Giavazzi et al. 2014). The same happens with attitudes toward the state, although the results are not robust to the sample when we add countries with more than 30 observations. Finally, two attitudinal statements, those referring to the relationship that a working mother can have with her children and to trust in police, do not seem to be strongly affected by attitudes in the country of origin either for first-generation migrants or for second-generation ones. Therefore, the findings suggest that the existing hypothesis in the literature may apply to different attitudinal questions.

12.2   Limitations of Cultural Economic Research

Probably the main conceptual concern in the cultural economic analysis is that of a need of some widely accepted definition of culture. Ideally, such a definition should try to seek some agreement across social sciences, although even within the social sciences views are difficult to reconcile. Nonetheless, besides the conceptualization of culture and preferences, any analysis of preferences and culture should consider the exogeneity of preferences. Postlewaite (1998) maintains the economic assumption of preference exogeneity, assuming standard deep preferences and suggesting that social norms affect reduced-form preferences. On the other hand, Guiso et al. (2006) assume away common prior beliefs and allow the choice of priors to be made on empirical observation. And, as suggested previously, Bowles boldly challenges the exogeneity of preferences by suggesting that markets exert a large influence on them. As Fernandez (2010) and Bowles (1998) point out, this is still an unsettled issue in the literature, and a relevant one, insofar as, if preferences are indeed endogenous, choices on institutions are likely to influence choices on culture, and vice versa.

Country of origin and destination culture change with migration, especially after large waves of migration that affect not only migrants themselves but also locals. Indeed, cultures and acculturation are dynamic processes. Hence, the question of acculturation is not only a question of assimilation but also a question of integration of bicultural or multicultural individuals.

There are also limits on the measuring of culture. For example, even if destination-country regulations (which are fixed effects) capture changes in citizenship laws, they do not treat everyone equally, and hence they may not capture the fact that some countries may give privileged access to citizenship to nationals of certain countries.

Another problem with studies of migrants is that they are a selected sample of the population. For instance, in the literature on health it is well known that migrants tend to be healthier than locals. The composition of migrants, the timing of migration, and the pattern of settlement groups matter. Even when potentially accounting for selection, one of the problems is the "acculturative stress" under which migrants suffer deteriorations in mental health as a result of changing environments (Berry 1980).

12.3   An Alternative Interpretation

Cultural Identity

The recent definitions and explorations of culture move the literature forward by interpreting culture as beliefs, some of which are sensitive to perception of generalized trust among other. However, these measures implicitly encompass a recognition of the importance of an acculturation process, and implicitly the molding of social identity (Fukuyama 2001; Akerlof and Kranton 2000, 2005). Indeed, the study of acculturation and cultural identity (Salant and Lauderdale 2003; Benhabib 2002) shows that conforming to an identity is what gives rise to "meaning" and social connections, beliefs, and rules guiding social behavior. In the mid twentieth century, however, such concepts fell out of favor; "it seemed like too nebulous a concept—one that was hard to identify and isolate" (Broga 2006). It is well documented that economic incentives alone have their limitations. For example, after Boston firemen had imposed on them a 15-day limit on paid sick days there was an increase in the number of sick days (Greenberger 2003). Instead, if we consider that social preferences and incentives have important influences on economic behavior, we can understand better how culture matters in providing social rather than solely economic rewards. Gorodnichenko and Roland (2010, 2011) argue that individualism emphasizes personal freedom and personal accomplishments (which, in turn, can lead to innovation). In contrast, collectivism reduces the transaction costs of group action.

Culture or Cultures?

The understanding of how culture changes is central to cultural economic debates. Cultural change may not be linear, as was predicted by earlier contributions to the literature (Gordon 1964). Cultures are formed through dialogue with other cultures, and migrants can be incorporated into the majority while retaining their values. However, today it is possible for values and cultures to be transmitted without migration: An individual may adopt values of a non-native society without leaving his or her own country. Thus, epidemiological studies need to account for the rate at which values in one society are transferred, copied, and adopted and hence begin to resemble one another rather than culture *per se*. Bowles (2011) distinguish among what they call boundary crossing, blurring, and shifting. The increasing interconnection and technological change implies that individuals can be plugged into different cultures at a time.

Swidler (1986) argues that cultural values don't drive action directly, but drive it indirectly so by equipping individuals with a "tool kit" of habits, skills, and styles from which they construct "strategies of action." Culture is given only an independent causal role, and it is by linking many sub-strategies that people are able to organize end goals (ibid.). The upshot of this is that one cultural system can lead to a large number of outcomes and actions, which aren't necessarily consistent with one another. If culture were to determine the tools with which people create strategies of action, end values would fade into the background. This brings us back to the assumption that cultures are long-lasting, persistent even while economic and structural frameworks change. Bibeau (1997) makes a similar point in arguing that actions precede beliefs and that the mere fact that an individual is seen to act a certain way does not preclude him from acting in a seemingly contradictory manner.

Culture as Priors

Another way to think about culture is to link it with findings of behavioral economics, more specifically with the role of culture in setting common reference points in a society. Guiso et al. (2006) write that priors in social interactions are difficult to change and are slow moving, which in some contexts can explain why the same economic policies do not yield equal outcomes everywhere. Priors were already part of Schelling's (1960) framework, defined as focal points in matching games, learned responses, and shared understandings to reduce conflict. Consistently, Helliwell et al. (2014) find a very similar result in trying to explain attitudes to generosity.

12.4   What Explains Cultural Change?

Rather than an "economic man" in a vacuum, one can argue for the existence of a "cultural man" as the central actor of an economy. Culture brings about social change by changing people's cultural identities and beliefs (even when as we find from empirical evidence that it cannot influence deep beliefs as effectively and rapidly as some economies need). Culture can be shaped through a number of mechanisms, including regulation (e.g., bans on smoking and the "ownership culture" in some European countries' housing markets) and education policy. Aspachs et al. (2008) find evidence that the language of education policy shapes the spatial identities of non-natives. Similarly, Cantoni et al. (2014) find that changes in textbook content and college entrance exams in China reflect government goals and appear to affect political participation, to affect trust, and to create skepticism about the market. Costa-Font and Cowell (2015) show how different forms of identity can influence preferences for redistribution.

From a policy perspective, new developments in social economics (or in sociology or economics) that endogenize culture as a policy variable can help to resolve a number of questions with which economics research has been struggling with, such as why people donate organs, why people participate in civic duties, and why people become willing to redistribute.

The simple empirical exercise we have carried out in this chapter reveals some of the challenges that the literature on culture and economics is facing. First, the concept of culture needs to be further specified and formalized. Some attitudinal questions may be actually measuring beliefs that are more likely to change when the environment changes, whereas other attitudinal questions may reflect some engrained values that a person has acquired during his or her "impressionable years" and which are likely to stay put (Giuliano and Spilimbergo 2014). In this respect, the work in which Shalom Schwartz conceptualizes the difference between values, attitudes, beliefs, norms, and traits can help us to understand better what we are empirically measuring. Second, the persistence of attitudes can be explained by competing theories. One theoretical explanation emphasizes the existence of an assimilation process by which most attitudes in the country of origin will, after some generations, stop influencing the attitudes of migrants. The other theory would emphasize the fact that some generations of migrants—for example, the second generation (Giavazzi et al. 2014)—might actually have a stronger preference to go back to their roots. If different explanations are valid for different attitudes, one avenue of research could focus on the types of attitudes that are more likely to be explained by one theory or the other.

Acknowledgments

We are grateful to the participants in the CESifo Conference on Social Economics. In addition, informal conversations with Berkay Ozcan, Paola Giuliano, and Alan Manning are appreciated.

Appendix

Table 12A.1
Descriptive statistics.

Variable	Description
Attitudes toward religion	
god	how important is God in your life
relig	are you a religious person
Attitudes toward trust	
trust	people can be trusted/can't be too careful
trusttu	how much confidence in: trade unions
trustpolice	how much confidence in: the police
trusteu	how much confidence in: European Union
Attitudes toward women, children, and work	
wneedch	women need children in order to be fulfilled
wkmum	working mother warm relationship with children
presch	pre-school child suffers if mother works
jbmen	jobs are scarce: giving men priority
chparents	children need both parents to grow up happily
family	how important in your life: family
abortion	abortion if couple doesn't want more children
Attitudes toward migration	
immibad	immigrants increase crime problems
immiwelfare	immigrants are a strain on welfare system
Attitudes toward labor ethics	
wklazy	people turn lazy not working
Attitudes toward the state	
stind	individual vs. state responsibility for providing

Source: European Values Study, 2008–2010.

Notes

1. For example, neoclassical growth theory (Solow 1956) and endogenous growth theory (Lucas 1988; Romer 1986) both assume perfect coordination of agents; the former does not even include technological advances in the modeling of growth.

2. For those variables that included a category "neither," we have generated two versions, one taking the observations with "neither" out and another adding the "neither" category. The results do not differ significantly.

3. The variables are "women need children to be fulfilled" (wneedch), "working mother cannot establish a warm relationship with her children" (wkmum), "pre-school child suffers if mother works" (presch), "if jobs are scarce men should have priority" (jbmen), and "children needs both parents to be happy" (chparents).

4. Schwartz understands beliefs as "ideas about how true it is that things are related in a particular way," and norms as standard rules for how members of society should behave. Some of the attitudes examined, such as whether a working mother can establish a warm relationship with her children or whether a pre-school child suffers if the mother works, seem to fall more into the category of beliefs, reflecting whether something is true, and therefore they are more malleable to a change of institutional environment.

References

Aghion, P., Y. Algan, P. Cahuc, and A. Shleifer. 2009. *Regulation and Distrust.* National Bureau of Economic Research.

Akerlof, G. A., and R. E. Kranton. 2000. Economics and identity. *Quarterly Journal of Economics* 115 (3): 715–753.

Akerlof, G. A., and R. E. Kranton. 2005. Identity and the economics of organizations. *Journal of Economic Perspectives* 19 (1): 9–32.

Alesina, A., and P. Giuliano. 2011. Family ties and political participation. *Journal of the European Economic Association* 9 (5): 817–839.

Alesina, A., and P. Giuliano. 2013. Culture and Institutions. Working Paper 19750, National Bureau of Economic Research.

Algan, Y., and P. Cahuc. 2006. Job protection: The macho hypothesis. *Oxford Review of Economic Policy* 22 (3): 390–410.

Aspachs-Bracons, O., I. Clots-Figueras, J. Costa-Font, and P. Masella. 2008. Compulsory language educational policies and identity formation. *Journal of the European Economic Association* 6 (2–3): 434–444.

Banks, J. A. Banks, and McGee, C. A. 1989. *Multicultural Education.* Allyn & Bacon.

Barro, R. J., and R. McCleary. 2003. *Religion and Economic Growth.* National Bureau of Economic Research.

Becker, G. S., and G. Stigler. 1977. De gustibus non est disputandum. *American Economic Review* 67 (2): 76–90.

Benhabib, S. 2002. *The Claims of Culture.* Princeton University Press.

Berry, J. W. 1980. Acculturation as varieties of adaptation. In *Acculturation: Theory, Models, and Some New Findings*, ed. A. Padilla. Westview.

Bibeau, G. 1997. At work in the fields of public health: The abuse of rationality. *Medical Anthropology Quarterly* 11 (2): 246–252.

Bowles, S. 1998. Endogenous preferences: The cultural consequences of markets and other economic institutions. *Journal of Economic Literature* 36 (1): 75–111.

Bowles, S. 2011a. A cultural-institutional market failure. Unpublished manuscript.

Bowles, S. 2011b. Is liberal society a parasite to tradition? Unpublished manuscript.

Broga, C. 2006. Culture and economics. *Region Focus* 10 (4): 7.

Cantoni, D., Y. Chen, D. Yang, N. Yutchman, and Y. J. Zhang. 2014. Curriculum and Ideology. Working Paper 4779, CESifo.

Costa-Font, J., and F. Cowell. 2015. Social identity and redistributive preferences: A survey. *Journal of Economic Surveys* 29 (2): 357–374.

David, P. A. 2007. Path dependence: A foundational concept for historical social science. *Cliometrica* 1 (2): 91–114.

De Jong, E. 2011. Culture, institutions and economic growth. *Journal of Institutional Economics* 7 (4): 523–527.

Evans-Pritchard, E. E. 1937. *Witchcraft, Oracles and Magic among the Azande.* Clarendon.

Falk, A., and A. Ichino. 2006. Clean evidence on peer effects. *Journal of Labor Economics* 24 (1): 39–57.

Fernandez, R. 2007. Culture and economics. In *The New Palgrave Dictionary of Economics*, second edition. Palgrave.

Fernandez, R. 2010. Does Culture Matter? Institute for the Study of Labor Discussion Paper 5122 (available at http://ftp.iza.org/dp5122.pdf).

Fernandez, R., and A. Fogli. 2006. Fertility: The role of culture and family experience. *Journal of the European Economic Association* 4 (2–3): 552–561.

Fernandez, R., and A. Fogli. 2009. Culture: An empirical investigation of beliefs, work, and fertility. *American Economic Journal: Macroeconomics* 1 (1): 146–177.

Fukuyama, F. 2001. Culture and economic development: Cultural concerns. In *International Encyclopedia of the Social and Behavioral Sciences*. Elsevier.

Giavazzi, F., I. Petkov, and F. Schiantarelli. 2014. Culture: Persistence and Evolution. Working Paper 20174, National Bureau of Economic Research.

Giavazzi, F., F. Schiantarelli, and M. Serafinelli. 2013. Attitudes, Policies and Work. *Journal of the European Economic Association* 11 (6): 1256–1289.

Giuliano, P. 2007. Living arrangements in Western Europe: Does cultural origin matter? *Journal of the European Economic Association* 5 (5): 927–952.

Giuliano, P., and A. Spilimbergo. 2014. Growing up in a recession. *Review of Economic Studies* 81 (2): 787–817.

Gordon, M. M. 1964. *Assimilation in American Life: The Role of Race, Religion, and National Origins.* Oxford University Press.

Gorodnichenko, Y., and G. Roland. 2010. Culture, Institutions and the Wealth of Nations. Discussion Paper No 8013, Center for Economic Policy Research, London.

Gorodnichenko, Y., and G. Roland. 2011. Which dimensions of culture matter for long-run growth? *American Economic Review* 101: 492–498.

Granovetter, M. 1985. Economic action and social structure: The problem of embeddedness. *American Journal of Sociology* 91 (3): 481–510.

Greenberger, S. S. 2003. Sick day abuses focus of fire talks. *Boston Globe,* September 17.

Greif, A. 1989. Reputation and coalitions in medieval trade: Evidence on the Maghribi traders. *Journal of Economic History* 49 (04): 857–882.

Guiso, L., P. Sapienza, and L. Zingales. 2003. People's opium? Religion and economic attitudes. *Journal of Monetary Economics* 50 (1): 225–282.

Guiso, L., P. Sapienza, and L. Zingales. 2006. Does culture affect economic outcomes? *Journal of Economic Perspectives* 20 (2): 23–48.

Guiso, L., P. Sapienza, and L. Zingales. 2009. Does local financial development matter? In *The Banks and the Italian Economy,* ed. D. Silipo. Physica-Verlag.

Helliwell, J. F., S. Wang, and X. Jinwen. 2014. How Durable Are Social Norms' Trust and Generosity in 132 Countries? Working Paper 19835, National Bureau of Economic Research.

Ichino, A., and G. Maggi. 2000. Work environment and individual background: Explaining regional shirking differentials in a large italian firm. *Quarterly Journal of Economics* 115 (3): 1057–1090.

Inglehart, R. F., M. Basanez, and A. Moreno. 1998. *Human Values and Beliefs.* University of Michigan Press.

Knack, S., and P. Keefer. 1997. Does social capital have an economic payoff? A cross-country investigation. *Quarterly Journal of Economics* 112 (4): 1251–1288.

Kluckhohn, C., and W. H. Kelly. 1945. The concept of culture. In *The Science of Man in the World Crisis,* ed. R. Linton. Columbia University Pres s.

Kroeber, A. L., and C. Kluckhohn. 1952. *Culture: A critical review of concepts and definitions. Paper 47.* Harvard University Peabody Museum of American Archeology and Ethnology.

La Porta, R., F. Lopez-De-Silane, A. Shleifer, and R. W. Vishny. 1996. *Trust in Large Organizations.* National Bureau of Economic Research.

Levin, P. 2008. Culture and markets: How economic sociology conceptualizes culture. *Annals of the American Academy of Political and Social Science* 619: 114–129.

Lederach, J. P. 1995. *Preparing for Peace: Conflict Transformation across Cultures.* Syracuse University Press.

Linton, R. 1945. The Cultural Background of Personality. Appleton-Century-Crofts.

Ljunge, M. 2014. Trust issues: Evidence on the intergenerational trust transmission among children of immigrants. *Journal of Economic Behavior & Organization* 106:175–196.

Lucas, R. E. 1988. On the mechanics of economic development. Journal of Monetary Economics 22 (1): 3–42.

Luttmer, E. F. P., and M. Singhal. 2011. Culture, context, and the taste for redistribution. American Economic Journal. Economic Policy 3 (1): 157–179.

Mantzavinos, C. 2001. Individuals, Institutions, and Markets. Cambridge University Press.

Murdock, George Peter. 1965. Culture and Society. University of Pittsburgh Press.

North, D. 1990. Institutions, Institutional Change, and Economic Performance. Cambridge University Press.

Postlewaite, A. 1998. The social basis of interdependent preferences. *European Economic Review* 42 (3): 779–800.

Pryor, F. L. 2007. Culture and economic systems. American Journal of Economics and Sociology 66 (4): 817–855.

Rao, V., and M. Walton. 2004. *Culture and Public Action.* Stanford University Press.

Redfield, R., R. Linton, and M. J. Herskovits. 1936. Memorandum for the study of acculturation. *American Anthropologist* 38 (1): 149–152.

Romer, P. M. 1986. Increasing returns and long-run growth. Journal of Political Economy 94 (5): 1002–1037.

Salant, T., and D. S. Lauderdale. 2003. Measuring culture: A critical review of the acculturation and health in Asia immigrant populations. Social Science and Medicine 57: 71–90.

Schelling, T. C. 1960. *The Strategy of Conflict.* Harvard University Press.

Schwartz, S. J., J. B. Unger, B. L. Zamboanga, and J. Szapocznik. 2010. Rethinking the concept of acculturation: Implications for theory and research. *American Psychologist* 65 (4): 237–251.

Solow, R. M. 1956. A contribution to the theory of economic growth. Quarterly Journal of Economics 70 (1): 65–94.

Swidler, A. 1986. Culture in Action: Symbols and Strategies. American Sociological Review 51 (2): 273–286.

Tabellini, G. 2008. Presidential address institutions and culture. *Journal of the European Economic Association* 6 (2–3): 255–294.

Titmuss, R. M. 1970. *The Gift Relationship: From Human Blood to Social Policy*. Allen & Unwin.

Uy, A. 2009. Can culture explain economic growth? A note on the issues regarding culture-growth studies. *Journal of Economics and Economic Education Research* 10 (3): 85–105.

Useem, J., R. Useem, and J. Donoghue. 1963. Men in the middle of the third culture: The roles of American and non-Western people in cross-cultural administration. *Human Organization* 22 (3): 169–179.

Williamson, C. R., and R. L. Mathers. 2011. Economic freedom, culture, and growth. Public Choice 148 (3–4): 313–335.

Wildavsky, A. 1987. Choosing preferences by constructing institutions: A cultural theory of preference formation. American Political Science Review 81 (1): 3–22.

Networks, Peer Pressure, and Social Interactions

13

The Role of Children in Building Parents' Social Networks

Odelia Heizler and Ayal Kimhi

Fertility is one of the most important decisions that a household makes. The economic literature has examined numerous aspects of fertility decisions: the optimal number of children, the tradeoff between quantity and quality of children, intergenerational transfers, old-age security and intra-family insurance, the effect of children on parents' labor supply, the effect of children on parents' marital stability, and so on (Browning 1992). However, despite the emerging economic literature on the important role played by social networks in various aspects of economic behavior (Jackson 2005; Birke 2009), little is known about the effect of family composition in general, and children in particular, on parents' involvement in social networks. The purpose of this chapter is to fill this gap in the literature.

Alesina and Giuliano (2010) found that families with strong ties participate less in the labor market but produce many more goods and services at home, including child care, cooking, caring for the elderly, and child education. Alesina and Giuliano (2013) studied the economic outcomes of family ties and found that strong family ties are negatively correlated with generalized trust; they imply more household production and less labor-market participation of women, young adults, and the elderly. Strong family ties are correlated with a lower interest in participating in political activities and lower participation in such activities. Families with strong ties prefer labor-market regulation and welfare systems based on the family rather than the market or the government.

The sociological literature highlights another home-produced good provided by the family: building social networks (Bubolz 2001). Social relationships are created both within and outside of the family. The internal and external social ties are interlinked; a family member establishes new linkages via other family members' outside contacts.

The literature provides extensive discussions of the influence of the parents' social network on the development of the child's social network. There are direct and indirect influences. Direct influences include face-to-face contact between the parents' network members and the child. Indirect influences are the effects of parents' characteristics on child behavior (Cochran et al. 1990, p. 17). Cardoso et al. (2010) showed that parents' decisions about the allocation of time affect the child's preferences and may enhance personal interaction skills when the child grows up. Coleman (1988) argued that the parents' social network is important for their children's educational development. Regarding the children's effect on the parents' social networks, however, the literature refers mainly to a negative indirect effect stemming from decreased leisure time for social activities in favor of child rearing (Fischer 1982, p. 253). Nevertheless, we assume that children can also affect their parents' social network positively in a direct way, by exposing the parents face-to-face to new contacts. Thus, the number of children is assumed to be an important determinant of social networks.

Parents' involvement in their children's education has become so popular in the United States that it is referred to as an "institutional standard." Many schools spend considerable resources and effort on encouraging parents to become more active in their children's education. Studies show that parents' involvement increases their child's achievement in school, and this involvement has therefore been classified as parents' investment in their children (Sheldon 2002). Parents' involvement reveals new linkages to teachers and other parents, and thus broadens their social network. However, when the age gap between the children in a family is small, there may be some overlap in the links that the parents obtain via the different children. Thus, the age gap between children is another likely determinant of parents' social networks.

Young children decrease their parents' involvement in social networks in two ways. First, they require more care and supervision than older children and therefore decrease the time that their parents can devote to social activities. Second, they affect their parents' participation in the labor market (Angrist and Evans 1998), and this affects social networks because the workplace is one of the main arenas for creating social networks. We therefore expect the age of the youngest child to affect parents' involvement in social networks.

This chapter examines the ways in which family composition affects a parent's social networks. The importance of understanding what affects social networks stems from the fact that social networks provide information about job and business opportunities, housing options, stock-market tips, and product quality. For example, Montgomery (1991) reviews a long list of research findings on the importance of social ties in the outcomes of job searches. In addition, social networks provide several basic non-economic services (Furman and Buhrmester 1985):

attachment—affection, security and intimate disclosure

reliable alliance—a lasting and dependable bond

enhancement of worth—affirmation of one's competence or value

social integration—companionship and the sharing of experiences

guidance—tangible aid and advice

opportunity for nurturance—taking care of another.

When an individual becomes a parent, his or her demand for network support functions, such as assistance with child rearing and practical or emotional help, increases (Cochran et al. 1990, p. 60).

The structure of the chapter is as follows. Section 13.1 reviews the literature on family composition and its economics implications. Section 13.2 presents hypotheses concerning the effects of family composition on a parent's social networks. Section 13.3 describes the data that we use, the empirical methodology, and the results. Section 13.4 contains a discussion of the results and some concluding comments.

13.1   Family Composition and Its Economic Implications

The economic literature refers to different kinds and different definitions of family composition (or family structure): intact and non-intact families, family size, birth order, and number of generations in the household. Emerging literature has examined the relationship between living in a non-intact family and children's achievements in school and in the labor market (Björklund et al. 2007). Mostly, researches show that children reared in non-intact families have less favorable educational outcomes than children reared in two-parent families, on average. Hill et al. (2001) specified the following family types: two-parent family, mother-only family, mother-with-stepfather family, mother-with-grandfather(s) family, and other living arrangements. They found that changes in family structure and the timing of changes affect children's educational attainments and non-marital births.

The literature also investigates the effect of family size and birth order on the children's future achievements (Kessler 1991). In general, family size affects child outcomes negatively, because large families have fewer resources to devote to each child. Regarding the effect of birth order on child outcomes, there is less agreement in the literature. On the one hand, the later-born children are born to older parents who have less energy, and they therefore receive less natural endowment. On the other hand, parents accumulate child-raising skills with their early-born children. Parents also accumulate financial resources that are useful in rearing children. Finally, having older siblings may be an asset for young children. Black et al. (2005) found a negative correlation between family size and children's educational attainment. However, when they included indicators for birth order, the effects of family size were reduced to almost zero.

Ogawa and Ermisch (1996), who referred to family structure as multi-generation household or nuclear household and investigated the effect of family structure on women's employment patterns using data from Japan, found that younger married women are more likely to take paid employment (particularly full-time employment) in multi-generation households than in nuclear-family households. This appears to stem from role of the woman's parents or parents-in-law in child care.

13.2   Hypotheses

In this chapter, family composition is represented by three characteristics: the number of children, the age of the youngest child, and the age gap between the children. In this section we outline hypotheses regarding the effects of these characteristics on social networking.

We assume that parents' social networks can be expanded and strengthened in two ways. The first is through allocation of time to social activities (parties and social events, hobby groups or garden clubs, religious or sport groups, literary or art discussions, fraternal groups, school fraternities or sororities, study groups, etc.) in which new acquaintances can be made. Glaeser et al. (2002) have shown that the number of organizations in which a person is a member can be a good measure of his or her social capital. The second is that parents can expand and strengthen social networks by being involved in their children's social life and by establishing contacts with other children's parents and with teachers and other school personnel. We assume that, conditional on an individual's work time, a parent allocates his or her free time between caring for children and social activities. As the number of the children increases, on the one hand, the individual has less time to social activities; on the other hand, he or she can create more social networks via children. Hence, we hypothesize that the effect of the number of children on the parents' level of social networks is ambiguous.

Kimmel and Connelly (2007) raised the question whether the time mothers spend caring for children is better categorized as home production time or as leisure. They suggested that it is somewhere in between. We distinguish between two kinds of the time taken to care for children: private time (time the parent spends with the child or children privately, e.g., feeding, washing, putting to bed, reading a story, and helping with homework) and social time (time the parent spends with the child or children and their friends). The child becomes more independent with age and requires less of a parent's time for routine activities such as feeding and washing. At the same time, the child's demand for social activities increases (Hofferth and Sandberg 2001; Folbre et al. 2005). In addition, the child's circle of friends expands with age, so that parents of older children may, through them, obtain more linkages. Hence, we hypothesize that the age of the youngest child has a positive effect on the parents' intensity of social networks.

As the age gap between the oldest and youngest child decreases, there is a larger likelihood of overlap between the members in the different child-specific social networks; in other words, friends that the parent knows via one child may also be the friends that the parent knows via the second child. Figure 13.1 illustrates this point. In the example, the parent has three children, each of whom links the parent to three individuals. The age gap between child 1 and child 2 is relatively large, whereas the age gap between child 2 and child 3 is relatively small. Child 2 and child 3 therefore have two common friends: individual no. 5 and individual no. 6. Thus the number of individuals that the parent knows via his or her children decreases from 9 to 7 as a result of to the overlap. Hence, we hypothesize that the age gap between the children has a positive effect on the parents' intensity of social networks.

13.3 Empirical Evidence

Data

The data for this research were taken from the Israeli Social Surveys for the years 2002–2006. These surveys are conducted by the Central Bureau of Statistics and are based on intensive one-on-one interviews. The sampling unit is a person rather than a household, although information about other members of the respondent's household is also

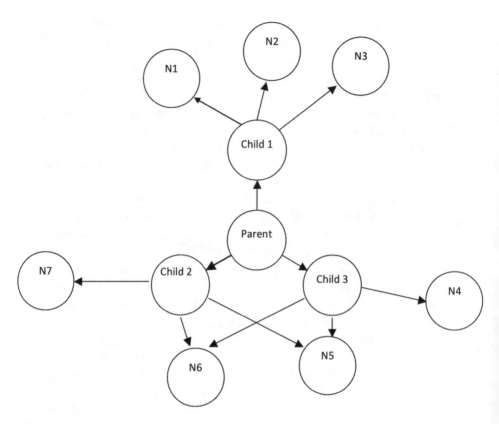

Figure 13.1
An illustration of the overlap in social networks due to different children.

collected. The questionnaire is exceedingly comprehensive, including hundreds of questions. It collects personal and socioeconomic details and covers various facets of life, such as self-defined national and religious identities, education, employment status, employment history, income, housing, health status and illnesses, habits of computer and Internet use, relations with family and friends (satisfaction from the relations and frequency of meetings), and engaging in voluntary and leisure activities. The survey also collects personal information on the respondent's family, including age, gender, education, relationship to the respondent, and marital status.

About 7,000 questionnaires are administered annually, and the original data set for the five years that we used included 36,562 records. We focused on households with the following characteristics: Jewish,) married parents, up to 50 years of age, up to five children (or no children), and no children over 18 years of age. We decided to focus on Jewish households because Israeli Muslims tend to live in villages with their extended families and thus the distinction between "friends" and "family relatives" is not always clear. We focused on married parents because we have information only on children who live with their parents. In the case of a divorced or widowed parent, the children sometimes do not live with a parent but can still affect a parent's social networks. We did not include households with more than five children, because almost all of them are ultra-orthodox (haredim) and their number is very small.[1] The age limitations are also a result of the fact that we only have information on children who live in the parents' household, whereas adult children who have left the house can also affect their parents' intensity of social networks. Overall, these constraints reduced the number of observations that we used to 8,411, including 4,156 males and 4,255 females. (Because households with five children make up less than 3 percent of the sample, we also reexamined our results using a sample of households with up to four children.)

We used the variables of having friends and frequency of contact with friends as proxies for level of social networks.[2] Specifically, we used two questions: "Do you have friends that you meet with or talk to on the phone (including fax and email)?" and "(If you have friends) how often do you meet these friends, or talk to them on the phone?" The respondents answered the latter question on a scale from 1 to 4, with 1 meaning daily or almost daily, 2 meaning once or twice a week, 3 meaning once or twice a month, and 4 meaning less than once a month. On the basis of the two questions, we created the variable "level of social networks," which includes four categories, 1 meaning "does not have any friends," 2 meaning "meets with friends twice a month or less," 3 meaning "meets with friends once or twice a week," and 4 meaning "meets with friends daily or almost daily."

Table 13.1 presents descriptive statistics of the dependent and explanatory variables by gender. The dependent variable is the level of social networks. Between 6 percent and 7 percent of the individuals in our sample declared that they do not have any friends at all; more than a third have strong social networks, meeting with their friends daily or almost daily. The difference between the levels of social networks for males and females does not seem to be quantitatively significant. The variables representing family composition are also quite similar for males and females. The average gap between the oldest and the youngest child is about 5.5 years.[3] The average age of the youngest child is about 4.5 years.

Table 13.1
Descriptive statistics.

Variable	Male	Female
Level of social network (%)		
Does not have any friends	6.02	6.67
Meets with friends once or twice a month or less	14.34	14.67
Meets with friends once or twice a week	41.84	39.27
Meets with friends daily, or almost daily	37.80	39.39
Number of children (%)		
0	14.51	14.48
1	20.21	19.79
2	31.74	32.17
3	22.81	22.66
4	8.01	7.94
5	2.72	2.96
Age gap between youngest and oldest child (mean)	5.64	5.54
Age of youngest child (mean)	4.31	4.70
Age (mean)	36.45	34.19
Ethnic group (%)		
New immigrants (1990+)	15.21	16.19
Old immigrants from Asia or Africa	4.57	3.67
Old immigrants from America or Europe	5.97	5.92
Religious group (%)		
Ultra-orthodox	9.70	10.74
Religious	11.09	10.69
Other		
Rural communities (%)	10.66	10.62
Academic education (%)	30.03	35.03
Work (%)	9.727	67.72
Good health (%)	6.59	6.58
Internet use (%)	62.92	56.26
Hobby (%)	18.41	29.07
Meets with family frequently (%)	25.29	30.15
Number of observations	4,156	4,255

Males in our sample are slightly older than females (about 36 versus about 34 years on average), but the difference is statistically significant. This may be a consequence of women's lower age at marriage. About 15 percent of our sample individuals are new immigrants.[4] We distinguished between old immigrants from Asia and Africa and old immigrants from America and Europe because of differences in their cultural backgrounds that might affect social behavior. Between 10 percent (males) and 11 percent (females) of our sample individuals are ultra-orthodox (haredim); about 11 percent are religious.[5] About 11 percent of our sample individuals live in rural communities.

Females are more educated than males in our sample. Almost 35 percent of the females have academic education, versus only 30 percent of the males. Males are employed more than females—almost 80 percent of the males and 68 percent of the females are employed. About 93 percent of the sample individuals declared that their health is very good. Internet use is much higher among males (63 percent, versus 56 percent among females). Hobby-group membership is much higher among females (29 percent, versus 18 percent among males). Females have a higher tendency to meet with family members frequently (30 percent, versus 25 percent for males).

Empirical Methodology

The Ordered Logit model was used to estimate the relationship between the level of a parent's social networks and a set of explanatory variables. An Ordered Response Model, of which the Ordered Logit is a special case, models the probability of observing outcome i as the probability that a linear function of the explanatory variables plus a random error is within the range of two corresponding cutoff points:

$$\Pr(outcome_j = i) = \Pr\left(k_{i-1} < \beta_1 x_{1j} + \beta_2 x_{2j} + \ldots + \beta_k x_{kj} + u_j \leq k_i\right), \quad i = 1, \ldots, I. \tag{1}$$

The coefficients $\beta_1, \beta_2, \ldots, \beta_k$ and the cutoff points, k_1, k_2, k_{I-1} were estimated jointly using Maximum Likelihood, where I is the number of possible outcomes and k_0 is taken as $-\infty$ and k_I as $+\infty$.

We estimated the model separately for males and females, because the literature points to essential differences in the time that fathers and mothers devote to child rearing. For example, Folbre et al. (2005) found that children spend 81 percent of their time spent with one parent with their mother and only 19 percent of that time with their father.

4.3   Results

The estimation results are presented in table 13.2. The effect of the number of children on the level of social network is different for males and females. Whereas each additional child decreases the mother's level of social network (the coefficient of age squared was found insignificant and hence excluded), the effect of the number of children on the father's social network has a U-shaped effect.

Figure 13.2 shows that the level of social networks declines with the number of children up to the second child and increases with additional children. Moreover, the level of social networks of fathers with four children is similar to that of males without children. Up to the third child, the level of the females' social network is higher than the level of the males' social networks, but that difference is reversed with more than three children. When we omit the ultra-orthodox from the sample, our results do not change.

We also found that the age gap between the oldest and the youngest child has a positive and significant effect on the parents' level of social networks. Note that as the number of the children increases, the age gap between the children is likely to increase too; that is, a parent with four children is likely to have a larger age gap than a parent with three children. When we calculated the total effect of the number of children on the parents' social networks (including the effect of the number of children and the effect of the age gap, which increases with the number of children), yet the effect of the number of children is not monotonic even for females. It means that the effect of the number of children on social network has a U-shaped effect for both males and females. These results were not affected by including households with more than five children.

Let us now discuss the coefficients of the other explanatory variables. As expected, an individual's age had a negative and significant effect on the level of social networks, meaning that the strength of the social networks deteriorates with age. New immigrants had significantly lower levels of social networks than native Israelis. Old immigrants from Asia and Africa had lower intensity of social networks than native Israelis but higher levels of social networks than new immigrants. There was no significant difference between the social network levels of old immigrants from America and Europe and those of native Israelis.[6]

Religious beliefs did not have a significant effect on the females' level of social networks, but this was not the case for males. Ultra-orthodox

Table 13.2
Ordered Logit results of the level of social networks.

Explanatory variables	Males		Females	
	Coefficient	Z value	Coefficient	Z value
Number of children	−0.441***	−2.90	−0.146***	−2.72
(Number of children)²	0.093***	3.54		
Age gap between children	0.025*	1.80	0.029**	2.09
Age of youngest child	−0.000	0.637	−0.000	−0.49
Age	−0.044***	−8.11	−0.013***	−2.67
Ethnic group				
New immigrant	−0.388***	−4.61	−0.458***	−5.69
Old immigrant from Asia or Africa	−0.354**	−2.47	−0.425**	−2.75
Old immigrant from America or Europe	−0.075	−0.61	−0.135	−1.09
Religious group				
Ultra-orthodox	0.486***	3.80	−0.141	−1.32
Religious	−0.421***	−4.30	−0.047	−0.49
Other				
Rural communities	0.196**	2.04	0.304***	3.18
Academic education	−0.185***	−2.71	0.273***	4.27
Work	−0.149*	−1.84	0.055	0.86
Good health	0.259**	2.06	0378***	3.10
Internet use	0.276	3.95	0.487***	7.54
LR χ² (p value)	277.95 (0.0000)		249.11 (0.0000)	
Pseudo R²	0.0285		0.0245	
Number of observations	4,156		4,255	

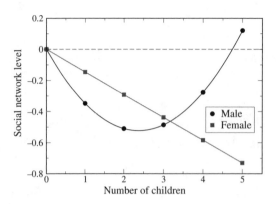

Figure 13.2
Level of social network as function of number of children.

men had higher levels of social networks than non-religious men, whereas religious men had lower levels of social networks than non-religious men. Ultra-orthodox men pray in the synagogue three times a day and meet for other religious activities, thereby strengthening their social networks. Ultra-orthodox females, on the other hand, are largely excluded from public religious activities (Berman 2000). Religious families, as opposed to the ultra-orthodox, are much more integrated in the non-religious society. The religious strictures (such as eating only Kosher food, not traveling or taking part in social activities on the Sabbath, and restrictions on males' and females' dancing together) negatively affect their levels of social networks. We do not have a good explanation for the fact that this affects religious men but not religious women.

Living in rural communities increased the level of social networks (more for females than for males), reflecting the common belief that relationships in large cities are less personal. (See, e.g., Coleman 1988.) We also tried to distinguish between larger and smaller cities, to examine the hypothesis that living in larger and more densely populated cities increases the level of social networks because of the greater opportunities of creating social contacts (Wahba and Zenou 2005). However, we could not find any significant difference.

The effect of academic education on an individual's level of social networks can be ambiguous. Many researchers have found that less educated people obtain much more help from friends in finding a job than more educated people, whereas educated people use mostly formal job-seeking channels and depend less on friends. (See, e.g., Holzer 1987.)

Moreover, the leisure time of more educated people is more expensive, so they might spend less time on social activities. These arguments lead to the expectation of a negative effect of academic education on the level of social networks. On the other hand, years spent in school are a prime period for creating social connections, and this may lead to a positive effect of academic education on the level of social networks. We found that academic education has a significantly negative effect on the males' level of social networks, but a significantly positive effect on the females' level of social networks.

Researchers have found a positive relationship between health status and level of social networks. (See, e.g., Cattell 2001.) We found that mothers who reported being in good health also reported significantly higher levels of social networks, but no significant differences were found for fathers. We found that Internet use affects the level of social networks positively and significantly, meaning that the Internet is not a substitute for friends, but rather complements them. Contacts made online may lead to subsequent face-to-face social relationships.

Work may decrease an individual's social networks by reducing the leisure time or may increase an individual's social networks by creating and maintaining social contacts with co-workers. We found that employment decreases males' level of social networks significantly, but does not significantly affect females' level of social networks.

Research has found that women with high earnings rely more on formal child-care services (see, e.g., Rosenbaum and Ruhm 2005), and thus spend less time with their children and are less exposed to social contacts through their children. We examined this hypothesis, but could not find different effects of children between the level of social networks of mothers with higher earnings and those of other mothers. Note that our results do not change when we omit households of ultra-orthodox (Haredim) from the sample.

The main results do not change qualitatively when we exclude people with no children (about 86 percent from our sample; see the appendix to this chapter): the effect of the number of children on the fathers' social networks has a U-shaped effect, while the effect of the number of children on the mothers' social networks is always negative. The effect of the age gap between the children is positive and significant. The effect of the age of the youngest child on the fathers' social networks is positive and significant. The age of the youngest child was not included in the females' model because of the high correlation between mother's age and the age of the youngest child, which follows from the biological limit on the age of childbearing which applies only to mothers. The effects of the other explanatory variables are qualitatively similar to the results presented above.

The essence of the results did not change either when we estimated the regression with dummy variables for each number of children, when we included two additional explanatory variables that might be endogenous to the level of social networks—participation in hobby groups and frequency of meeting family, and when we omitted large households with five children from the sample.

13.4   Discussion and Conclusion

A considerable volume of economic literature exists on the effects of family composition on various outcomes, including wealth, parents' time allocation between child care and market work, children's education, abilities and outcomes, and so on. (See, e.g., Gong and van Soest 2002; Kalenkoski et al. 2007.) There is also a well-established body of economic literature on the role of social networks in communicating valuable information (Montgomery 1991). This chapter represents the first attempt to combine these two important lines of research by examining the relationship between family composition and social networks. In particular, we examine empirically the effect of family composition on parents' level of social networks, using a sample of Jewish married couples derived from the Israeli Social Survey for 2002–2006. We focus on the effects of three variables which represent family composition: the number of children, the age gap between the oldest and youngest child, and the age of the youngest child. The richness of our data enables us to control for a wide range of explanatory variables, including age, belonging to a minority group, belonging to a religious group, place of residence, education, employment, health status, Internet use, taking part in hobby groups, and relationships with other family members.

Our main finding is a positive effect of the age gap between children on the level of social networks. This is because the overlap between the social links created through the different children decreases as the age gap increases. The children have two opposed effects on the individuals' social networks: children decrease the parents' time for leisure activities but increase the number of new linkages made through them. We found that the effect of the number of children on the fathers' level of social network is U-shaped; i.e., the fathers' level of social networks initially decreases with the number of children, but increases after a certain number of children. However, for mothers, only the negative effect of the number of children on the level of social networks is statistically significant. This may follow from the fact that mothers dedicate relatively more time to physical activities of child rearing and less time to social activities with the children than fathers.

In this chapter we assume that the effects of sons and daughters on the parents' social network are identical. It would be interesting to relax this assumption in future research. Specifically, it will not be surprising if we find that fathers' social networks are affected more by the presence of sons, and mothers' social networks more by the presence of daughters.

Appendix

Table 13A.1
Ordered Logit results of the level of social networks, excluding people with no children.

Explanatory variables	Males		Females	
	Coefficient	Z value	Coefficient	Z value
Number of children	−0.512***	−3.34	−0.145***	−2.66
(Number of children)^2	0.103***	3.88		
Age gap between children	0.041***	2.81	0.028**	1.99*
Age of youngest child	0.047***	4.12	—	—
Age	−0.060***	−7.56	−0.011**	−2.02
Ethnic group				
New immigrant	−0.458***	−4.88	−0.490***	−5.53
Old immigrant from Asia or Africa	−0.310**	−2.09	−0.445***	−2.78
Old immigrant from America or Europe	−0.100	−0.76	−0.220*	−1.66
Religious group				
Ultra-orthodox	0.467***	3.33	−0.176	−1.51
Religious	−0.349***	−3.33	−0.070	−0.67
Other				
Rural communities	0.207**	2.03	0.329***	3.26
Academic education	−0.129*	−1.74	0.306***	4.41
work	−0.130	−1.48	−0.021	0.31
Good health	0.284**	2.13	0.455***	3.47
Internet use	0.237***	3.17	0.458***	6.66
LR χ^2 (*p* value)	193.33 (0.0000)		212.01(0.0000)	
Pseudo R^2	0.0228		0.0242	
Number of observations	3,553		3,639	

***, **, and * denote significance at 1%, 5%, and 10%, respectively.

Table 13A.2
Ordered Logit results of the level of social networks, using dummy variables for number of children.

Explanatory variables	Males		Females	
	Coefficient	Z value	Coefficient	Z value
Number of children				
2	−0.173*	−1.80	−0.177**	−1.87
3	−0.193	−1.42	−0.281**	−2.09
4	−0.044	−0.24	−0.569***	−3.11
5	0.561**	2.15	−0.416*	−1.64
Age gap between children	0.042***	2.86	0.029**	2.02
Age of youngest child	0.046***	4.10	—	—
Age	−0.060***	−7.75	−0.011**	−2.01
Ethnic group				
New immigrant	−0.461***	−4.90	−0.490***	−5.51
Old immigrant from Asia or Africa	−0.309**	−2.08	−0.436***	−2.72
Old immigrant from America or Europe	−0.099	−0.75	−0.214	−1.62
Religious group				
Ultra-orthodox	0.462***	3.29	−0.188	−1.60
Religious	−0.343***	−3.27	−0.068	−0.65
Other				
Rural communities	0.208**	2.04	0.329***	3.25
Academic education	−0.129*	−1.73	0.303***	4.36
work	−0.129	−1.47	0.024	0.35
Good health	0.280**	2.10	0.454***	3.46
Internet use	0.237***	3.16	0.457***	6.63
LR χ² (p value)	194.27 (0.0000)		214.70 (0.0000)	
Pseudo R²	0.0229		0.0245	
Number of observations	3,553		3,639	

***, **, and * denote significance at 1%, 5%, and 10%, respectively.

Table 13A.3
Ordered Logit results of the level of social networks, including hobby and family contacts.

Explanatory variables	Males		Females	
	Coefficient	Z value	Coefficient	Z value
Number of children	−0.503***	−3.27	−0.143***	−2.63
(Number of children)^2	0.101***	3.80		
Age gap between children	0.042***	2.82	0.029**	2.02
Age of youngest child	0.045***	3.95	—	—
Age	−0.058***	−7.18	−0.011**	−1.99
Ethnic group				
New immigrant	−0.439***	−4.65	−0.446***	−5.01
Old immigrant from Asia or Africa	−0.325**	−2.18	−0.414*	−1.64
Old immigrant from America or Europe	−0.093	−0.70	−0.218	−1.39
Religious group				
Ultra-orthodox	0.542***	3.84	−0.163	−1.39
Religious	−0.312**	−2.97	−0.051	−0.49
Other				
Rural communities	0.160	1.56	0.315***	3.11
Academic education	−0.143*	−1.90	0.262***	3.72
Work	−0.127	−1.44	0.011	0.17
Good health	0.253*	1.88	0.430***	3.28
Internet use	0.204***	2.71	0.428***	6.18
Hobby	0.463***	5.53	0.390***	5.49
Meets with family frequently	0.475***	6.37	0.204***	2.92
LR χ^2 (*p* value)	263.58 (0.0000)		251.18 (0.0000)	
Pseudo R^2	0.0311		0.0287	
Number of observations	3,553		3,639	

***, **, and * denote significance at 1%, 5%, and 10%, respectively.

Table 13A.4
Ordered Logit results of the level of social networks, households with up to four children.

Explanatory variables	Males Coefficient	Z value	Females Coefficient	Z value
Number of children				
2	−0.188**	−1.94	−0.196**	−2.04
3	−0.220	−1.60	−0.318**	−2.32
4	−0.072	−0.38	−0.609***	−3.26
Age gap between children	0.045***	2.98	0.035**	2.33
Age of youngest child	0.046***	4.01	—	—
Age	−0.059***	−7.28	−0.013**	−2.32
Ethnic group				
New immigrant	−0.453***	−4.74	−0.554***	−6.13
Old immigrant from Asia or Africa	−0.332**	−2.19	−0.491***	−2.97
Old immigrant from America or Europe	−0.099	−0.74	−0.222*	−1.65
Religious group				
Ultra-orthodox	0.416***	2.87	−0.269**	−2.20
Religious	−0.351***	−3.25	−0.103	−0.94
Other				
Rural communities	0.204**	1.97	0.355***	3.43
Academic education	−0.141*	−1.88	0.294***	4.18
work	−0.120	−1.34	0.023	0.34
Good health	0.274**	2.02	0.459***	3.41
Internet use	0.222**	12.93	0.440***	6.28
LR χ^2 (*p* value)	156.30 (0.0000)		218.97 (0.0000)	
Pseudo R^2	0.0190		0.0260	
Number of observations	3,440		3,513	

***, **, and * denote significance at 1%, 5%, and 10%, respectively.

Notes

1. Our results did not change qualitatively when we included larger families.

2. Frequency of contact is one of the ways to measure social networks. (See, e.g., Jennings et al. 1991; Allen 2000.) Another possible proxy is the size of the social network, but we do not have information on that. It should be noted that these proxies are positively correlated.

3. The age gap was computed only when there were two or more children.

4. The year 1990 marks the beginning of a large wave of immigration from the former USSR to Israel. Hence, we define "new immigrants" as those who immigrated since 1990. Pre-1990 immigrants are defined as "old immigrants."

5. Although haredim certainly are religious, the Social Survey questionnaire uses religious as a distinct category, meaning "religious but not haredim." We keep this terminology here.

6. We also tried to distinguish natives whose parents came from America or Europe from natives whose parents came from Asia or Africa, but did not find any significant differences.

References

Alesina, A., and P. Giuliano. 2010. The power of the family. *Journal of Economic Growth* 15 (2): 93–125.

Alesina, A., and P. Giuliano. 2013. Family Ties. IZA Discussion Paper 7376.

Allen, W. D. 2000. Social networks and self-employment. *Journal of Socio-Economics* 29: 487–501.

Angrist, J. D., and W. N. Evans. 1998. Children and their parents' labor supply: Evidence from exogenous variation in family size. *American Economic Review* 88 (3): 450–477.

Berman, E. 2000. Sect, subsidy, and sacrifice: An economist's view of ultra-orthodox Jews. *Quarterly Journal of Economics* 115 (3): 905–953.

Birke, D. 2009. The economics of networks—a survey of the empirical literature. *Journal of Economic Surveys* 23 (4): 762–793.

Björklund, A., D. K. Ginther, and M. Sundström. 2007. Family structure and child outcomes in the USA and Sweden. *Journal of Population Economics* 20: 183–201.

Black, S. E., P. J. Devereux, and K. G. Salvanes. 2005. The more the merrier? The effect of family size and birth order on children's education. *Quarterly Journal of Economics* 120 (2): 669–700.

Browning, M. 1992. Children and household economic behavior. *Journal of Economic Literature* 30 (3): 1434–1475.

Bubolz, M. M. 2001. Family as source, user, and builder of social capital. *Journal of Socio-Economics* 30: 129–131.

Cardoso, A. R., E. Fontainha, and C. Monfardini. 2010. Children's and parents' time use: Empirical evidence on investment in human capital in France, Italy and Germany. *Review of Economics of the Household* 8 (4): 479–504.

Cattell, V. 2001. Poor people, poor places, and poor health: The mediating role of social networks and social capital. *Social Science and Medicine* 52: 1501–1516.

Cochran, M., M. Larner, D. Riley, L. Guunarsson, and C. R. Henderson Jr. 1990. *Extending Families: The Social Networks of Parents and Their Children.* Cambridge University Press.

Coleman, J. S. 1988. Social capital in the creation of human capital. *American Journal of Sociology* 94: S95–S120.

Fischer, C. S. 1982. *To Dwell among Friends: Personal Networks in Town and City.* University of Chicago Press.

Folbre, N., J. Yoon, K. Finnoff, and A. S. Fuligni. 2005. By what measure? Family time devoted to children in the United States. *Demography* 42 (2): 373–390.

Furman, W., and D. Buhrmester. 1985. Children's perceptions of the personal relationships in their social networks. *Developmental Psychology* 21 (6): 1016–1024.

Glaeser, E. L., D. Laibson, and B. Sacerdote. 2002. An economic approach to social capital. *Economic Journal* 112: 437–458.

Gong, X., and A. van Soest. 2002. Family structure and female labour supply in Mexico City. *Journal of Human Resources* 37 (1): 163–191.

Hill, M. S., W. J. Yeung, and G. J. Duncan. 2001. Childhood family structure and young adult behaviors. *Journal of Population Economics* 14 (2): 271–299.

Hofferth, S. L., and J. F. Sandberg. 2001. How American children spend their time. *Journal of Marriage and the Family* 63 (2): 295–308.

Holzer, H. J. 1987. Informal job search and black youth unemployment. *American Economic Review* 77 (3): 446–452.

Jackson, M. O. 2005. A survey of network formation: Stability and efficiency. In *Group Formation in Economics: Networks, Clubs, and Coalitions*, ed. G. Demange and M. Wooders. Cambridge University Press.

Jennings, D. J., V. Stagg, and R. E. Connors. 1991. Social networks and mothers' interactions with their preschool children. *Child Development* 62 (5): 966–978.

Kalenkoski, C. M., D. C. Ribar, and L. S. Statton. 2007. The effect of family structure on parents' child care time in the United States and the United Kingdom. *Review of Economics of the Household* 5 (4): 353–384.

Kessler, D. 1991. Birth order, family size, and achievement: Family structure and wage determination. *Journal of Labor Economics* 9 (4): 413–426.

Kimmel, J., and R. Connelly. 2007. Mothers' time choices: Caregiving, leisure, home production, and paid work. *Journal of Human Resources* 42 (3): 643–681.

Montgomery, J. D. 1991. Social networks and labor-market outcomes: Toward an economic analysis. *American Economic Review* 81 (5): 1408–1418.

Ogawa, N., and J. E. Ermisch. 1996. Family structure, home time demands, and the employment patterns of Japanese married women. *Journal of Labor Economics* 14 (4): 677–702.

Rosenbaum, D. T., and C. J. Ruhm. 2005. The Cost of Caring for Young Children. IZA Discussion Paper 1860.

Sheldon, S. B. 2002. Parents' social networks and beliefs as predictors of parent involvement. *Elementary School Journal* 102 (4): 301–316.

Wahba, J., and Y. Zenou. 2005. Density, social networks and job search methods: Theory and application to Egypt. *Journal of Development Economics* 78: 443–473.

14

Individual Fundraising: The Power of the Personal

Abigail Payne, Kimberley Scharf, and Sarah Smith

In recent years, individual fundraising through online platforms has become a mass activity, raising substantial sums for many charities. Through JustGiving, the UK's biggest charity fundraising platform, more than a million people have raised £1.5 billion for over 13,000 charities and causes since the website was set up in 2001.[1] Recent figures suggest that online donations, of which individual fundraising is only a part, are still a relatively small part of the total (an estimated 7 percent of the total dollar amount given in the US[2]) and that online fundraising platforms are used by 7 percent of UK donors.[3] But online and text giving are growing at a faster rate than total donations, indicating that this share will grow.

Individual online fundraising typically works as follows: Individual fundraisers decide on a fundraising activity to raise money for their chosen charity (these activities often involve a sporting event such as running a marathon or swimming the English Channel, but also include "novelty activities," such as head shaving). The fundraisers then set up personalized webpages on a platform such as JustGiving and invite people to make donations to their chosen charities. As we show below, most of the donations come from the fundraiser's friends, family members, and colleagues. Almost all are made online via the fundraising page and are passed directly by the fundraising website to the charity. The online donations are listed on the fundraising page, the most recent first. Information on how much has been given, and by whom,[4] is visible to the fundraiser and also visible to each donor who subsequently arrives at the fundraising page.

In this chapter we present new insights on individual fundraising from micro-econometric analysis of JustGiving data. The analysis exploits a number of different data sub-samples. The largest comprises 416,313 fundraisers who were active JustGiving users at the time of an online survey that ran from October 2010 to April 2011. We also analyze data on 10,597 fundraisers who ran in the 2010 London Marathon and from a sample of 39,238 fundraisers who had linked their fundraising pages to their Facebook page. Details on all these samples are given in an appendix.

A "typical" individual fundraising page (the median) attracts 14 donations and raises £245. But, as table 14.1 shows, there is substantial variation in the number of donations and the amounts raised. The top 10 percent of pages raise £1,343 or more, the bottom 10 percent less than £38. In this chapter we show that at least some of this variation can be linked to specific factors having to do with the individual's fundraising strategy (for example, the type of event and whether or not a fundraising target is set). We also argue that social interactions are crucially important in individual fundraising. Such fundraising is highly personal—at least in the UK, where it typically involves asking people one knows to give to a charity. Recent evidence (Castillo et al. 2014; Lacetera et al. 2016) indicates that peer-to-peer fundraising may not be highly successful at generating new donations. Individual fundraising, by contrast, which is a particular form of peer-to-peer fundraising, appears to be much more effective in eliciting donations. One important difference is that fundraising platforms and fundraising pages make donations very visible within social networks, so the fundraiser can see whether or not a person who was asked has given. A second crucial difference is the fundraising activity itself: the fundraiser is engaging in an activity rather than just asking a friend to make donation. Whereas previous studies on charitable giving have emphasized the relationship between the donor and the charity, we argue that individual fundraising may be motivated by the donor's "relational altruism" toward the fundraiser and by how much the fundraiser raises.

14.1 Why Fundraise?

Why do individuals choose to do fundraising events and to raise money for charity? Table 14.2 summarizes self-reported motivations for individual fundraising. The main motivation reported by fundraisers is to help charities, either by raising money and/or by increasing awareness. Taking part in a fundraising event, though not the main factor, is "very important" for about one fourth of fundraisers. In the UK, charities exploit the popularity of mass sporting events, such as the over-subscribed London Marathon, to buy tickets, which they then allocate to people in return for contributions in excess of £1,000. Other charities have successfully organized their own fundraising events (mass-participation events), such as the Race for Life (a series of 5-kilometer running races at different locations), which have become very popular

Table 14.1
Summary statistics on 39,238 JustGiving fundraising pages.

	Mean	Tenth percentile	Median	Ninetieth percentile
Page level				
Number of donations	21	3	14	46
Average donation amount	23.97	9.09	17.50	40.35
Total amount raised	565.86	38.00	245.00	1,343.22
Donation level				
Amounts donated	26.92	5	20	50

in their own right, attracting hundreds of thousands of people who will pay to take part.

In most cases, the initiative for fundraising comes from the individuals themselves. Being asked by someone else (a friend, people at work, a charity) has been shown to play an important role in explaining why people volunteer (Freeman 1997), but appears to be much less important in explaining why people fundraise.

14.2   Individual Fundraising Strategies

Individual fundraisers have to make a number of choices. Big decisions include how to raise money (run a marathon, grow a moustache, stay dry for a month, ask people to make contributions for an anniversary) and what charity to support (a specific cause, a big national charity, a small local organization). In the case of mass-participation events—either charity tickets to sporting events or charity-organized events—the choices may be related. Looking across our largest sample of 416,313 JustGiving fundraisers (who among them have more than 500,000 pages), we estimate that 38 percent of fundraising pages are for charity-organized mass events (such as the Race for Life), and that 45 percent are for other-organized mass events (such as the London Marathon). The remaining 17 percent are lone fundraisers who do not appear to be fundraising with other people in conjunction with a mass event but have chosen their own individual event and charity.

We show in table 14.3 that the numbers of donations and the amounts raised differ strikingly between lone fundraisers and mass-event fundraisers. Lone fundraisers tend to attract more donations than people taking

Table 14.2
Individual motivations for fundraising: responses to "Generally how important to you were each of the following factors in deciding to fundraise?"

	Very important	Somewhat important	Not very important	Not at all important
I wanted to raise as much money for charity as possible	50.4%	41.4%	7.2%	1.0%
I wanted to raise awareness of a particular charity or cause	40.2%	40.8%	13.1%	5.9%
I wanted to do more for charity than just give my own money	37.9%	47.9%	12.1%	2.2%
I wanted to raise money for a cause that was related to a personal event or tragedy that affected me or someone I know	35.0%	27.5%	17.6%	20.0%
I wanted to participate in an event that required me to fundraise for charity	25.6%	33.0%	23.2%	18.2%
I wanted to do a particular activity, and though it would be nice to raise some money in the process	24.2%	35.5%	20.9%	19.3%
I wanted to raise money in memory of someone	23.4%	23.6%	24.0%	29.0%
I wanted to set a good example so others would see the importance of fundraising	10.7%	32.8%	24.9%	31.5%
My fundraising page was a part of a group of pages done with my friends/colleagues/family members	8.5%	18.7%	20.7%	52.1%
I was asked to host a fundraising page for a particular charity	4.6%	11.1%	25.5%	58.9%
I was asked to host a fundraising page by my work/corporate responsibility scheme	2.8%	7.7%	23.2%	66.4%

Source: Online survey of JustGiving donors, fundraisers and sponsors carried out from October 2010 to April 2011. Sample size: 13,784.

part in mass events, and they tend to raise more money. This suggests that there may be important distinctions in fundraising behavior between the two kinds of fundraisers.

One possibility is that some mass-event fundraisers may be attracted by the activity as well as, or even instead of, by the particular cause. As table 14.2 shows, the activity is a very important motivating factor for about one fourth of fundraisers. Lone fundraisers, by contrast, may be more likely to be motivated by the desire to raise money for a particular charity or cause. A higher level of commitment to the charity or cause may, then, be one reason why they tend to raise more than mass fundraisers.

Another difference, however, is that mass-event fundraisers may find themselves competing for donations—they are not the only ones raising funds for a particular charity at a particular time. The competition may be particularly intense in the case of local events that attract people from the same social networks (a local Race for Life, for example). On the other hand, the publicity surrounding a mass event may help to increase awareness of the cause and encourage a greater response from donors. Lone fundraisers do not have to compete with other fundraisers doing the same activity for the same charity at the same time; however, they have to do all their own promotion, as there isn't as much publicity attached to their event.

More generally, lone fundraisers may find it more costly in time and effort to organize a fundraising activity—they can't simply turn up on the day of an event. And although it may be personally rewarding to raise

Table 14.3
Lone fundraising versus mass-event fundraising.

	% sample (fundraisers)	Number of donations per fundraiser	Total amount raised per fundraiser	% of fundraisers who fundraise again
Individual-led	17.1%	25	£853	15.0%
Mass event	44.8%	22	£588	19.0%
Charity-organized mass event	38.1%	16	£439	19.5%

Analysis based on 546,637 fundraising pages. Individual-led: individual is the sole fundraiser in a unique event. Mass event: many fundraisers, many possible charities (e.g., London Marathon). Charity mass event: many fundraisers, one charity (Race for Life). "Fundraise again" refers to following 12 months money for one's preferred charity or cause, a lone fundraiser may miss out on some of the fun of taking part in an event alongside thousands of other fundraisers. This may affect how lone fundraisers feel about fundraising and whether they choose to repeat the experience. Although lone fundraisers tend to raise more money, they are less likely to fundraise again within the next 12 months.

14.3   The Power of the Personal

For charities, individual fundraising can have a number of advantages over conventional fundraising methods.

First, individual fundraising can be highly cost-effective in comparison with alternatives such as professional face-to-face fundraising. (The estimated break-even point for professional fundraising comes after 26–28 months of donations.[5]) Mass-participation events (such as Races for Life) can be costly if they are organized by the charity or if the charity has to pay for fundraising places in externally organized events (such as the London Marathon). But many fundraising events have been devised and organized by an individual at relatively little or no cost to the charity. And even when it bears the costs of an event up front, a charity can often pass some of those costs on to the individual fundraisers by charging individuals to take part or by setting a high fundraising target.

Second, individuals can be highly effective fundraisers. The fact that an individual takes the time and effort to fundraise on behalf of a charity provides it with a personal endorsement. This may not matter for a large, well-known charity, but could potentially be important for smaller, less well known charities. The economics literature on charitable giving takes the importance of signals as verifiers of the quality of a charity very seriously. (See, for example, Vesterlund 2003.) Such signals—often in the form of large, leading donations—have been shown to increase subsequent giving. In a world in which hundreds of thousands of charities are competing for attention and money, signals in the form of personal effort may be important.

Also important is the personal nature of the "ask" in individual fundraising. As table 14.4 shows, most people who give to individual fundraising pages are likely to be members of the fundraiser's existing social network of friends, family members, and colleagues. Not only are sponsorship requests more likely to come from within the immediate social network of family members, friends, and colleagues (rather than from people in more distant relationships, such as friends of friends), but these requests are also more likely to be met with a positive response.

The importance of personal relationships mirrors previous findings in the empirical economics literature. For example, Meer (2011) shows that a personal "ask" is much more effective in alumni fundraising; he compares cases in which alumni raising money for their university asked for contributions from people with whom they had roomed in college against cases in which they asked for contributions from people they didn't know. The attraction of individual fundraising for charities is that fundraisers are able to exploit their personal relationships with family members, friends, and colleagues to raise money.

However, the findings from a two recent experimental studies indicate that it may be relatively hard to spread donation activity through social networks with a simple, personal "ask" (peer-to-peer fundraising). Castillo et al. (2014) looked at what happened when donors giving through a donation portal were given the opportunity to ask others in their social network to join them in supporting the same charity. The donors could ask others by posting on their Facebook wall or by sending a message to a single friend (the two options were offered randomly). More donors chose to post to their wall rather than to send a private message, but few did either (7 percent and 4 percent, respectively). The response

Table 14.4
Responses to "Which of the following types of acquaintances have asked you to sponsor them and have you given when asked?"

	Always gave when asked	Sometimes gave when asked	Never gave when asked	Never asked
Family member	72.6%	11.0%	0.5%	16.0%
Friend	64.0%	32.2%	0.3%	3.5%
Colleague	42.5%	45.4%	1.2%	11.0%
Son or daughter of someone I know	25.1%	23.6%	3.3%	48.1%
Neighbor	22.3%	21.4%	1.7%	54.6%
Friend of someone I know	10.6%	37.0%	7.3%	45.2%
Parent of friend or schoolmate of my child	10.4%	20.3%	5.4%	63.9%
Charity representative	5.9%	45.9%	17.2%	31.1%

Source: Online survey of JustGiving donors, fundraisers and sponsors carried out from October 2010 to April 2011. Sample size: 18,163.

rate—measured by the number of number of cases of a wall post or a personal suggestion in which a donation was actually made—was very low. Only 1.9 percent of the wall posts, and none of the personal messages, generated a donation. Putting the two together (and focusing on the more effective wall post) indicates that it would take about 750 donors (and their social networks) to yield a single extra donation.

Lacetera et al. (2016) illustrate the potential risks of "slacktivism" in online giving. Rather than donate to a charity, people are happy to engage in visible, but less costly, online activities, such as "liking" or sharing information about a charity. Lacetera et al. studied responses to an online fundraising campaign intended to encourage donations to a charity and to spread giving through online social networks. They found that 10.5 percent of those who received one of the sponsored stories or advertisements clicked on it, 5 percent "liked" it, and 0.5 percent shared it or commented on it. However, only 0.05 percent pledged to donate. From among those who pledged, they randomly selected half to automatically broadcast to their wider social network of more than 2,000 people, but no further donations were forthcoming. Of course, this is only one example of a charity campaign, but it does suggest potential limitations to simple peer-to-peer fundraising.

Individual fundraising is much more effective at generating donations. In our sample of fundraisers who "broadcast" their fundraising page on their Facebook page, the median number of Facebook friends is 251 and the median number of donations is 9—an implicit response rate of 3.5 percent. At least two features of individual fundraising are likely to be important: that there is a fundraising activity (and often a fundraising target) set by the fundraiser and that donations are directly visible to the fundraiser (and to other donors). In contrast with cases in which people ask members of their social network to donate to a third party, the donation is made to a page set up by the fundraiser.

A standard approach to modeling motivations for giving is to assume that donors care directly about the goods and services that are being provided by the charities (Bergstrom et al. 1986). In the context of individual fundraising, however, fundraisers may care about the charity and about how much they raise, but donors may be motivated by their relationship with the fundraiser. We can therefore think of this as *relational altruism*, because it comes directly from the relationship between the fundraiser and the donor.

Table 14.5 provides information on the relative importance of various factors in determining how much people give in the context of individual fundraising. The first two factors reflect standard motivations for giving—individual donations are affected by a sense that the money will be used efficiently and effectively and by the charity's cause or mission. However, the relational altruism also matters—the fourth most important factor on the list is the donor's personal relationship to the fundraiser. That factor comes before tax relief, which is typically thought to provide an important financial incentive to encourage donations.

14.4   Social Interactions—Fundraisers and Donors

The fundraiser's personal relationship with the donor is an important aspect of the behavior of donors. Most donations to a fundraising page come from the fundraiser's existing social group—the fundraiser's network of friends, family members, and work colleagues. In practice, the size of this social network will vary—some fundraisers have extensive networks, others have a much smaller social group. The extent of this variation is clear from looking at the number of Facebook friends that fundraisers have—arguably a plausible indicator of a relevant social network, not least because links to fundraising pages are posted to Facebook pages.

In our sample of JustGiving donors with links to Facebook, the median number of Facebook friends is 252, but the tenth percentile of the distribution is 77 friends and the ninetieth percentile is 654 friends. Some fundraisers are making "asks" to wider network than others. An obvious question is whether these differences in size of social group translate into variation in fundraising success. Insofar as personal relationships matter, do people with large networks and more friends tend to raise more money?

Of course, size of social group may be correlated with other characteristics of the fundraisers (and the donors). Young people tend to have more Facebook friends than older people; they also tend to give less. Without controlling for age, we would get a spurious correlation between size of social group and size of donations. Table 14.6 illustrates the variation in fundraising behavior and number of Facebook friends. The demographic information comes from JustGiving and is based on a household-specific market-research classification. In our analysis of the effect of size of social group on fundraising behavior, we control for the fundraiser's gender, age, and income,[6] the type of event, and the gender of the donor.

The raw relationships between size of social group and donations to the fundraising page are shown in figure 14.1. The three graphs in that

Table 14.5
Factors that determine how much people give (self-reported).

	Very important	Somewhat important	Not very important	Not at all important	Not applicable
A sense that my money will be used efficiently or effectively	56.1%	35.0%	6.9%	1.6%	0.6%
The charity's cause or mission	45.1%	44.1%	8.4%	1.9%	0.6%
My income and what I can afford	45.3%	42.3%	9.0%	2.5%	0.8%
A personal connection to the fundraiser	41.5%	43.4%	10.6%	3.5%	1.1%
The fundraiser's reason for fundraising	38.0%	48.0%	10.1%	3.0%	1.0%
The reputation of the charity	32.7%	47.5%	15.3%	3.4%	1.0%
Tax relief (e.g., Gift Aid)	21.7%	34.8%	23.5%	14.3%	5.8%
Type of fundraising event	14.4%	45.8%	29.8%	8.6%	1.5%
Name of the charity	14.1%	39.4%	32.5%	12.1%	1.9%
Total amount the fundraiser is seeking to raise	3.3%	28.0%	38.9%	24.9%	5.1%
How much other people have given to the fundraiser	2.7%	21.6%	39.0%	33.1%	3.7%
An individual amount suggested by the fundraiser	1.4%	15.9%	39.6%	29.9%	13.2%

Source: Online survey of JustGiving donors, fundraisers and sponsors carried out from October 2010 to April 2011. Sample size: 17,989.

figure show number of donations to a page, average amount given, and total amount raised. Size of social group—captured by the number of Facebook friends of the fundraiser—is shown along the horizontal axis. These figures illustrate correlations that remain significant when we control for characteristics of fundraisers.[7]

The main message is that the size of the fundraiser's social group makes a difference both to the number of donations received and to the average donation size:

- People with larger social groups receive more donations. The effect is not large—on average (including a full set of controls), someone with 250 Facebook friends receives one more donation than someone with 100—but it is statistically significant.

- The average size of donations is smaller in larger social groups. When someone with 250 Facebook friends is compared against someone with 100 (including a full set of controls), each donation is £3 smaller. This is not simply a result of the "marginal donation" being smaller and bringing down the average. In larger groups, we find that the very first donation to a page is smaller; we also find that the maximum donation to a page is smaller. Taken together, these findings provide strong evidence that donors who are members of larger social groups give less.

- Our final outcome is the total amount raised. We find no significant relationship with size of social group, which suggests that the effect on the number of donations and the effect on donation size roughly cancel out. We also show that this relationship holds for pages both with and without targets. Target setting is more likely in larger social groups, which is a reasonable response if fundraisers anticipate smaller donations, but size of social group has a negative effect on the probability that the target is met and on the proportion of the target that is reached.

To what extent can we treat group size as exogenous and so interpret these relationships as causal? The number of Facebook friends is measured at the start of the fundraising campaign, and thus it will not be affected by individual fundraising activity. Our results are robust to controlling for the fundraiser's gender, age, and income. It is possible that there are other characteristics of the fundraiser or the members of his or her social group that we cannot control for and that may be correlated with both the number of Facebook friends (size of social group) and how much is donated. The psychology literature suggests a number of factors

Table 14.6
Variation in fundraising, by fundraiser and donor characteristics.

	Proportion of sample	Number of donations	Total amount raised (£)	Mean donation (£)	Number of friends
Male fundraiser	0.473	16.2	328.6	18.3	342.6
Female fundraiser	0.526	13.0	246.4	16.9	315.2
Fundraiser's age					
18–25	0.149	13.1	231.6	15.6	481.5
26–30	0.172	14.4	265.5	16.7	361.6
31–35	0.149	15.6	300.0	17.6	311.8
36–40	0.166	15.0	303.0	18.1	266.3
41–45	0.137	14.6	304.9	18.7	273.5
46–50	0.094	14.5	312.0	19.0	297.0
51–55	0.050	14.4	313.5	19.2	276.2
56–60	0.028	14.6	301.7	18.7	255.5
61–65	0.018	13.4	289.2	19.4	304.7
66–70	0.012	13.6	282.5	17.8	314.8
71–75	0.007	13.2	261.1	17.5	317.8
76+	0.018	15.5	296.9	17.1	335.0
Fundraiser's household income					
< £10K	0.071	12.3	215.5	15.7	372.4
£10K–£15K	0.036	12.1	213.6	15.9	403.2
£15K–£20K	0.151	13.0	235.4	16.0	367.0
£20K–£25K	0.178	13.2	247.6	16.7	333.3
£25K–£30K	0.164	14.1	267.4	17.0	315.8
£30K–£40K	0.120	15.3	299.9	17.5	302.2
£40K–£50K	0.078	15.4	305.8	18.0	300.2
£50K–£60K	0.120	16.7	358.0	19.3	295.3
£60K–£75K	0.064	18.2	436.3	21.6	313.9
£75K+	0.016	21.1	526.8	23.2	316.9

Table 14.6 (continued)

	Proportion of sample	Number of donations	Total amount raised (£)	Mean donation (£)	Number of friends
Donor's gender					
Male	0.311			20.0	
Female	0.393			15.3	
Anonymous	0.073			12.8	
Unknown	0.222			20.5	

Sample: 39,238 fundraising pages linked to a Facebook page.

that may affect size of social group, including popularity, narcissism, and brain size, but none of these can plausibly explain the strong negative relationship between group size and contributions. We therefore interpret our findings as saying something meaningful about the effect of group size on donations to a fundraising page.

At first sight, the fact that people in larger social groups give less seems like a classic free-riding result for a public good: When there are more people to give to a charity, each person can get away with giving a bit less. But this does not hold up under closer scrutiny. Many of the fundraising pages are for large, national charities, such as Cancer Research UK. For such a charity, the donation of any single individual to an individual fundraising page is a drop in the ocean whether there are 80 or 800 potential donors in a fundraiser's social network.

The free-riding argument makes sense only if donors care about the total amount raised for the charity on the particular fundraising page, not (just) about how much the charity gets in total. If people in the fundraiser's social network care about the fundraiser and how much the fundraiser raises, then, in larger social groups, each donor will give a little less. But note that this is a new approach to the public-good free-riding argument; it assumes that donors care not only about the charity but also about the fundraiser, and it brings the relationship between donors and the fundraiser (the relational altruism) into explanations of donors' behavior.

14.5   Social interactions—peer pressure

One reason why public fundraising platforms may be more effective than simple "asks" is that they provide a public setting for donations in which

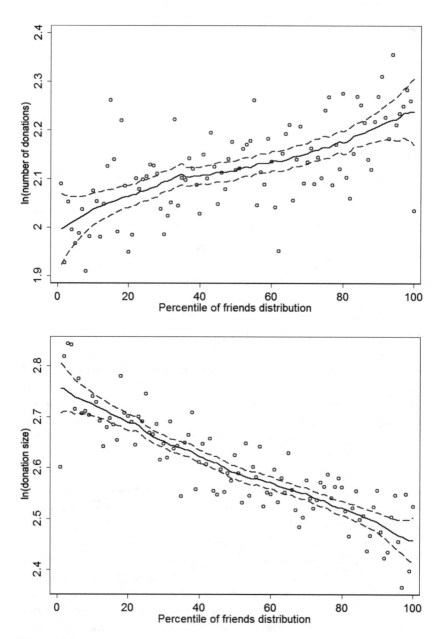

Figure 14.1
Relationship between size of social group and donations. The graphs plot the means of the
ln(number of donations per page), the per-page mean ln(donation size), and ln(total
amount raised per page) by the percentile of the distribution of the number of Facebook
friends (shown by the scatter points), together with smoothed running lines and 95%
confidence intervals.

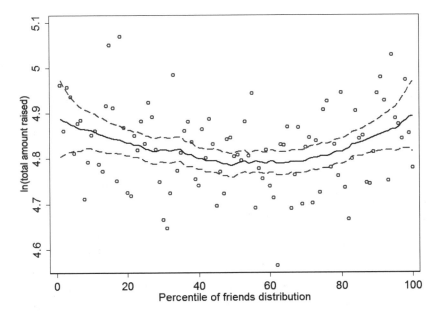

Figure 14.1 (continued)

donors know that their donations will be seen by others. Fundraisers know whether or not members of their social group responded, and how much they gave. This public setting also shapes giving behavior. Donations made in public have been shown to be larger than donations made in private. Information on how much other people have given also affects whether and how much people give.

JustGiving donors report that how much other people have given is a relatively unimportant factor in determining how much they give (table 14.5). In practice, it turns out to affect donor behavior.[8]

There are a number of possible ways in which donors may be influenced by how much other people have given:

- Donors may be affected by "shining knights" (i.e., large donations to a page). The idea of "competitive altruism" suggests that people compete to be the most generous if it is advantageous to do so (e.g., because it sends a message about their wealth or their generosity).

- Donors may also be affected by "widows' mites" (i.e., small donations to a page) if they want to avoid the social stigma of being the meanest on the page.

- There may be "herd behavior" as donors desiring to conform try to target the modal amount.

- There may also be benchmarking as donors use the information about donations already made to gauge how much they should give.

Analysis of giving patterns on JustGiving suggests that all of these behaviors are relevant. To illustrate this, figure 14.2 shows levels of giving before and after a large donation to a fundraising page (defined as one that is more than twice the page's mean and at least £50), before and after a small donation (defined as less than half the page's mean), and before and after a change in the modal donation. Each bar represents the average donation size (averaged across all pages). Negative numbers represent donations before the event (where the event is someone making the large donation or the small donation). Zero captures the large or small donation or the change in modal donation. Positive numbers represent donations after the event.

The figures powerfully demonstrate how donors respond to how much other people give. The donations that follow a single large donation are significantly greater, on average, than the donations that came before. Further analysis shows that different-sized large donations (twice previous mean, three times previous mean, five times previous mean, and more than ten times previous mean) trigger different-sized responses. The opposite effect occurs in the case of a small donation—the donations that come after a small donation are significantly smaller than the donations that precede it. The size of the average donation also moves up or down after an increase or a decrease in the modal donation.

Further analysis shows that the effects appear to be fairly persistent, affecting donation size for at least ten donations that follow. This is due in part to the fact that both large and small donations trigger other similar-sized donations (other large and small donations). But there are also long-term effects, even on "regular-sized" donations. Our estimates imply that a single £100 donation results in a £10 increase in subsequent donations. This implies that a single £100 donation will "pay back" in ten donations' time.

We find no adverse spillover effects from donors' giving more in response to a large donation on one fundraising page to how much they give on other fundraising pages. There may be a concern that a large donation to one page crowds out donations to other pages. Exploiting the fact that within the JustGiving sample we can identify donors who give to more than one fundraising page, we confirm that there is a positive own-page effect, but we find that the estimated spillover effect on donations by the same donor to other fundraising pages is positive, though insignificant.

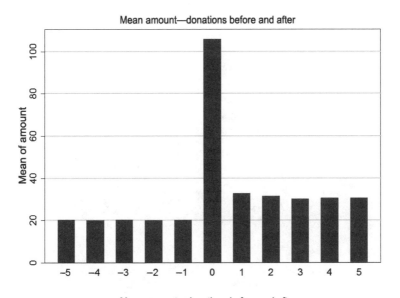

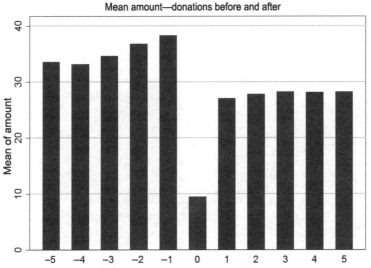

Figure 14.2
Donors' responses to how much other people have given. The analysis was based on a sample of 10,597 fundraisers who ran in the 2010 London Marathon. On the *x* axis, negative numbers donate the donations *before* the large or small donation/change in mode; positive numbers donate the donations *after*. A large donation is defined as twice the page mean and at least £50. A small donation is half the page mean. We focus on the first large or small donation or change in mode to occur on a page, excluding those within the first three donations.

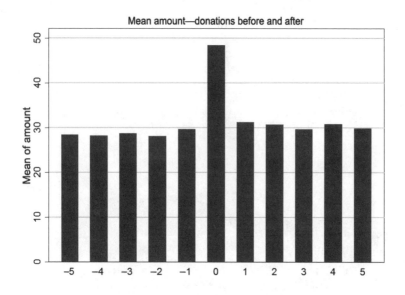

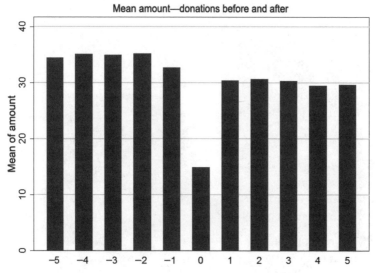

Figure 14.2 (continued)

Further analysis shows that the effects of donation amounts on subsequent donation size are equal for pages with and pages without a target and for large, established charities and newer, smaller ones (suggesting that large donations do not provide a signal of charity quality in this case). Our preferred explanation is benchmarking—donors want to position themselves at the appropriate place within the distribution of donations on a page, depending on factors such as their relationship to the fundraiser, their income, and their support for the cause. Looking at how much other people have given provides information on how much it is appropriate to give. This is consistent with the observed pattern of behavior, including donors' responses to large and small donations as well as to changes in modal donations. It is also consistent with the fact that a single large or small donation has less effect if it appears later on the page. The explanation for this is that it provides less additional information than if it appears earlier on the page. The intuition that fundraisers want a large donation early on their fundraising page is well supported by the data.

We also find no evidence that large donations might put people off donating altogether. We can't see whether people visit a fundraising page without giving, but we can measure the rate at which people arrive at a page and make a donation (the arrival rate, captured by number of donations per day) and can test whether this is affected by a large or a small donation. We find no evidence that large or small donations have any effect on the arrival rate.

Summary

Analysis of fundraising data provides the following insights into an important and growing source of income for many charities, and into motivations for charitable giving more generally:

- Individual fundraising comes in different guises—from large-scale mass events to lone fundraisers doing a very personal challenge. The nature of the fundraising seems to matter for how much people raise. People doing mass events tend to raise less individually, but are more likely to do more fundraising in the future. The fact that fundraisers doing the same event may have to compete for donations may be one explanation for the lower amounts raised, although more work is needed to test this further.

- Individual fundraising introduces new social dynamics (new in comparison with traditional fundraising by charities) into fundraising. Most sponsors are members of the fundraiser's existing social network. One reason they give is because they care about the fundraiser (and not just about the charity). Individual fundraising appears to be more effective than simple peer-to-peer fundraising. We argue that this is attributable both to the fundraising activity and to the fundraising platform (which makes the donations visible to the fundraiser and to other donors).

- In this public setting, donors also look closely at what other donors give and use other people's donations to benchmark the amount that they give. Encouraging early, large donations really is a sure-fire way for fundraisers to help increase their total.

Acknowledgments

This chapter draws on a number of separate analyses of JustGiving data. Thanks are due to staff at JustGiving, especially to Liz Kessick and Mike Bugembe, for helping to make the data available. We also thank Olesya Kolyachkov and Edmund Wright for excellent research assistance.

Appendix

The analysis in the chapter is based on three samples of JustGiving data that were used for separate projects. We briefly describe each of the samples and provide comparative descriptive statistics.

Large Sample of JustGiving Fundraisers

Our largest sample consists of 416,313 fundraisers who were active JustGiving users at the time of an online survey that ran from October 2010 to April 2011. This was based on a randomly selected sample from the wider population of all active JustGiving fundraisers. In our analysis we focus on the pages set up by these fundraisers in 2009 and 2010 (a total of 546,821 pages). We exclude any pages which received no donations. Data for this sample are presented in table 14.A.1.

London Marathon Fundraising Data

Our initial sample contained information from more than 12,000 fundraising pages. The data were captured on April 30, 2010, five days after the marathon took place. Table 14.A.2 provides a summary of the sample. Note that we exclude pages which have single donations of more than £1,000. We also exclude pages with fewer than ten donations (1,783 pages) or more than 100 donations (212 pages). With these exclusions, our sample is 10,597 pages.

Facebook Fundraisers

Our sample for analysis comprises 566,240 donations made to 39,238 pages where the fundraiser linked their fundraising page to their Facebook page. This is after some cleaning. We remove 3,817 pages where we cannot identify the charity registration number for England and Wales. We also remove 30 pages with zero friends and 364 with zero amounts donated. We remove outliers, including pages with individual donations of more than £170 (the top 1 percent), pages that raised more than £3,241 (the top 1 percent), and pages with fundraising targets of £100,000 or more (37 pages). Data for this sample are presented in table 14.A.3.

Table 14.A.1

	Mean	Tenth percentile	Median	Ninetieth percentile
Number of donations	21	3	14	46
Amount raised	£566	£38	£245	£1,343

Sample: 416,313 fundraisers, 546,821 pages.

Table 14.A2

	Mean	Tenth percentile	Median	Ninetieth percentile
Number of donations	37	14	33	65
Amount raised	£1,115	£291	£892	£2,129

Sample: 10,597 pages.

Table 14.A3

	Mean	Tenth percentile	Median	Ninetieth percentile
Number of donations	14.5	2	9	20
Amount raised	£347.4	£35	£134	£792

Sample: 39,238 fundraising pages.

Notes

1. Source: JustGiving.

2. Source: https://www.blackbaud.com/files/resources/downloads/2012
.CharitableGivingReport.pdf.

3. Source: https://www.cafonline.org/PDF/UKGiving2012Full.pdf.

4. Donors can choose to donate anonymously. Around 10 percent choose to do
so. Large and small donations are more likely to be made anonymously, as
might be expected.

5. Source: http://www.pfra.org.uk/face-to-face_fundraising/do_you_object_to
_chuggers/money_doesnt_go_to_charity/.

6. Ideally we would want to control for characteristics of donors, but we have
information only on characteristics of fundraisers. However, under the
assumption of network homophily (i.e., that people in social groups share
characteristics) it is reasonable to assume that the fundraiser characteristics are
a proxy for donor characteristics.

7. Full regressions are available in Scharf and Smith 2014.

8. This analysis of peer effects summarizes Smith et al. 2015.

References

Bergstrom, T., L. Blume, and H. Varian. 1986. On the private provision of
public goods. *Journal of Public Economics* 29 (1): 25–49.

Castillo, M., R. Petrie, and C. Wardell. 2014. Fundraising through online social
networks: A field experiment on peer-to-peer solicitation. *Journal of Public
Economics* 114:29–35.

Freeman, R. 1997. Working for nothing: The supply of volunteer labor. *Journal
of Labor Economics* 15 (1), part 2: S140–S166.

Lacetera, N., M. Macis, and A. Mele. 2016. Viral altruism? Generosity and
social contagion in online networks. *Sociological Science*. March 24. https://
www.sociologicalscience.com/articles-v3-11-202/.

Meer, J. 2011. Brother, can you spare a dime? Peer pressure in charitable
solicitation. *Journal of Public Economics* 95 (7–8): 926–941.

Scharf, K., and S. Smith. 2014. Relational Altruism and Giving in Social Groups.
Working Paper 10059, Centre for Economic Policy Research.

Smith, S., F. Windmeijer, and E. Wright. 2015. Peer effects in giving: Evidence
from the (running) field. *Economic Journal (Oxford)* 125 (585): 1053–1071.

Vesterlund, L. 2003. The informational value of sequential fundraising. *Journal
of Public Economics* 87:627–657.

Contributors

Sjoerd Beugelsdijk, University of Groningen

Mireia Borrell-Porta, London School of Economics and Political Science

Joan Costa-Font, London School of Economics and Political Science

Elwyn Davies, University of Oxford

Julio Jorge Elias, Universidad del CEMA

Marcel Fafchamps, Stanford University

Luigi Guiso, Einaudi Institute for Economics and Finance

Odelia Heizler, Tel-Aviv–Yaffo Academic College

Ayal Kimhi, The Hebrew University of Jerusalem

Mariko J. Klasing, University of Groningen

Martin Ljunge, Research Institute of Industrial Economics

Mario Macis, Johns Hopkins University

Mark Ottoni-Wilhelm, Indiana University–Purdue University Indianapolis

Abigail Payne, McMaster University

Kelly Ragan, Stockholm School of Economics

Jana Sadeh, University of Southampton

Azusa Sato, Asian Development Bank

Kimberley Scharf, Warwick University

Sarah Smith, University of Bristol

Mirco Tonin, Free University of Bozen-Bolzano

Michael Vlassopoulos, University of Southampton

Evguenia Winschel, University of Mannheim

Philipp Zahn, University of St. Gallen

Index